The Nature and Value of Knowledge

The Nature and Value of Knowledge

Three Investigations

Duncan Pritchard
Alan Millar
Adrian Haddock

OXFORD
UNIVERSITY PRESS

OXFORD

UNIVERSITY PRESS

Great Clarendon Street, Oxford OX2 6DP

Oxford University Press is a department of the University of Oxford.
It furthers the University's objective of excellence in research, scholarship,
and education by publishing worldwide in

Oxford New York

Auckland Cape Town Dar es Salaam Hong Kong Karachi
Kuala Lumpur Madrid Melbourne Mexico City Nairobi
New Delhi Shanghai Taipei Toronto

With offices in

Argentina Austria Brazil Chile Czech Republic France Greece
Guatemala Hungary Italy Japan Poland Portugal Singapore
South Korea Switzerland Thailand Turkey Ukraine Vietnam

Oxford is a registered trade mark of Oxford University Press
in the UK and in certain other countries

Published in the United States
by Oxford University Press Inc., New York

British Library Cataloguing in Publication Data

Data available

Library of Congress Cataloging in Publication Data
Library of Congress Control Number: 2010920357

Typeset by Laserwords Private Limited, Chennai, India
Printed in Great Britain
on acid-free paper by
MPG Books Group, Bodmin and King's Lynn

ISBN 978-0-19-958626-4

Preface

This book is an outcome of a project on the value of knowledge in which each of us was a participant. The aim of the project was to investigate whether light could be shed on the nature of knowledge by reflecting on whether, and if so why, knowledge is of value to us. The core issue about value was, of course, not whether knowledge is better than ignorance, but whether knowledge is better than true belief, or states implicating true belief but falling short of knowledge. The topic is opportune for at least two reasons.

The first connects with the fact that there are widely differing views on the nature of knowledge, and on how to pursue the theory of knowledge. The epistemological mainstream aspires to a reductive account of knowledge in terms of true belief plus the satisfaction of further conditions. But a growing number of philosophers, most notably Timothy Williamson, challenge this aspiration. They in turn face a challenge concerning whether it is possible to provide an illuminating general account of knowledge once the aspiration is abandoned. Whoever is right in this situation, one might expect to make some progress by considering the interplay between issues concerning what knowledge is and issues concerning why, if at all, knowledge is of value to us. An epistemology that fails to make sense of why knowledge is of value, if it is, would be unsatisfactory. But the fact that philosophers make a fuss about the difference between knowledge and states implicating true belief but falling short of knowledge would be puzzling if this difference turned out to be of little importance for human enquiry or for the social transmission of the results of enquiry.

The second reason why the project is opportune is that, provoked by Jonathan Kvanvig's *The Value of Knowledge and the Nature of Understanding* (Kvanvig 2003), there has been considerable discussion in the literature as to whether knowledge really can be more valuable than true belief or states implicating true belief but falling short of knowledge. Perhaps the best way to secure true belief is to secure something better than true belief, such as knowledge, but once we have true belief as to whether something is so, why should it matter that we know or have a justified belief on the matter? This and related issues are pursued in different ways in this volume and in a collection of articles entitled *Epistemic Value* (Haddock, Millar, and Pritchard [eds.] 2009), which is another output of the project.

Each of us shares the conviction that the matters raised above merit much further attention. We hope and believe that this volume will contribute to that end. The book is a collaborative effort borne out of much discussion and much critical interplay between us over several years. We have not attempted to provide a unified text to which each of us subscribes. Collaborative outputs of that kind, whilst frequently successful, do not provide the only model for collaborative work. Philosophers are typically individualistic in their approach to philosophical problems. Even so, as we have found, those who differ can sometimes fruitfully collaborate within a framework provided by overall aims and shared themes. We trust that these contributions will be of interest both for their detailed content, and for the contrasts and similarities that their juxtaposition makes evident.

The first investigation, 'Knowledge and Understanding' (Part I), by Duncan Pritchard, provides, amongst other things, a close analysis of problems concerning the value of knowledge and a critical examination of a conception of the value of knowledge within the framework of virtue-theoretic epistemology. Pritchard believes that we have a widely shared intuition that knowledge has a distinctive value—final value—and that a form of virtue theory that represents knowledge as a cognitive achievement provides the most promising account available of that value. Nonetheless, he finds the theory wanting and argues that there is a cognitive state—understanding—which is similar to, but different from, knowledge, and which has final value.

In the second investigation, 'Knowledge and Recognition' (Part II), Alan Millar argues that there is a tension between the assumption that knowledge admits of a reductive analysis along traditional lines, and the roles that knowledge and thought about knowledge play in our lives. He presents accounts of perceptual knowledge, knowledge from indicator phenomena, and knowledge from testimony, in each of which recognitional abilities feature prominently. These abilities, he claims, enable us to have a better understanding of how it can be that we are as good as we are at telling what we and others know. This in turn helps us to understand how knowledge can matter to us in the ways he thinks it does.

The third investigation, 'Knowledge and Action' (Part III), by Adrian Haddock, focuses on the relationship between perceptual knowledge and knowledge of our own intentional actions. He argues for an account of knowledge and justification to which a certain kind of second-order knowledge is central. He illustrates his account for the case of human perceptual knowledge, and suggests that, as against others, it enables us to make sense of the distinctive value of knowledge. Building on the groundbreaking work of G. E. M. Anscombe, he applies the account to the case of knowledge of our intentional actions.

Each of us believes that there is scope for further work to explore the similarities and contrasts between the philosophical stances that are manifested in these investigations. Both Pritchard and Millar acknowledge the importance for epistemology of conceptions of abilities and competences but have differing views about how the abilities or competences are individuated. There are affinities between Millar and Haddock over how to account for perceptual knowledge but differences over exactly how to characterize the role of justification in relation to knowledge.

The project from which this book has arisen was generously funded by a Research Grant provided by the United Kingdom's Arts and Humanities Research Council. We are very grateful to the Council for funding this project.

Several conferences and workshops were held under the aegis of the project at the Universities of Stirling and Edinburgh. We would like to thank everyone who attended these events for the stimulus which they contributed. Above all we would like to thank Wayne Riggs, Ernest Sosa, and Jennifer Hornsby for their detailed comments on drafts of our contributions to this book at a workshop organized for this purpose. The book has benefited greatly from their excellent comments. We are grateful too for support provided by the University of Stirling and its Department of Philosophy, and in particular to Yvonne McClymont for assistance with financial and other administrative matters and to Nikki Leavitt for her assistance in organizing conferences and workshops. Warm thanks are due to Steinvör Thöll Árnadóttir, who provided invaluable help in preparing the text, and to Tom Cunningham for preparing the index. Finally, we would like to thank Peter Momtchiloff for his encouragement and for his understanding of the character of the project.

Adrian Haddock, Alan Millar, and Duncan Pritchard

Stirling and Edinburgh
August 2009

Contents

I

KNOWLEDGE AND UNDERSTANDING

Duncan Pritchard

PART I

ANALYTICAL TABLE OF CONTENTS

Chapter 1. The Value Problem for Knowledge

The primary value problem. The secondary value problem. The tertiary value problem. The swamping problem applied to reliabilism about knowledge. The swamping problem generalized as posing a difficulty for a certain conception of epistemic value. Fundamental and non-fundamental epistemic goods. Fundamental epistemic goods distinguished from finally valuable epistemic goods. Epistemic value T-monism. The swamping problem expressed as a possible *reductio* of epistemic value T-monism. The swamping problem contrasted with the primary value problem. The practical response to the swamping problem. The monistic response to the swamping problem. The pluralist response to the swamping problem. The relevance of final value.

Chapter 2. Knowledge and Final Value

Robust versus modest virtue epistemology. The achievement thesis. The knowledge as achievement thesis. The value of achievements thesis. The robust virtue epistemologist's argument for the final value of knowledge. Robust virtue epistemology as a potentially reductive account of knowledge. *Contra* the knowledge as achievement thesis (I): the problem of environmental luck and cases of achievement without knowledge. *Contra* the knowledge as achievement thesis (II): cases of knowledge without achievement. *Contra* robust virtue epistemology. Knowledge is not finally valuable.

Chapter 3. Anti-Luck Virtue Epistemology

Two master intuitions about knowledge: the ability intuition and the anti-luck intuition. Robust anti-luck epistemology and robust virtue epistemology are unable to accommodate both intuitions. Anti-luck virtue epistemology. Anti-luck virtue epistemology as a potentially reductive account of knowledge. A genealogical diagnosis of the structure of knowledge. A response to the primary and secondary value problems, and to the swamping problem.

Chapter 4: Understanding

The problem of easy achievements. The strong achievement thesis. The final value of (strong) achievements. The final value of (strong) cognitive achievements. Understanding why X is the case. The factivity of understanding. Understanding is incompatible with 'Gettier-style' epistemic luck. Understanding is compatible with environmental epistemic luck. Understanding without knowledge. Knowledge without understanding. All understanding involves (strong) cognitive achievement. Understanding is finally valuable. Potential implications of the final value of understanding thesis for (i) the proper target of the problem of radical scepticism, and (ii) the goal of enquiry.

1

The Value Problem
for Knowledge

1.1. The Value Problem

It is widely held that knowledge is of distinctive value. Presumably, this is
the reason why knowledge—and not, say, justified true belief—has been the
principal focus of generations of epistemological theorising. Understanding just
why knowledge is distinctively valuable, however, has proved elusive, and this
has led some to question whether it is distinctively valuable at all. Call this the
value problem. The goal of this chapter is to set out what this problem involves.
As we will see, this is far from being a straightforward matter, and part of
the difficulty here is that there is a related problem—the so-called *swamping
problem*—which, while being superficially similar to the value problem, in fact
presents a more specific challenge.

1.2. Unpacking the Value Problem

Part of the difficulty posed by the value problem involves getting clear about
just what it means to say that knowledge is distinctively valuable. One minimal
reading of this claim is that knowledge is more valuable than mere true belief.[1]
Call the challenge to explain why knowledge is more valuable than mere
true belief the *primary value problem*.[2] Clearly there is more to showing that

---

[1] Note that where I draw these contrasts between, as in this case, knowledge and mere true belief, I
have in mind a mere true belief that appropriately corresponds to the true belief at issue in the instance
of knowledge. For example, one is comparing a situation in which an agent knows a proposition with
an exactly analogous situation in which that agent merely truly believes this proposition.

[2] Of course, if you think, like Sartwell (1992), that knowledge just is true belief, then it follows that
knowledge cannot be more valuable than mere true belief. For other sources of scepticism about the
claim that knowledge is more valuable than mere true belief, see Stich (1990: 122–3), Hawley (2006),
and Goldman and Olsson (2009: §1).

knowledge is distinctively valuable than answering this problem, and we will consider what additional demands a response to the value problem needs to satisfy in a moment. What ought to be clear, however, is that if we are unable to account even for why knowledge is more valuable than mere true belief then the very project of answering the value problem is a lost cause.

On the face of it, there is a very straightforward answer to the primary value problem—viz., that knowledge is more valuable than mere true belief because it tends to be of greater practical value. Of course, there may be particular propositions which, for some special reason, one would prefer to merely truly believe rather than know (perhaps in knowing them one would incur a penalty which one wouldn't incur if one merely truly believed them), but in general you are more likely to achieve your goals with knowledge than with mere true belief.

Indeed, this was precisely the way that Socrates answers the primary value problem in the *Meno*. Why should you prefer knowledge of the correct way to Larissa rather than mere true belief, given that both will, on the face of it, ensure that you get to your destination? Socrates' answer is that knowledge has a 'stability' which mere true belief lacks. Mere true belief, argues Socrates, is like one of Daedalus' self-moving statues untethered, in that it is liable to be lost. Knowledge, in contrast, is like one of those statues tethered. For while a mere true belief may well enable you to achieve your goals as well as knowledge, one will be far more insulated from failure by possessing knowledge.

Suppose, for example, that the road to Larissa takes an unexpected course. Someone with mere true belief—where the belief is based on just a hunch, say—may well at this point lose all faith that she is on the right track and turn back. Someone who knows that this is the right way to go, however—perhaps because she consulted a reliable map before her departure—will not be so shaken by this turn of events.

Even supposing that we are able to respond to the primary value problem in this way, however, there would still be more to do to secure our intuition that knowledge is distinctively valuable. At the very least, we would need to answer the *secondary value problem* of explaining why knowledge is more valuable than that which falls short of knowledge.

In order to see this, suppose that one answered the primary value problem by, for example, pointing to a necessary condition for knowledge which in general added practical value (the justification condition, say), but suppose further that the satisfaction of this condition, in conjunction with true belief, was not sufficient for knowledge. Perhaps, for example, when one knows that p it is the fact that one's belief that p is thereby justified that ensures that knowledge has a greater practical value than mere true belief that p alone.

One would thereby have answered the primary value problem while leaving the secondary value problem unanswered. Moreover, let us take it as given that there is no further feature of knowledge which is value-conferring, such that the secondary value problem is regarded not just as unanswered, but as unanswerable.

On the face of it, this lacuna might not seem that problematic, since just so long as one can show that knowledge is more valuable than mere true belief then that would seem to satisfy our intuition that knowledge is of some special value to us (on this view it is, after all, the kind of thing that we should prefer to mere true belief, all other things being equal). The problem, however, is that if the distinctive value of knowledge is due to some feature of knowledge which, with true belief, falls short of knowledge, then it seems that what we should seek is not knowledge as such, but rather that which falls short of knowledge (i.e. true belief plus the value-conferring property X, in this case justification). But if that's right, then why do we regard knowledge as distinctively valuable at all?[3]

The primary value problem thus naturally leads to the secondary value problem, and it seems that both will need to be answered if we are to account for the distinctive value of knowledge. Even if we can offer a response to the secondary value problem, however, it is still not clear that we have accounted for the distinctive value of knowledge.

This is because the secondary value problem leaves open the possibility that the difference of value at issue is merely one of degree rather than kind. To say that knowledge is of *distinctive* value, however, appears to suggest that the difference in value between knowledge and that which falls short of knowledge is not just a matter of degree, but of *kind*. After all, if one regards knowledge as being more valuable than that which falls short of knowledge merely as a matter of degree rather than kind, then this has the effect of putting knowledge on a kind of continuum of value with regard to the epistemic, albeit further up the continuum than anything that falls short of knowledge. The problem with this 'continuum' account of the value of knowledge, however, is that it

---

[3] Elsewhere, I've called this 'Kaplan's problem'. Kaplan (1985) famously argues that the conclusion to be drawn from the Gettier counterexamples to the tripartite account of knowledge (i.e. knowledge as justified true belief) is that knowledge is not a distinctively valuable epistemic standing. Instead, what we should seek is justified true belief, something which the Gettier counterexamples demonstrate falls short of knowledge. Given the further claim that justified true belief is more valuable than mere true belief, Kaplan thus in effect answers the primary value problem while arguing that the secondary value problem does not need to be answered. In a similar vein, Kvanvig (2003) has recently argued that knowledge is not more valuable than any proper subset of its parts because there is no Gettier counterexample-excluding theory of knowledge available which could account for the greater value of knowledge over any non-Gettier counterexample-excluding proper subset of its parts.

fails to explain why the long history of epistemological discussion has focused specifically on the stage in this continuum of value that knowledge marks rather than some other stage (such as a stage just before the one marked out by knowledge, or just after). Accordingly, it seems that accounting for our intuitions about the value of knowledge requires us to offer an explanation of why knowledge has not just a greater *degree* but also a different *kind* of value than whatever falls short of knowledge. Call this the *tertiary value problem.*

Further support for the tertiary value problem comes from the fact that we often treat knowledge as being, unlike lesser epistemic standings, *precious*, in the sense that its value is not merely a function of its practical import. But if that is correct, then knowledge must be the kind of thing that, unlike that which falls short of knowledge, is valuable for its own sake. That is, it must be non-instrumentally—i.e. *finally*—valuable.[4]

Most of those who have explored the issue of the value of knowledge have tended to focus their attentions on the primary value problem, to the exclusion of the other two problems. As noted above, there is a good rationale for a focus of this sort, since if one is unable to answer the primary value problem then, *a fortiori*, one will be unable to answer the secondary and tertiary problems as well. This rationale can be turned on its head, however, since it equally follows that if one could offer a response to the tertiary value problem then one would thereby be able to deal with the primary and secondary value problems as well.

In essence, then, the challenge we face in trying to account for the distinctive value of knowledge is to find a way of demonstrating that knowledge, unlike that which falls short of knowledge, is finally valuable. This is precisely the possibility that I will be exploring in the next chapter.

1.3. The Swamping Problem

Before we can get down to the nitty-gritty of exploring how one might account for the final value of knowledge, however, it is first necessary to consider a problem that on the face of it is a variant of (if not simply a subspecies of) the primary value problem. This difficulty is the so-called 'swamping problem', as defended most prominently by Jonathan Kvanvig (e.g. 2003), but also put forward in various forms by Ward Jones (1997), Richard Swinburne (1999,

---

[4] Final value, and in particular its relation to intrinsic value, is discussed in more detail in the next chapter.

2000), Wayne Riggs (2002), Linda Zagzebski (2003), and John Greco (2009), amongst others. Interestingly, the standard way of expressing this problem is not as posing a general epistemological difficulty which faces all theories of knowledge—which is how the value problem is usually understood—but rather as posing a problem for particular epistemological proposals, such as reliabilism.[5] With the argument so directed, here is how it goes.[6]

Imagine two great cups of coffee identical in every relevant respect—they look the same, taste the same, smell the same, are of the same quantity, and so on. Clearly, we value great cups of coffee. Moreover, given that we value great cups of coffee, it follows that we also value reliable coffee-making machines—i.e. machines which regularly produce good coffee. Notice, however, that once we've got the great coffee, then we don't then care whether it was produced by a reliable coffee-making machine. That is, that the great coffee was produced by a reliable coffee-making machine doesn't contribute any additional value to it. In order to see this, note that if one were told that only one of the great identical cups of coffee before one had been produced by a reliable coffee-making machine, this would have no bearing at all on the issue of which cup one preferred; one would still be indifferent on this score. In short, whatever value is conferred on a cup of coffee through being produced by a reliable coffee-making machine, this value is 'swamped' by the value conferred on that coffee in virtue of it being a great cup of coffee.

The supposed import of this example to reliabilist theories of knowledge—theories which hold that knowledge is reliably formed true belief—is that it follows, by analogy, that if we are faced with two identical true beliefs, one of them reliably formed and one not, it shouldn't make any difference to us which one we have. After all, we only value reliable belief-forming processes as a means to true belief, just as we only value reliable coffee-making machines as a means to great coffee, and so once we have the good in question—true belief or great coffee—then it shouldn't matter to us whether that good was in addition acquired in a reliable fashion. Intuitively, though, it *is* better to have reliable true belief rather than just mere true belief. Moreover, if, as the reliabilist maintains, reliable true belief is knowledge, then this intuition is stronger still. For surely, many of us have the intuition that it would be better to have knowledge rather than mere true belief.

More generally, the axiological claim implicit in the coffee-cup case is that if a property (like being reliably formed, when it comes to beliefs, or being

---

[5] Though see Riggs (2002).
[6] The following discussion closely follows that offered by Zagzebski (2003).

reliably produced, when it comes to coffee) is only instrumentally valuable relative to some further good (e.g. true belief or great coffee), then in cases in which the further good in question is already present, no further value is conferred by the presence of the instrumentally valuable property. This is, of course, a general thesis about value. Moreover, as the coffee-cup example illustrates, there seems every reason to think that it is true.

Interestingly, once we recognize that what is driving the swamping argument is this general thesis about value, then it ceases to become plausible that it should only affect reliabilist views. After all, the general value thesis just described will have an impact on *any* epistemological proposal which has the same relevant features as reliabilism—viz., which treats the epistemic standing in question as instrumentally valuable only relative to the good of true belief. Moreover, once the point is put in this way it also becomes clear that what is at issue in the swamping argument is not the greater value *simpliciter* of knowledge over mere true belief, but rather the greater *epistemic* value of knowledge over mere true belief. Let us take these points in turn.

In order to see the first point, suppose, for example, that we only value justification because it is a means to true belief—i.e. we only value it instrumentally relative to the good of true belief. If that is right, then we could just as well run the swamping argument for justification as we can for reliability, since if the swamping argument works at all then any value that is conferred on a belief in virtue of its being justified will be swamped by the value conferred by the belief's being true. The problem, then, is not specific to reliabilism but instead applies to any view which treats the value of an epistemic standing as being instrumental value relative only to the good of true belief.[7]

In order to see the second point, notice that there is on the face of it very little to be gained by responding to the swamping problem by arguing that the epistemic standing in question generates a practical value that mere true belief lacks.[8] For example, suppose one responded to the swamping problem by arguing that knowledge is more valuable than mere true belief because knowledge entails justification and justification is practically valuable. Justified true belief, we might say—in a broadly Socratic fashion (see §1.2 above)—has

---

[7] Indeed, the problem isn't specific to externalist epistemological proposals more generally either. The argument that was just run as regards justification would work with equal force whether the notion of justification in question were cashed-out in an externalist or internalist fashion. All that matters is that justification has the target property in question (i.e. that it is only instrumentally valuable relative to the epistemic good of true belief).

[8] Since something could be both practically and epistemically valuable, note that in what follows, unless I specify otherwise, when I talk of something being practically valuable I have in mind a practical *non-epistemic* value.

a 'stability' that mere true belief lacks, and this means that it is more practically useful to us in attaining our goals. The problem with this response, however, is that it doesn't appear to engage with the swamping problem at all. After all, the difficulty that the swamping problem poses concerns how to make sense of the idea that knowledge is more valuable than mere true belief because it involves an epistemic standing which better serves our specifically *epistemic* goals—in particular, the epistemic goal of true belief. Thus, the kind of value that is at issue is specifically an epistemic value. Accordingly, even if it is true that knowledge has more all-things-considered value because it entails an epistemic standing which adds practical value to true belief, the problem would still remain that, on the face of it, knowledge is not *epistemically* more valuable than mere true belief.

Of course, one response to this could be to argue that it is so much the worse for the swamping problem that it turns specifically on epistemic value in this way. After all, if the swamping problem is consistent with the greater all-things-considered value of knowledge over true belief, then how seriously should we take it? Call this the *practical response* to the swamping problem. On this view, the right reaction to the swamping problem is to recognize that its conclusion is in fact harmless. We will explore this response to the swamping problem in more detail below. First, though, we need to do more to pick apart the different moving parts of the argument.

1.4. Fundamental and Non-fundamental Epistemic Goods

If the swamping argument is indeed concerned with specifically epistemic value—i.e. a value which specifically concerns epistemic goods—then that prompts the question of what particular view of epistemic value it challenges.[9] In order to formulate the value thesis in question, we first need to introduce a distinction between *fundamental* and *non-fundamental* epistemic goods. Call a fundamental epistemic good any epistemic good whose epistemic value is at least sometimes not simply instrumental value relative to a further *epistemic*

---

[9] The observant reader will have a spotted a kind of circularity in play here. On the one hand, one's account of epistemic value will have a bearing on what one counts as an epistemic good. On the other hand, one will evaluate a theory of epistemic value by considering how well it accords with the intuitive class of epistemic goods. Such circularity is unavoidable, but it is not vicious. Here, as elsewhere in philosophy, the solution is to seek a reflective equilibrium, where that might involve, for example, regarding some goods which one intuitively supposed as epistemic as being non-epistemic.

good. That is, such an epistemic good is at least sometimes epistemically valuable entirely for its own sake. Call a non-fundamental epistemic good any good which is not a fundamental epistemic good—i.e. any good whose epistemic value is always instrumental value relative to a further epistemic good (and which is thus never epistemically valuable entirely for its own sake).

Clearly, the very idea of there being such a thing as epistemic value—of assessing the value of something relative to specifically epistemic goals—presupposes that some epistemic goods are fundamental. Something, after all, needs to act as the terminus for the instrumental regress of epistemic value. Nonetheless, one might be puzzled as to why this distinction is being put in the way that it is, since why can't we just talk about instrumental and non-instrumental—i.e. *final*—value?

The problem is that something can be a fundamentally epistemic good and yet not be finally valuable. For while a fundamental epistemic good can act as the terminus of the instrumental regress of epistemic value, this is entirely compatible with that good not being finally valuable *simpliciter*. After all, it could be that the value of the fundamental epistemic good in question is only instrumental value relative to some further non-epistemic goods (e.g. practical goods). For example, suppose that true belief is a fundamental epistemic good—a possibility which we will explore in more detail in a moment. If that is right, then we won't instrumentally value this good relative to any further epistemic good, such as, say, justified belief. Nevertheless, it could be that true belief is not itself finally valuable *simpliciter*, but is instead only instrumentally valuable relative to a further non-epistemic good—e.g. it serves some practical purpose.

There is also a further difference between final and fundamental epistemic value, in that when we describe a good as finally valuable we are claiming that it is in the *nature* of the good in question to be valuable in this way. In contrast, in calling an epistemic good a fundamental epistemic good we are merely saying that at least *sometimes* it has non-instrumental epistemic value. On the face of it at least, this is entirely compatible with the good in question not being in its nature of fundamental epistemic value at all.

So fundamental epistemic value does not entail final value *simpliciter*. Interestingly, however, final value *simpliciter does* entail fundamental epistemic value. After all, if an epistemic good has a value which is not an instrumental value then, *a fortiori*, it has a value which is not an instrumental epistemic value either, and hence the reverse direction of fit holds. This might initially seem surprising. After all, one might think that final value is *sui generis* and hence the sort of thing that by definition cannot be thought of as specifically epistemic. I think this worry subsides, however, once one clarifies the claim in play here.

For suppose, for the sake of argument, that knowledge has final value. This means that knowledge has a value which is independent of all other considerations. But if this is right then, *a fortiori*, knowledge has a value which is independent of all *epistemic* considerations too, and hence it is a fundamental epistemic good. That is, from a purely epistemic point of view where only epistemic considerations are taken into account, knowledge has a value which is not an instrumental value relative to a further epistemic good. It is only in this sense that the final value of an epistemic standing entails that this epistemic standing is a fundamental epistemic good. Note, however, that there is no conflict between this claim and the idea of final value as being *sui generis*. For to say that the final value of an epistemic standing entails that this epistemic standing is a fundamental epistemic good is not to qualify the final value in question, but merely to note its axiological implications for a particular domain.

One last point is in order regarding our distinction between fundamental and non-fundamental epistemic goods and its relation to final value. Given how weakly the notion of a fundamental epistemic good is understood, such that an epistemic good need only *sometimes* have an epistemic value which is non-instrumental in order to qualify, it ought to be clear that an epistemic standing need only be sometimes of final value in order to ensure that it is a fundamental epistemic good. In particular, it need not, for example, be in the nature of the epistemic standing in question that it is finally valuable. For suppose, for instance, that knowledge only sometimes has final value—i.e. that it is not in the nature of knowledge to be valuable in this way, though it sometimes is. Even then, it will follow that there are occasions on which knowledge retains a value independently of all other considerations, and hence independently of all other epistemic considerations too. Thus, even on this relatively weak supposition about the value of knowledge, it will still count as a fundamental epistemic good.[10]

1.5. The Relevance of Epistemic Value Monism

With this distinction in mind, we can now formulate the thesis about epistemic value that is really at issue in the swamping argument, which is a

---

[10] Sosa (2007: ch. 4) draws a similar distinction between fundamental and non-fundamental epistemic goods to that marked out here, though (if I've read him correctly anyway) our presentation of this distinction diverges in some important details.

variety of epistemic value monism where the fundamental epistemic value is true belief:

> *Epistemic Value T-Monism*
> True belief is the sole fundamental epistemic good.[11]

The driving idea behind epistemic value T-monism is that there is only one fundamental epistemic good (this is the 'monism' part) and that this good is true belief (this is the 'T' part). Accordingly, the epistemic value of all other epistemic goods is instrumental value relative to this epistemic good. So, for example, on this picture the epistemic value of an epistemic standing like justification is to be understood purely instrumentally relative to the fundamental epistemic good of true belief. That is, justification is epistemically valuable, but only because it is a means to true belief; it is not, unlike true belief, epistemically valuable in its own right.[12]

I take it that many epistemologists would be attracted to epistemic value T-monism, at least pre-theoretically (i.e. independently of considering any problems that a commitment to this thesis would generate). Indeed, one might go so far as to hold that it is a mere truism that the ultimate epistemic good just is the good of true belief, and hence that all other epistemic goods must be understood relative to this ultimate epistemic good. Epistemic value T-monism is clearly an immediate consequence of a picture of epistemic value of this sort.

So why does the swamping problem presuppose epistemic value T-monism? The key point in this regard is that the setting up of the problem demands that whatever epistemic value is contributed by the epistemic standing in question—reliability, justification, etc.—that value is only instrumental epistemic value relative to the further good of true belief. Moreover, since the swamping argument is meant to be a decisive strike against the greater epistemic value of knowledge over mere true belief, it is clearly being presupposed here that the additional value cannot be generated in any further fashion, and thus it is being taken for granted that the conception of epistemic value at issue is a monistic one regarding the value of true belief. In effect, then, the claim made by the swamping problem is that with this conception of epistemic value in play, it follows that knowledge cannot be more valuable than mere true belief.

---

[11] Note that sometimes this view is expressed in terms of the thesis that it is *truth* (rather than true belief) which is the only ultimate fundamental epistemic good (see e.g. Kvanvig 2003: ch. 2). The difference between these two views is complex and raises some subtle questions. However, since nothing is lost for our purposes by focusing on the version of epistemic value T-monism set out here, I will ignore this complication in what follows.

[12] Given that this is a monistic proposal, the epistemic value of true belief must *always* be non-instrumental.

More formally, we can express the swamping argument in terms of an inconsistent triad of claims. The first claim is just the thesis of epistemic value T-monism, which we will for convenience rephrase as (1):

(1) The epistemic value conferred on a belief by that belief having an epistemic property is instrumental epistemic value relative to the further epistemic good of true belief.[13]

The second claim is the general thesis about value that we noted in §1.3:

(2) If the value of X is only instrumental value relative to a further good and that good is already present, then it can confer no additional value.

The difficulty posed by the swamping problem, however, is that (1) and (2) entail that there cannot be an epistemic standing which is epistemically more valuable than mere true belief. After all, whatever epistemic value an epistemic standing contributes could only, given (1), be instrumental epistemic value relative to the epistemic good of true belief. But (2) makes clear that this value gets swamped by the value of true belief. Thus, there can never be a true belief which, in virtue of possessing an epistemic property, is epistemically more valuable than a corresponding mere true belief.

In order to get our inconsistent triad, then, all we require is a thesis to the effect that there is an epistemic standing that is at least sometimes epistemically more valuable than mere true belief. For the sake of simplicity, we will here focus on the epistemic standing of knowledge, since as I noted above we have the strong intuition that knowledge is more valuable than mere true belief. We thus get (3):

(3) Knowledge that p is sometimes more epistemically valuable than mere true belief that p.

In short, then, (1), (2), and (3) are jointly inconsistent because it straightforwardly follows from (1) and (2) that (3) is false. Thus, if we accept (1) and (2), we are thereby committed to the denial of (3). Given that this is an inconsistent triad, it follows that one must reject one of the claims that make up this triad.

Now that we have more clearly set out the swamping problem, it should be easier to see that the challenge it poses differs from the superficially similar challenge at issue in the primary value problem as we formulated it above. For while the latter poses a general problem about how knowledge is more

---

[13] Clearly I am here taking truth not to be an epistemic property of one's beliefs. If one wishes to think of truth as an epistemic property of belief, then one should reformulate this claim accordingly.

valuable than mere true belief, the swamping problem instead issues in a far more restricted difficulty, one that is focused specifically on epistemic value and which, as a result, should not be considered, at least not without qualification, to simply be a variant on the primary value problem. As we noted in §1.3, one could answer the primary value problem by appealing to the greater practical value of knowledge over mere true belief. Given that the swamping problem is explicitly expressed in terms of epistemic value, however, the issue of whether this approach to the primary value problem can be extended to the swamping problem—i.e. the practical response—is clearly moot. At the very least, one would need to supplement this proposal in some way to make it effective for both value problems.

With this point in mind, we can now consider the question of how one should go about responding to this problem.

1.6. Responding to the Swamping Problem I: The Practical Response

One option, of course, is just to reject the general claim about value expressed as (2). Unfortunately, I can see no way of objecting to this claim, nor am I aware of any good objections to this thesis in the literature (typically, responses to the swamping argument in effect focus on other elements of the argument than this claim). Accordingly, in what follows I am going to take this thesis for granted and focus instead on the status of the other two members of this triad, since this is where I think the real promise of responding to this problem lies.

Let me start with the option of denying (3).[14] This will be the strategy favoured by the proponent of the practical response to the swamping problem that we described at the end of §1.3. We have just noted that merely arguing for the greater practical value of knowledge over mere true belief would not in itself engage with the swamping problem, since the issue at hand specifically concerns epistemic value. However, although this point by itself does not gain any purchase on the swamping problem, it may be possible to supplement this claim in such a way that it does have an impact. In particular, if one wished to respond to the swamping problem by denying (3), then one might use this

---

[14] This view has been expressed to me in conversation by both Michael Lynch and Mike Ridge. See also Petersen (2008). Kvanvig (2003) could also be read as responding to the swamping problem by denying (3). As I note below, however, I think that ultimately he is best read as rejecting (1).

claim as part of a diagnostic story about why we tend to suppose that (3) is true. On this view, the greater practical value of knowledge over mere true belief—a non-epistemic value which, accordingly, cannot be swamped by the value of true belief—is meant to account for our initial conviction that (3) is true. The idea is that once we make the distinction between practical and specifically epistemic value clear—and once, in addition, we realize that knowledge is of greater practical value when compared with mere true belief—we are meant to see that there is no harm in denying (3). Moreover, there is a key advantage of this approach, in that by denying (3) the swamping problem is completely blocked and hence one is free, on this score at least, to endorse epistemic value T-monism.

We thus get the practical response to the swamping problem whereby one responds to the swamping problem by arguing that if this problem is indeed specifically focused on epistemic value then that in itself should serve to undermine its plausibility, in that so long as knowledge is generally practically more valuable than mere true belief then it is harmless to concede that knowledge is not epistemically more valuable than mere true belief. Indeed, one might go so far as to maintain that to insist on epistemic value in the absence of practical value in this way is to succumb to a kind of theoretical fetishism. Is this view sustainable?

In order to evaluate the merits of this position, it is worth first reflecting on just how weak (3) is—it merely holds that knowledge is *sometimes* of greater epistemic value than mere true belief. Given the weakness of this claim, to deny it is to endorse a very strong thesis: that knowledge is *never* of greater epistemic value than mere true belief. Indeed, recall that our focus on knowledge was arbitrary, in that we could have easily focused on *any* epistemic standing. More generally, then, the detractor of (3) has to argue that *no* epistemic standing is *ever* of greater epistemic value relative to true belief. This is strong stuff indeed.

Nevertheless, the proponent of this strategy will no doubt be prepared to accept this consequence of their position. Of course, in order for their view to be plausible it will be essential that they are able to offer an adequate response to the more general primary value problem which we outlined in §1.2. After all, it is only if knowledge is indeed of greater practical value when compared with mere true belief that the proponent of this response to the swamping problem can offer her crucial diagnostic story of why we might (wrongly) be initially inclined to regard (3) as true. Still, as we saw in §1.1, it is plausible to hold that such a story is forthcoming.

Interestingly, note that the revisionism of the proposal does not end with the denial of (3), since the proponent of this view must also argue that the tertiary value problem is a pseudo-problem. Recall that the tertiary value problem demands an explanation of why knowledge is more valuable, not merely as a matter of degree but of kind, than that which falls short of knowledge, and we noted in §1.2 that this meant that knowledge, unlike that which falls short of knowledge, must be of final value. Recall, however, that we also noted above that if knowledge has final value then it follows that it is a fundamental epistemic good. Hence the thesis that knowledge has final value is inconsistent with epistemic value T-monism. It follows that the defender of the practical response to the swamping problem must regard knowledge as lacking in final value, and hence must reject the intuitions that led to the tertiary value problem.

Will the proponent of the practical response be troubled by this? I suspect not. For their view is meant to be a 'de-mystifying' stance which can extend even to the tertiary value problem. That is, they will argue that just as we can be tempted into thinking that knowledge has greater epistemic value than mere true belief because we confuse practical value with epistemic value, so we can be tempted into thinking that knowledge has final value by reifying the practical value that it possesses.

Rather than engage with this proposal directly, I want to instead explore the relative plausibility of alternative proposals. For if an alternative response to the swamping problem is available—one that is compatible with a positive answer to the tertiary value problem—then this would go a long way towards mitigating the attraction of this view. Given that one accepts (2) and (3), the only remaining alternative is to deny (1).

1.7. Responding to the Swamping Problem II: The Monistic Response

Interestingly, there are two very different ways of denying (1). In particular, while any response to the swamping problem which denied (1) would be committed to denying epistemic value T-monism, it does not follow that in denying this thesis one is thereby endorsing epistemic pluralism.

The reason for this is that there are different ways of being an epistemic value monist than being a T-monist. Consider, for example, someone like Timothy Williamson (e.g. 2000), who has explicitly argued for what he calls a 'knowledge-first' epistemology. Although (as far as I am aware), he has not endorsed such a view in print, presumably he would be very attracted, given his wider epistemological views, to an epistemic value monism of the following form:

Epistemic Value K-Monism
Knowledge is the sole fundamental epistemic good.

According to this view, there is only one fundamental epistemic good and that is knowledge, which means that the value of all other epistemic goods is to be understood along instrumental lines relative to this fundamental good.

On this view, there is no reason to assent to (1), and thus the argument cannot even get started. Moreover, notice that one cannot run a swamping argument against this view. For what is crucial to the swamping argument described above is that we are comparing mere true belief with a more elevated epistemic standing, and asking the question of why the latter epistemic standing should be epistemically more valuable. With epistemic value K-monism in play, however, the question of why knowledge is more valuable than mere true belief has a straightforward answer: because knowledge, unlike mere true belief, is a fundamental epistemic good. Call this response to the swamping problem the *monistic response*.

In order to motivate such a position one would need to give it the further theoretical support that it requires. That is, one would need to re-examine the intuitions that drive epistemologists to commit themselves to epistemic value T-monism and offer an alternative diagnosis of what is going on here. More generally, insofar as epistemic value K-monism is wedded to a knowledge-first epistemology, then it will represent a far more revisionary approach to our contemporary thinking about epistemology. That said, of course, perhaps such revisionism is required, in which case one should not shirk from it.

Indeed, notice that taking this line might also enable one to make some progress with the value problem more generally. For one thing, if knowledge is the sole fundamental epistemic value then one might plausibly contend that one can resolve the secondary value problem, and thereby the primary value problem, on account of how on this view it follows immediately that knowledge is of greater epistemic value than any epistemic standing that falls short of knowledge. Given the plausible additional claim that no lesser epistemic standing is of greater non-epistemic (e.g. practical) value than knowledge, then the secondary problem is completely neutralized.

What about the tertiary value problem? Here matters are not so clear. We noted earlier that it does not follow from the fact that an epistemic good is fundamental that it is thereby of final value. Given that demonstrating that knowledge has final value is key to answering the tertiary value problem, it follows that one will need to do more to answer the tertiary value problem than simply defend epistemic value K-monism. If this further argumentation is not forthcoming, then it would be incumbent upon the proponent of the monistic response to explain why the tertiary value problem need not be answered.

1.8. Responding to the Swamping Problem III: The Pluralist Response

The only remaining option available to us is to deny claim (1) not by advancing a distinct form of epistemic value monism but rather by advocating an appropriate form of epistemic value pluralism.

To begin with, notice that simply opting for a form of epistemic value pluralism might not be enough by itself to rescue our intuition that knowledge is at least sometimes epistemically more valuable than mere true belief. Consider, for example, a form of epistemic value pluralism which maintained that both true belief and a further epistemic property—let's call it 'X'—are fundamental epistemic goods. Simply arguing for such a position would not, however, be enough to ensure the truth of (3). After all, suppose that it were the case that, necessarily, when one knows a proposition, one's belief *cannot* exhibit the target epistemic property, X. Although this may be unlikely, this doesn't seem to be a possibility that we can rule out in advance *a priori*, since it depends upon one's wider epistemological commitments (in particular, what theory of knowledge one endorses). If this were the case, however, then clearly that X is an epistemic property which, in addition to true belief, is fundamentally epistemically valuable would not suffice to ensure that knowledge is sometimes epistemically more valuable than mere true belief, and hence (3) would still be in question. The whole point of denying (1) in the face of this inconsistent triad, however, is surely so that one is able to consistently endorse (2) and (3).

Accordingly, what is required of this strategy is some way of denying (1) so that (3) gets the support that it requires. In particular, what is needed is a form of epistemic value pluralism which can account for why knowledge is sometimes of greater epistemic value than mere true belief by appeal to the fact that knowledge, in addition to true belief, is of fundamental epistemic value.[15] Call this the *pluralist response* to the swamping problem.

---

[15] Note that one might further claim that there are other epistemic standings which are of fundamental epistemic value. Since what is crucial to the view (*qua* response to the swamping problem at least) is only that knowledge and true belief are fundamental epistemic goods, I will set this complication to one side in what follows.

Consider, for example, the kind of epistemic value pluralism endorsed by Kvanvig (e.g. 2003). Kvanvig argues that there are several fundamental epistemic goods other than true belief, the chief example that he offers in this respect being understanding. Interestingly, however, Kvanvig does not offer his epistemic value pluralism as a means of rescuing the intuition that knowledge is epistemically more valuable than mere true belief, since he instead uses the swamping argument to demonstrate that we are mistaken in thinking that knowledge is a particularly valuable epistemic standing, as opposed to understanding. Accordingly, it would seem that Kvanvig responds to our inconsistent triad by rejecting *both* (1) and (3).[16]

I don't think that this can be the full story, however, for while Kvanvig argues that understanding is not a species of knowledge, he does not argue for the stronger claim that it is *never* the case that when one knows a proposition one's true belief also has the relevant epistemic property of understanding. Indeed, although the details of his view are too involved to be usefully expounded here—we will be discussing understanding more fully in Chapter 4—his conception of understanding and its relationship to knowledge in fact strongly suggests that it is quite often the case that when one has what he calls 'propositional' understanding, one will also have knowledge of the corresponding proposition.[17] If this is right, though, then Kvanvig ought to be willing to accept (3) after all, and thereby accept that knowledge is at least sometimes epistemically more valuable than mere true belief, since in those cases where knowledge and understanding coincide, the known true belief in question will have an epistemic value which is greater than the epistemic value of the corresponding mere true belief. The ultimate problem posed by the swamping argument on Kvanvig's view, then, is thus not for (3) at all, but rather for epistemic value T-monism (i.e. (1)).

Nevertheless, I think that Kvanvig is on to something here when he seems to, in effect, treat the swamping argument as ultimately undermining both (1) and (3). For suppose that one argues for the negation of (1) by appeal to a form of epistemic value pluralism which treats knowledge as sometimes

---

[16] Of course, evaluations of this sort are inevitably moot, given that Kvanvig wasn't responding to the swamping problem in the specific form that is presented here. What follows should be read with this caveat in mind.

[17] For example, consider one's true belief that one's house burned down because of faulty wiring. It seems entirely plausible that it could be the case that this belief both has the epistemic property of knowledge and the epistemic property of understanding (i.e. that one both knows and understands that one's house burned down because of faulty wiring). As just noted, we will be discussing understanding more fully in Chapter 4. In the meantime, for more on Kvanvig's conception of understanding, see Grimm (2006), Brogaard (2007b), Elgin (2009), Kvanvig (2009), and Pritchard (2008c; forthcoming c); for more on the notion of understanding more generally, see Zagzebski (2001) and Riggs (2003).

epistemically more valuable than mere true belief because of the fundamental epistemic value of an epistemic property which is only sometimes present when one has knowledge (such as understanding). Indeed, just to make this point particularly vivid, suppose that one argues for the negation of (1) by appeal to a form of epistemic value pluralism which treats knowledge as *always* epistemically more valuable than mere true belief because of the fundamental epistemic value of an epistemic property which is *always* present when one has knowledge, even though it is not sufficient, with true belief, for knowledge (i.e. the epistemic property in question is merely necessary for knowledge). Would we regard such a stance as demonstrating that knowledge has the kind of epistemic value that we typically suppose it to have?

I think not. In order to see this, notice that part of what is at issue in the wider debate about epistemic value is the central role that knowledge plays in epistemological enquiry. If it were to turn out, however, that knowledge is only of greater epistemic value than mere true belief because of the greater epistemic value of a necessary component of knowledge (still less, a non-necessary component), then that would surely threaten the central role that knowledge plays in epistemological theorizing almost as much as the claim that knowledge is *never* of greater epistemic value than mere true belief. After all, why should we now care whether we have knowledge, specifically, rather than just true belief plus the extra fundamentally valuable epistemic property? (The observant reader will spot that this is essentially a variant of the secondary value problem outlined in §1.2 as applied to the specific issue of epistemic value raised by the swamping problem.)

Ideally, then, what we want is a defence of (3) which is able to support our wider intuition that knowledge is worthy of the central focus that it enjoys in epistemological theorizing. The most straightforward way of doing this within the model of epistemic pluralism would simply be to argue that knowledge is itself a fundamental epistemic value, in addition to the fundamental epistemic good of true belief. The trouble with this suggestion, however, is that once one grants that true belief is a fundamental epistemic good then it is hard to see why knowledge should in addition be a fundamental epistemic value also, rather than being an epistemic standing which is instrumentally epistemically valuable relative to the epistemic good of true belief.

Moreover, the point raised earlier against epistemic value K-monism that the fundamental epistemic good in question needs to have final value if this response to the swamping problem is to extend to the value problem more generally is equally applicable here. For if the greater value of knowledge turns out to ultimately just be a greater non-epistemic instrumental value, then the pluralist response to the swamping problem will not extend to the tertiary value problem. Conversely, however, if one could show that knowledge is finally valuable, then one would thereby have shown that knowledge is fundamentally epistemically valuable as well.[18]

So if one wishes to extend the pluralist response to the swamping problem to the tertiary value problem, it is essential that one is able to demonstrate that knowledge is not only fundamentally epistemically valuable but also finally valuable. Alternatively, if such additional argumentation is not forthcoming, then it will be incumbent upon the proponent of the pluralist response to explain away the tertiary value problem—i.e. demonstrate that this is a pseudo-problem that does not require a response.[19]

1.9. Concluding Remarks

In this chapter we have examined the value problem for knowledge: the problem of accounting for the distinctive value of knowledge. We have found that there are three 'levels' of response required in this regard. The primary value problem demands that one show that knowledge is more valuable than mere true belief. The secondary value problem demands that one show that knowledge is more valuable than that which falls short of knowledge. And finally the tertiary value problem demands that one show that knowledge is more valuable than that which falls short of knowledge not merely as a matter of degree but of kind. We argued that any adequate response to the tertiary value problem must be able to defend the claim that knowledge has final value.

In addition, we also examined a problem concerning the value of knowledge which is superficially similar to the primary value problem—viz., the swamping problem. As we saw, this problem in effect arises from the fact that three highly intuitive claims are collectively inconsistent. These claims are: (1) epistemic value monism regarding true belief (epistemic value T-monism); (2) a general claim about value; and (3) the thesis that knowledge is at least sometimes of greater epistemic value than mere true belief.

We found that there are three prima facie plausible responses to the swamping problem. The first—the practical response—appeals to the practical value of knowledge in order to explain why knowledge is not epistemically more

---

[18] For further discussion of the idea that final value is relevant to our understanding of the swamping problem, see Brogaard (2007a) and Pritchard (2007b; 2007d; 2009; forthcoming c; forthcoming e). A precursor to this approach can be found in Percival (2003).

[19] For more on the debate between epistemic value pluralists and epistemic value T-monists, see the exchange between David (2005) and Kvanvig (2005).

valuable than mere true belief after all. This view is entirely compatible with epistemic value T-monism. The other two responses, in contrast, maintain that knowledge is a fundamental epistemic good and hence reject epistemic value T-monism. The first approach—the monistic response—argues that knowledge is the only fundamental epistemic good, and hence blocks the swamping problem by appeal to a different form of epistemic value monism (epistemic value K-monism). The second approach—the pluralist response—instead puts forward a form of epistemic value pluralism which holds that both knowledge and true belief are fundamental epistemic goods.

We noted that the swamping problem poses a distinct problem to the value problem for knowledge. Indeed, it poses a distinct problem even when compared to the primary value problem for knowledge. Since ideally we want an account of the value of knowledge that can deal with both difficulties, it is thus incumbent upon us to consider how a response to the one problem bears on the other problem. In particular, since any response to the value problem for knowledge requires us to defend the thesis that knowledge is finally valuable, we need to consider how the three responses to the swamping problem would fit with this claim.

Interestingly, we noted that the practical response to the swamping problem is incompatible with the thesis that knowledge is finally valuable, and hence must regard the tertiary value problem as a pseudo-problem. In contrast, the monistic and pluralist responses to the swamping problem are compatible with the final value of knowledge. Thus, if one can show that knowledge is finally valuable, then this would put these two views at an advantage when compared with the practical response. Conversely, if it were to turn out that knowledge is not finally valuable, then the practical response to the swamping problem could not be faulted on account of its inability to deal with the tertiary value problem.

The central question raised by this chapter is thus whether knowledge is finally valuable, and this question will be the concern of the next chapter.[20]

---

[20] For a recent survey of research on both the value problem for knowledge and the swamping problem, see Pritchard (2007b; cf. Pritchard 2007d). See also Baehr (2009) and Pritchard (forthcoming d; forthcoming e).

2

Knowledge and Final Value

2.1. Introduction

We saw in the last chapter that in order to answer the value problem we need to explain why knowledge is more valuable, not only as a matter of degree but also as a matter of kind, than any epistemic standing that falls short of knowledge. We noted that offering such an explanation requires us to explain why knowledge, unlike that which falls short of knowledge, has *final* value. Moreover, we saw that if one could account for the final value of knowledge then one would thereby have a resolution to the swamping problem as well (in the form of either a monistic or pluralist response to this difficulty). The goal of this chapter is to examine the best—indeed, the *only*—response to the value problem in the contemporary literature which proceeds by arguing that knowledge has final value. As we will see, this response to the value problem is ultimately unsuccessful, though the failure of this account of epistemic value highlights some important epistemological morals, both as regards the problem of epistemic value and also regarding the very project of understanding knowledge.

2.2. Robust Virtue Epistemology

The account of knowledge which has the best shot at accounting for the final value of knowledge is a type of virtue epistemology, what I will refer to as a *robust* virtue epistemology. This is the sort of virtue theoretic account of knowledge that is offered by, for example, Ernest Sosa (1988; 1991; 2007), Linda Zagzebski (1996; 1999), and John Greco (e.g. 2003; 2007a; 2007b; 2009). What makes such a virtue-theoretic proposal robust is the fact that it attempts to exclusively analyse knowledge in terms of a true belief that is the product of epistemically virtuous belief-forming process.

The big attraction of virtue-theoretic accounts of knowledge is that they capture our strong intuition that knowledge is the product of one's reliable cognitive abilities.[1] A true belief that is gained in a way that is completely unconnected with one's cognitive abilities, even if that belief is reliably formed or would count as justified by the lights of certain conceptions of justification, just would not count as knowledge. We will explore the motivation for virtue epistemology in greater detail in the next chapter (and also examine some specific cases that lend support for the view). For now, however, this rather schematic presentation of the view will suffice, even though it glosses over the many important differences between different types of virtue epistemic proposal (for example, depending on what one builds into one's conception of an epistemic virtue, one will be led to adopt a very different kind of virtue epistemology). As we will see in a moment, we do not need to worry about the specifics of different robust virtue-theoretic accounts, since what is salient for our purposes is simply the *structure* of these proposals.

On the face of it, robust virtue epistemology does not look particularly promising because of the difficulty of specifying the virtue-theoretic condition on knowledge in such a way as to deal with the problem of knowledge-undermining epistemic luck—e.g. of the sort found in Gettier-style cases. After all, no matter how reliable an epistemic virtue might be, it seems possible that it could generate a belief which is only true as a matter of luck.

Consider, for example, the case of 'Roddy'.[2] Using his highly reliable cognitive faculties, Roddy the shepherd forms a true belief that there is a sheep in the field that he is looking at. Unbeknownst to Roddy, however, the item that he is looking at in the field is not a sheep at all, but rather a sheep-shaped object—a rock, say—albeit one which is obscuring from view a genuine sheep that is hidden behind (and which ensures that his belief is true). Here, then, we appear to have a true belief that is the product of the agent's epistemic virtue and yet which does not qualify as knowledge because of the presence of knowledge-undermining epistemic luck.

With cases like this in mind, one might naturally be tempted to opt for a *modest* virtue epistemology, one that does not try to completely analyse knowledge in terms of a virtue-theoretic condition but which is instead willing to endorse in addition a further codicil that can deal with Gettier-style cases.[3]

In contrast, robust virtue epistemology attempts to get around this problem by, in effect, 'beefing-up' the virtue-theoretic demand on knowledge. Rather than allowing that knowledge is merely true belief that arises out of the agent's

---

[1] Note that henceforth I will take it as given that a genuine cognitive ability is reliable.

[2] This example is adapted from one offered by Chisholm (1977: 105).

[3] For example, in early work, Greco (1999; 2000) took just this line. As we will see in a moment, these days he advocates a robust form of virtue epistemology.

cognitive abilities—which, as we have just seen, is compatible with Gettier-style cases—the strengthened virtue-theoretic thesis is that knowledge only results when the agent's true belief is *because of* the operation of her cognitive abilities.

How are we to read the 'because of' relation here? There is as yet no consensus amongst robust virtue epistemologists on this score, but the most developed view in the literature in this regard—due to Greco (2007*a*; 2007*b*)—takes the causal explanatory line that a true belief is because of an agent's cognitive abilities when it is *primarily* creditable to the agent that her belief is true.[4] Although this way of reading the because of relation does generate some surprising results, we will set these potential problems to one side in order to give the account the best run for its money.[5]

So construed, this strengthened proposal certainly deals with the case of Roddy, since while his true belief is indeed produced by his cognitive abilities, it is not the case that his belief is true *because of the operation of* his cognitive abilities in the relevant sense, since we would not count his true belief as being primarily creditable to his cognitive abilities. Instead, his belief is true because of a helpful quirk of the environment—that there happened to be a sheep behind the sheep-shaped object that he was looking at. In contrast, had he actually been looking at a sheep (in normal circumstances), then his belief *would* have been true because of the operation of his cognitive abilities. Moreover, what goes for Roddy will intuitively also go for other Gettier-style cases, since they each share the same relevant properties (i.e. the cognitive success in question is not properly attributable to the agent's cognitive abilities, but rather to some other factor outwith our hero's cognitive agency).

It seems, then, that robust virtue epistemology may well have the resources to deal with the kind of knowledge-undermining epistemic luck in play in Gettier-style cases. If that is right, then there is no need to add a codicil to

---

[4] Those familiar with the literature in this respect will recognize that often virtue epistemologists like Greco (e.g. 2003) make a stronger claim in this regard. That is, they do not simply argue that the true belief in question is primarily creditable to the knowing agent but also that it is *of credit* to the knowing agent that she believes truly (i.e. that she is deserving of some sort of praise, at least when assessed from a purely epistemic point of view). I think this is a mistake, and I explain why in §2.4.

[5] One surprising consequence—noted in Greco (2007*b*; 2008*a*)—is that robust virtue epistemology becomes committed to a kind of attributer contextualism due to the context-sensitivity of causal explanations. As it happens, Greco welcomes this result, but as I have argued elsewhere—e.g. Pritchard (2008*b*)—he is unwise to do so. But if one does not analyse the because of relation in causal explanatory terms, then what are the alternatives? This is unclear. Zagzebski (e.g. 1999) ultimately treats this relation as a primitive, though she notes that a good approximation is the sensitivity principle (i.e. if the proposition believed had not been true then the agent would not have believed it). Perhaps the best alternative account on offer is that put forward by Sosa (2007), who argues that we should think of the relation in terms of the exercise of a power. For further discussion of Sosa's proposal, see n. 21.

one's virtue-theoretic account of knowledge in order to make it Gettier-proof. From a theoretical point of view this is very satisfying, since having such a codicil in one's account of knowledge looks ad hoc. Why should knowledge have this structure such that the virtue-theoretic component captures almost all the cases, but not quite? Robust virtue epistemology thus appears to have a lot going for it.

2.3. Knowledge and Achievement

As Greco (2009) points out, a further advantage of understanding knowledge along robust virtue-theoretic lines is that it seems to capture the idea of knowledge as being a kind of cognitive achievement. That is, we might broadly think of achievements as being successes that are because of one's ability (i.e. primarily creditable to the exercise of one's ability), and virtue epistemology seems to be offering the epistemic analogue of this claim—on this view, knowledge is cognitive success that is because of one's cognitive ability. As we will see, that knowledge turns out to be a type of achievement on this view is key to its defence of the final value of knowledge.

In order to see the plausibility of this general account of achievement, consider the following case. Suppose that our hero—let's call him 'Archie'—selects a target at random and uses his bow to fire an arrow at that target with the intention of hitting it. Suppose further that he does indeed hit the target. If, however, the success in question is purely a matter of luck—if, for example, Archie does not possess the relevant archery abilities—then we would say that this success is not an achievement on Archie's part. Similarly, even if Archie has the relevant archery abilities and is in addition successful in hitting the target, we still wouldn't count his success as an achievement if the success was not *because of* Archie's archery abilities (i.e. where his success is not primarily creditable to his archery abilities but rather to some further factor).

This is important because of the possibility that the success in question is 'Gettierized'. If, for example, a dog ran on to the range and grabbed the arrow (which was heading towards the target) in mid-flight and proceeded to deposit it on the target, then we would not regard this successful outcome as Archie's achievement, even if the original firing of the arrow had been highly skilful. Instead, what is required for an achievement is that Archie's hitting of the target is *because of* the exercise of his relevant archery abilities, where this means that his success is primarily creditable to his abilities rather than to some factor independent of his abilities. Call this the *achievement* thesis.

There are some prima facie problems with the achievement thesis. In particular, there are grounds for thinking that as it stands it is too permissive. After all, we tend to think of achievements in such a way that they involve the overcoming of an obstacle of some sort, and yet it seems consistent with the achievement thesis that the mere success-through-agency at issue in this thesis need involve nothing of the sort. Relatedly, it seems an essential part of achievements that they involve certain motivational states on the part of the subject with regard to the success in question—in particular, that the subject is actively seeking to bring this success about. But since the achievement thesis makes no mention of such motivational states, it seems to allow that achievements could be entirely passive. More generally, the problem is that the achievement thesis seems to count as achievements successes which are just too easy to legitimately fall into this category.

We will come back to the problem of easy achievements in Chapter 4, since it raises issues that are not directly relevant to our present concerns. For now, we will take it that the achievement thesis is on roughly the right lines in order to give the robust virtue epistemologist's argument for the final value of knowledge the best run for its money. What is important for our present purposes is that if this account of achievement is right then it follows that knowledge, by the lights of the robust virtue epistemologist at any rate, is just a specifically cognitive type of achievement. That is, achievements are successes that are because of ability, and yet knowledge, according to the robust virtue epistemologist, is just cognitive success (i.e. true belief) that is because of cognitive ability (i.e. epistemic virtue, broadly conceived). The achievement thesis when combined with robust virtue epistemology thus entails the claim that knowledge is a type of achievement, what we will call the *knowledge-as-achievement* thesis, or KA for short.

The reason why the KA thesis is important for our purposes is because achievements are, plausibly, distinctively valuable. More specifically, it is plausible to hold that the kind of successes that count as achievements are valuable for their own sake because of how they are produced (i.e. they are finally valuable because of their relational properties). If this is right, and we can show that knowledge (unlike that which falls short of knowledge) is a type of achievement, then we may be in a position to thereby show that knowledge has a kind of value—final value—which that which falls short of knowledge lacks, and hence show that it is distinctively valuable.[6]

---

[6] While epistemic virtue theorists are aware that they may be able to account for the distinctive value of knowledge by appeal to the value of an achievement, they unfortunately mis-characterize the kind of value in question, since they hold that it is *intrinsic value* rather than final value that is at

In order to see why achievements might be thought to be finally valuable, consider again the case of 'Archie'. This time, though, suppose that Archie—in the manner of Robin Hood—is trying to escape from an adversary and the target he is firing at is a mechanism which will drop the drawbridge in front him, thereby ensuring that he gets to safety. From a practical point of view, it may not matter whether the hitting of the target is because of Archie's archery abilities or through dumb luck (e.g. by a lucky deflection). Either way, it still results in the dropping of the drawbridge, thereby enabling Archie to escape. Nevertheless, we would value Archie's success very differently if it were the product of luck (even when the relevant ability is involved, but the success in question is 'Gettierized'), rather than it being because of his ability such that it is an achievement. In particular, we would regard Archie's achievement of hitting the target through ability as, in this respect, a good thing in its own right, regardless of what other instrumental value it may accrue.

Moreover, what goes here for Archie's achievement of hitting the target seems to be equally applicable to achievements more generally: achievements are finally valuable. Imagine, for example, that you are about to undertake a course of action designed to attain a certain outcome and that you are given the choice between merely being successful in what you set out to do, and being successful in such a way that you exhibit an achievement. Suppose further that it is stipulated in advance that there are no practical costs or benefits to choosing either way. Even so, wouldn't you prefer to exhibit an achievement? And wouldn't you be right to do so? If that is correct, then this is strong evidence for the final value of achievements.

Indeed, that achievements are valuable in this way is hardly surprising, once one reflects that they constitute the exercise of one's agency on the world. A life lacking in such agential power, even if otherwise successful (e.g. one's goals are regularly attained), would clearly be severely impover-ished as a result. A good life is thus, amongst other things, a life rich in

issue. See e.g. Greco (2009: §4). Crucially, however, intrinsic value is not the same as final value. This is because intrinsic value concerns only the value generated by the intrinsic properties of the target item, and yet something can be finally—i.e. non-instrumentally—valuable because of its *relational* (and hence non-intrinsic) properties. Think, for example, of the first book produced on the first ever printing-press. Moreover, it is important to our discussion that we focus on final value rather than intrinsic value, because on the account of the value of knowledge under consideration it is clearly because of the *relational* properties of the true belief in question—i.e. that it is true belief that is skilfully attained—that it constitutes a cognitive achievement and hence on this view accrues a distinctive kind of value. Thus, the additional value that is generated is final value, not intrinsic value. For more on this point see Pritchard (forthcoming *d*: §2). Brogaard (2007*a*) is one commentator who has recognized this point. See also Percival (2003). For two recent, and influential, discussions of the intrinsic value/final value distinction, see Rabinowicz and Roennow-Rasmussen (1999; 2003).

achievement. Call the claim that achievements are finally valuable the *value of achievements* thesis.[7]

Now, if knowledge is simply a type of achievement, and achievements are finally valuable, then it immediately follows that knowledge has final value too. Robust virtue epistemology, when combined with a claim about the nature of achievements (the achievement thesis) and a claim about the final value of achievements (the value of achievements thesis), thus entails the thesis that knowledge has final value. More formally, we can express the reasoning in play here as follows:

From Robust Virtue Epistemology to the Final Value of Knowledge

(P1) Achievements are successes that are because of ability (Achievement thesis);

(P2) knowledge is a cognitive success that is because of cognitive ability (Robust Virtue Epistemology);

(C1) so, knowledge is a cognitive achievement (KA thesis);

(P3) achievements are finally valuable (Value of Achievements thesis);

(C2) so, knowledge has final value.

Since the inferences in play here are clearly valid, if one wishes to object to this argument then one will need to deny one of the premises in play.

Let's start with the two premises concerning achievements more generally, (P1) and (P3). We have already noted that there is a prima facie worry regarding (P1) which concerns 'easy' achievements. In order to give this argument the best run for its money, however, we will let this premise stand for now (we will consider the status of (P1) in more detail in Chapter 4).

That brings us to (P3), the value of achievements thesis. One worry that one might have about this thesis is that some achievements seem to have very little value—or are even *dis*valuable—because, for example, they are pointless or just plain wicked. Are even achievements of this sort of final value? Note, however, that the value of achievements thesis, properly construed, is only that achievements have final value *qua* achievements. This is entirely consistent with the undeniable truth that some achievements may have no practical value, and may even accrue *dis*value, perhaps because of the opportunity cost incurred by seeking the pointless achievement over a more substantive achievement or because of the wicked nature of the achievement in question. Indeed, there may well be situations in which the all-things-considered value of Archie's success of hitting the target when it is due to luck is much

---

[7] I discuss the relevance of achievements to the problem of the meaning of life in Pritchard (forthcoming *a*).

greater than the all-things-considered value of a corresponding success attained because of Archie's ability. It is important to recognize that the value of achievements thesis when properly understood is entirely consistent with this possibility.[8]

This point is also important when it comes to understanding the way in which this thesis that knowledge, *qua* cognitive achievement, accrues final value can help us answer the tertiary value problem. In particular, we need to note that the mere fact that knowledge (unlike that which falls short of knowledge) is, *qua* cognitive achievement, of final value will not necessarily be enough to resolve the tertiary value problem. This is because of the possibility that that which falls short of knowledge is generally of greater non-final value than knowledge. If this were so, then it could still be true that knowledge is generally of less all-things-considered value than that which falls short of knowledge, even granting the fact that knowledge, in contrast to that which falls short of knowledge, is finally valuable. Nevertheless, it is plausible to suppose that knowledge is not generally of *less* instrumental value than that which falls short of knowledge. And with this assumption in play the final value of knowledge would ensure that the tertiary value problem is met and, with it, the primary and secondary value problems too. In what follows we will let this assumption stand.

In any case, while we will reconsider the status of (P3) in more detail in Chapter 4 when we look again at (P1), we have sufficient grounds for taking this premise to be well founded. This leaves only (P2), which is the robust virtue epistemological account of knowledge itself. As we will see in a moment, this thesis faces some fairly severe problems. Primarily, we will be arguing against this claim by showing that the KA thesis (i.e. (C1)) that it (along with (P1)) generates is false. Ultimately, however, the way that we will be arguing against (C1) should leave no one in any doubt that whatever other difficulties the other premises in this argument might face, it is (P2) that is the key weak link in the robust virtue epistemologist's argument for the final value of knowledge. As a result, this argument fails to demonstrate its conclusion (C2).

---

[8] An alternative way of dealing with this problem would be to argue that it can be in the nature of something to be finally valuable even though sometimes it isn't. For example, one might argue that pleasure is in its nature finally valuable even though some pleasures (i.e. the 'bad' ones) lack final value. According to this proposal, then, it would be in the nature of achievements to be finally valuable even though some of them (i.e. the wicked or trivial ones) lack final value. I am grateful to Mike Ridge for this suggestion.

2.4. Interlude: Is Robust Virtue Epistemology a Reductive Theory of Knowledge?

We noted in the last chapter in our discussion of the swamping problem that there are two prima facie plausible responses to that problem which are consistent with the final value of knowledge. What is key to both responses is that they reject the epistemic value T-monism that is essential to the setting up of the swamping problem and argue instead that knowledge is a fundamental epistemic good. The first proposal (the monistic response) advances a form of epistemic value monism—epistemic value K-monism—which treats knowledge as the only fundamental epistemic good. The second proposal (the pluralist response) is a form of epistemic value pluralism which treats knowledge as a fundamental epistemic good in addition to true belief

We noted in the last chapter that if knowledge is finally valuable then it thereby follows that it is a fundamental epistemic good. As a result, if the robust virtue epistemic defence of the final value of knowledge is successful, then it will on the face of it lend support to *both* of these responses to the swamping problem. (It will also constitute a decisive strike against the third response to the swamping problem that we considered—the practical response—since this was inconsistent with the final value of knowledge.) This raises the question of whether the robust virtue epistemic account of knowledge is more naturally allied with one of these responses to the swamping problem over the other.

In order to answer this question, we need to decide whether robust virtue epistemology offers a reductive account of knowledge. That is, is the proposal meant to 'decompose' knowledge into constituent parts which can be understood independently of knowledge? The reason why this question is important in this regard is that we saw in the last chapter that epistemic value K-monism is naturally wedded to a 'knowledge-first' account of knowledge whereby knowledge is treated as a primitive relative to which other epistemic standings are defined (rather than vice versa, as is the case with reductive accounts of knowledge). This is not to suggest that it would be in principle incoherent to advance epistemic value K-monism while nevertheless endorsing a reductive account of knowledge. The point is rather that if one does not already accept knowledge-first epistemology then it is unclear where the motivation for this form of epistemic value monism comes from.

I take it that most, if not all, robust virtue epistemologists regard their account of knowledge as a reductive account, and this certainly seems the default reading to take of the view (i.e. the reading that we should take unless we have grounds for the contrary). If that is right, then this response to the value problem is naturally allied to the pluralist response to the swamping problem. Moreover, on the face of it, it does seem right to conceive of robust virtue epistemology in this way. After all, prima facie at least, it does seem possible to define cognitive abilities independently of knowledge—e.g. as, roughly, the stable, reliable, and cognitively integrated belief-forming traits of the agent.

Still, the devil is in the detail, and it certainly might well turn out on closer inspection that ultimately one is unable to define cognitive abilities without making appeal to knowledge. Indeed, in the extreme case, it may turn out that cognitive abilities need to be defined as those belief-forming traits which are knowledge-conducive, and if that is the case then clearly robust virtue epistemology cannot be a reductive theory of knowledge. The robust virtue-theoretic response to the value problem would then be more naturally allied to the monistic response to the swamping problem.

Notice, however, that we do not need to take a stand on this issue here, since either way, so long as the robust virtue epistemological account can demonstrate the final value of knowledge, then it will be in a position to answer both the value problem and the swamping problem. The issue of whether the view constitutes a reductive account of knowledge merely influences what kind of conception of epistemic value is in play. That said, although this issue may not be important for our present purposes, one might still regard this issue as salient in light of broader epistemological concerns. For example, one might for various reasons be antecedently suspicious of reductive accounts of knowledge, and hence regard any view which was committed to such a reduction as being prima facie implausible. It is because of these broader epistemological concerns that I have flagged this issue here.

2.5. Achievement without Knowledge

In any case, despite the surface appeal of the robust virtue epistemologist's argument for the final value of knowledge, it faces some critical problems. In particular, the key concern lies with the intermediate conclusion (C1), the KA thesis. As we will see, this claim is highly problematic on closer inspection. In particular, there are instances of knowledge which do not involve the corresponding cognitive achievement, and there are cognitive achievements which are not also instances of knowledge. Moreover, as we will see, the case against the KA thesis in no way depends on the specific account of achievement in play, and thus although there are two premises involved in the argument for the KA thesis—the achievement thesis (P1), and the robust virtue epistemological account of knowledge (P2)—it is the second premise that is the problem. Crucially, however, without the KA thesis the robust virtue epistemologist's argument for the final value of knowledge will fail to go through. In this section we will be focusing on the left-to-right entailment that makes up the KA thesis—viz., the idea that it is sufficient for knowledge that one exhibit the corresponding cognitive achievement.

Consider again the case of Archie, who selects a target at random from a target-range and then successfully fires an arrow at that target. We noted above that if Archie lacks any kind of archery skill, such that his success is entirely lucky, then we would not count his success as being an achievement. Similarly, even if Archie has plenty of skill at archery but his success is 'Gettierized'—such that it is not *because of* his skill—then we would not count it as an achievement. So far so good.

But now consider a third case, in which Archie again selects a target at random, skilfully fires at this target, and successfully hits it because of his skill. On the account of achievement on the table, his hitting of the target is a genuine achievement. Suppose, however, that unbeknownst to Archie there is a force-field around each of the other targets such that, had he aimed at one of these, he would have missed. It is thus a matter of luck that he is successful, in the sense that he could very easily have not been successful. Notice, however, that luck of this sort does not seem to undermine the thesis that Archie's success is a genuine achievement. Indeed, we would still ascribe an achievement to Archie in this case even despite the luck involved. It is, after all, *because of* his skill that he is successful, even though he could very easily have not been successful in this case. That is, his success in this case is still primarily creditable to his archery abilities, even despite the luck involved in that success.

The problem that cases like this pose for the robust virtue epistemologist is that if we allow Archie's success to count as an achievement, then we seem compelled to treat *cognitive* successes which are relevantly analogous as also being achievements. Given the KA thesis, however, this would mean that we would thereby be compelled to regard the cognitive achievement in question as knowledge, even despite the luck involved.

In order to see why this is a problem for those virtue epistemologists who defend the KA thesis, consider the case of 'Barney', which is structurally analogous to the 'Archie' case. Barney forms a true belief that there is a barn in front of him by using his cognitive abilities. That is, unlike a Gettier-style case—such as the case of 'Roddy' described above—Barney does not make any cognitive error in forming his belief in the way that he does. Accordingly, we would naturally say that Barney's cognitive success is because of his cognitive ability, and so we would, therefore, attribute a cognitive achievement to Barney. That is, his cognitive success in this case is primarily creditable to his cognitive abilities. According to the KA thesis, then, we should also treat Barney as knowing that what he is looking at is a barn. The twist in the tail, however, is that, unbeknownst to Barney, he is in fact in 'barn façade county', where all the other apparent barns are fakes. Intuitively, he does not have knowledge in this case because it is simply a matter of luck that his belief is true.[9]

Cases like that of 'Barney' illustrate that there is a type of knowledge-undermining epistemic luck—what we might call *environmental* epistemic luck—which is distinct from the sort of epistemic luck in play in standard Gettier-style cases like that of 'Roddy'.[10] In particular, the kind of epistemic luck in play in standard Gettier-style cases 'intervenes' between the agent and the fact, albeit in such a way that the agent's belief is true nonetheless (i.e. Roddy is not looking at a sheep at all, even though he reasonably believes that he is, but his belief that there is a sheep in the field is true nonetheless). In contrast, in cases of environmental epistemic luck like that involving Barney, luck of this intervening sort is absent—Barney really does get to see the barn and forms a true belief on this basis—although the epistemically inhospitable nature of the environment ensures that his belief is nevertheless only true as a matter of luck such that he lacks knowledge.

In short, then, robust virtue epistemology is only able to exclude Gettier-style epistemic luck and not also environmental luck. The moral to be drawn is thus that there is sometimes *more* to knowledge than merely a cognitive achievement, contrary to what the robust virtue epistemologist (who defends the KA thesis) argues. That is, there can be cases in which (environmental) knowledge-undermining luck is involved where the luck does not in the process undermine the achievement in question. Merely exhibiting a cognitive achievement will not suffice to exclude all types of knowledge-undermining epistemic luck. Call this the problem of *environmental luck*.

How might the defender of the KA thesis respond to this problem? One response might be to try to evade it by reformulating the achievement thesis, and thus (P1). On the face of it, this might seem like a viable way of dealing

---

[9] This case was originally offered by Goldman (1976), although he credits the example to Carl Ginet.

[10] In Pritchard (2005: ch. 5) I delineate the core kind of knowledge-undermining epistemic luck and label it 'veritic luck'. Both environmental epistemic luck and Gettier-style 'intervening' epistemic luck fall under the more general category of veritic luck.

with this issue since there are, after all, two premises—the achievement thesis (P1), and the robust virtue epistemic account of knowledge (P2)—being used to generate the KA thesis (C1). In order to see why such a strategy would be hopeless, however, we only need to note that the 'Barney' case is a counterexample *both* to the KA thesis and to the more specific robust virtue epistemological claim that knowledge is cognitive success that is because of cognitive ability (i.e. (P2)). After all, it is both true that (i) Barney exhibits a cognitive achievement but does not possess the corresponding knowledge, and that (ii) Barney's cognitive success is because of his cognitive ability and yet he lacks the corresponding knowledge. There may well be good reasons to reformulate the achievement thesis—indeed, we will consider some reasons on this score in Chapter 4—but this issue is by-the-by here, given that however the achievement thesis is formulated a key premise in the robust virtue epistemologist's argument for the final value of knowledge is blocked.

A second response to the problem that is superficially appealing is to argue that abilities need to be understood relative to suitable environments in a far more fine-grained way than we standardly suppose. One could thus argue that neither Archie nor Barney exhibit an achievement in cases where there is environmental luck in play, since contrary to intuition they are not exercising the relevant abilities. Accordingly, the 'Barney' case can pose no problem for the KA thesis.[11]

Now it is undeniable that abilities should be understood relative to suitable environments. In crediting you with the ability to play the piano, for example, we are not thereby supposing that you can play the piano underwater. Even so, I take it that we tend to understand what constitutes a suitable environment in a very coarse-grained fashion. Intuitively, for example, Archie is employing the very same archery ability in the case in which there is environmental luck present as he does in corresponding cases where such luck is absent, and the same point goes for Barney's exercise of his barn-spotting ability in barn façade and corresponding non-barn façade environments.

Still, the proponent of the KA thesis might well extract from the problem of environmental luck the moral that a more fine-grained conception of the relativization of abilities to suitable environments is required in order to deal with this problem. I think this would be a very theory-driven way of responding to the problem of environmental luck, and I also think that it would ultimately generate a very counterintuitive conception of abilities, one

---

[11] This strategy forms a key part of the response to the problem of environmental luck offered by Greco (2007*b*: §5).

that is in the final analysis extremely fine grained indeed.[12] Still, if the proposal worked then this might be a price worth paying in order to have a response to the problem. The key difficulty facing this response to the problem of environmental luck, however, is that it completely fails to understand what the source of this difficulty is.

In order to see this, consider again the ability to play the piano. We noted above that we would not evaluate the possession of such an ability relative to an environment in which the agent is underwater. Whatever ability our agent is exhibiting, or trying to exhibit, in such a case, it is not her ordinary ability to play piano. Imagine, however, that, unbeknownst to our agent, she is in an environment in which she could very easily have been underwater right now but in fact is not. It is thus a matter of luck that she is not presently underwater. (Perhaps, say, she is standing in an empty chamber which in most nearby possible worlds is full of water right now.) While standing there, she sits down at her piano and begins to play. What ability is she exhibiting? Intuitively, the ability on display here is the very ability to play the piano that she exhibits in normal circumstances. After all, although she could very easily be underwater right now, in fact she is not.[13]

The point of this case is that, no matter how fine grained we might want to make the relativization of abilities to suitable environments, we surely do not want to hold that our piano-player is not manifesting her ordinary piano-playing abilities in a case like this. What this demonstrates is that, while it is undoubtedly true that abilities should be understood relative to suitable environments, however that point is to be understood it must be compatible with the fact that it can be a matter of luck that one is in a suitable environment to exercise one's ability in the first place. Critically, however, that is just to allow that the presence of environmental luck is compatible with one exercising one's normal abilities (i.e. the abilities one exercises in corresponding cases which don't involve environmental luck). After all, what is key to cases of environmental luck is that while circumstances were indeed, as it happens, propitious for the exercise of the relevant ability, they could so very easily have not been. Properly understood, then, the issue in hand is not the degree to which abilities should be understood relative to suitable environments, but only whether it is possible for it to be a matter of luck that one is in suitable conditions to exercise one's ability. As we have seen,

---

[12] For more discussion of this point, see Pritchard (2008b; cf. Pritchard 2008f) and Kvanvig (2009).

[13] Moreover, notice that since our agent is unaware of how modally close she is to disaster, it is not as if her awareness of this danger could have a bearing on whether this environment is suited for the exercise of this ability.

it can be, and hence, however one relativizes abilities to suitable conditions, one must allow that environmental luck—and thus environmental *epistemic* luck—is compatible with the exercise of the target ability. Responding to the problem of environmental luck by appeal to the relativization of abilities to suitable environments is thus a theoretical dead-end.[14]

With these options rejected, the prospects for the defender of the KA thesis look somewhat dim. One possibility might be to argue that there is something special about the cognitive achievement at issue in knowledge which ensures that it is resistant to even this type of luck, even though non-cognitive achievements are entirely compatible with this kind of luck. There may be a case that can be made for this, though it will obviously face the charge of being ad hoc. Alternatively, one might simply insist that achievements exclude luck, and thus that we should not, contrary to intuition, treat Archie's success as an achievement when his success is lucky in the relevant fashion. The problem facing this proposal, however, is to explain why our intuitions about achievements are so off-the-mark in this case.[15]

Perhaps the robust virtue epistemologist who wishes to retain the KA thesis could make one of these strategies—or some third strategy, such as denying the intuition that knowledge is incompatible with environmental epistemic luck[16]—stick. I don't think the result would be a happy one, but it is often the case that our theories force us to make awkward theoretical moves in order to save the theory, so the fact that such a move is not all that compelling need not be a decisive count against the view. The more fundamental problem, however, is that there is a further difficulty on the horizon for a view of this sort. Once these two objections for the KA thesis are taken together,

[14] One can strengthen this point by noting that it is in fact incidental to both the 'Archie' and 'Barney' cases that the relevant deception is *actually* occurring in the subject's environment, albeit in such a way that it does not affect the exercise of the target ability. That is, one could re-describe both cases as involving no deception in the actual world but only in most nearby possible worlds and the cases would still demonstrate the same point. Interestingly, Sosa (2007) is one philosopher who has recognized that what is at issue here is the 'fragility' of the exercise of one's abilities (i.e. that it can be a matter of luck that one is in a position to exercise them). His response has been to argue that an agent like Barney *does* have knowledge—i.e. he claims that knowledge is entirely compatible with environmental epistemic luck of this sort. Given the strong intuitions which support the barn façade case, such an approach will inevitably be highly contentious. For further discussion of Sosa's view in this regard, see Pritchard (forthcoming *b*). See also n. 21.

[15] Greco (2003: §3; cf. 2009: §5) takes the line that achievements are by their nature luck-excluding (with the consequence, presumably, that Archie's success is not an achievement in the case in which the other targets have the arrow-excluding force-fields around them). Elsewhere, in Greco (2007*b*: §5), he argues that there is something peculiar about knowledge which ensures that it is luck-excluding in a more exacting fashion than non-cognitive achievements. For further discussion of Greco's response(s) to the problem of environmental luck, see Pritchard (2008*b*; cf. 2008*f*) and Kvanvig (2009).

[16] As noted in n. 14, this is the line taken by Sosa (2007).

though, they suggest not a mere 'patching-up' of the original proposal, but a radical rethink.

2.6. Knowledge without Achievement

Consider the following example, due to Jennifer Lackey (2007: §2). Our protagonist, whom we will call 'Jenny', arrives at the train station in Chicago and, wishing to obtain directions to the Sears Tower, approaches the first adult passer-by that she sees. Suppose further that the person that she asks has first-hand knowledge of the area and gives her the directions that she requires. Intuitively, any true belief that Jenny forms on this basis would ordinarily be counted as knowledge. Relatedly, notice that insofar as we are willing to ascribe knowledge in this case then we will be understanding the details of the case such that the true belief so formed is non-lucky in all the relevant respects (i.e. it is not subject to either Gettier-style or environmental epistemic luck). For example, we are taking it as given that there is no conspiracy afoot among members of the public to deceive Jenny in this regard, albeit one which is unsuccessful in this case.

The moral that Lackey draws from this example is that sometimes one can have knowledge without the success in question being of credit to the agent. I think this conclusion is ambiguous. In particular, we need to make a distinction between a true belief being *of credit* to an agent, in the sense that the agent is deserving of some sort of praise for holding this true belief, and the true belief being *primarily creditable* to the agent, in the sense that it is to some substantive degree down to her agency that she holds a true belief. Lackey's focus when employing this example is on the former claim,[17] and this is not surprising, since a number of commentators—see, for example, Greco (2003) in particular—have expressed their view in such a way that it seems to straightforwardly support this thesis. That said, strictly speaking, the robust virtue-theoretic proposal is the latter claim.

Now this may initially seem to be an idle distinction, in that one might naturally suppose that in every case in which the former description holds the latter description holds, and vice versa—viz., that when your belief is primarily creditable to your cognitive agency then it is of credit to you, and where it is of credit to you then it is primarily creditable to your cognitive agency. The

---

[17] The title of the paper in which this example appears is 'Why We Don't Deserve Credit for Everything We Know'.

problem, however, is that closer inspection of these two formulations reveals that they in fact make very different demands. Moreover, one kind of case in which they come apart is precisely scenarios like the 'Jenny' example where an agent gains knowledge by to a large degree trusting the word of another.

In order to see this, we just need to note that it is of *some* credit to Jenny that she has a true belief in this case. It is, after all, a *person* that she asks for directions, and not, say, a lamp-post or a dog. Moreover, the person she asks is not a small child, or someone who one might reasonably expect to be unreliable on this score (e.g. someone who is clearly a tourist). In addition, if the testimony which Jenny received were obviously false, then we would expect her to be sensitive to this fact. If, for example, the informant told her that she should get back on the train and go home to New York, then we would expect her to treat these directions as entirely spurious. So the moral to be drawn from this case is not that sometimes knowledge can be possessed even though the cognitive success in question is of no credit to the agent concerned.[18]

Nevertheless, what is true is that it is not *primarily creditable* to Jenny that she has formed a true belief in this case, and this is where the true moral of these cases resides. More specifically, that Jenny has a true belief in this case does not seem to be *because of* her cognitive abilities, but rather because of the cognitive abilities of the informant who knows this proposition on a non-testimonial basis. One can thus have a true belief that is deserving of credit and yet that true belief not be primarily creditable to one's cognitive agency.[19]

Given that the true belief needs to be primarily creditable to the agent in order for it to count as a cognitive achievement, it follows that while Jenny has knowledge in this case she does not exhibit a cognitive achievement. Again, then, we have seen that there is a problem associated with the idea that knowledge is to be identified with cognitive achievement.

It is not obvious how the proponent of the KA thesis can respond to cases of this sort. As before, notice that there is no mileage in trying to pin the blame here on the achievement thesis (P1). This is because, as with the 'Barney' case, the 'Jenny' case is a counterexample *both* to the KA thesis and to the more

---

[18] A second type of case that Lackey (2007) offers—that of innate knowledge—might fare better in this regard. After all, if there is such a thing as innate knowledge then it would presumably be such that it involves a true belief which is *neither* of credit to the agent nor primarily creditable to the agent. For my own part, I do not hold that innate knowledge is even possible, but this is an issue that cannot be usefully engaged with here.

[19] Moreover, the distinction between creditworthy true belief and true belief that is primarily creditable to one also comes apart in the other direction. There could, after all, be true beliefs that are primarily creditable to one's cognitive agency and yet for which you are deserving of no credit at all (e.g. where the cognitive achievement in question is very easy).

specific robust virtue epistemological claim that knowledge is cognitive success that is because of cognitive ability (i.e. (P2)). After all, it is both true that (i) Jenny has knowledge while failing to exhibit the corresponding cognitive ability, and that (ii) Jenny has knowledge even though her cognitive success is not because of her cognitive ability. As we noted above, there may well be good reasons to reformulate the achievement thesis but this issue is entirely by-the-by here, given that however the achievement thesis is formulated a key premise in the robust virtue epistemologist's argument for the final value of knowledge is blocked.

But if this response to the 'Jenny' case doesn't work, then what other options are there? None that are particularly palatable, that's for sure. On the one hand, one might bite the bullet and concede that Jenny lacks knowledge after all. On the other hand, one might try to resist this counterintuitive commitment by maintaining that it is primarily creditable to her that her belief is true, and thus that she is exhibiting a bona fide achievement after all (and hence has knowledge too). Both strategies involve denying some pretty strong intuitions about this case, and so anyone taking either line will face a tough uphill struggle.

Indeed, notice that taking the latter line will almost certainly commit one to a very restrictive account of testimonial knowledge, a view that is usually known as global reductionism. Although this view does have some adherents—most notably Elizabeth Fricker (e.g. 1995)—it is very unpopular, and most in the literature on the epistemology of testimonial belief regard it as a position to be avoided at all costs.[20] It is perhaps for this reason that Greco (2007b) opts for the former line, although he does not make a very strong case for it.

By analogy, he argues that one might score a very easy goal as a result of that goal being set up by a display of tremendous skill. He maintains that the skill involved in setting up this easy goal does not undermine the achievement of the agent who scores the goal. Given that we grant the account of achievement in question—such that achievements are nothing more than successes that are primarily creditable to one's agency—then I think that Greco's claim that this easy goal constitutes an achievement is correct (though remember that we will be questioning the adequacy of this account of achievement in the next chapter). The problem, however, is that this case is not relevantly analogous to the case of 'Jenny'. After all, what is crucial to that example is not that someone appropriately skilful helps Jenny, but rather more specifically that Jenny gains her true belief by (for the most part at least) *trusting* this other person. This is

---

[20] This is not the place to explore this issue in more detail. For more on the epistemology of testimony, see Adler (2006).

why, for example, other cases in which we depend on the skills of others—as when one takes an inner-city road-sign at face value—do not generate the same epistemological moral. In such cases my knowledge depends on—i.e. is made easy by—the skills of others, but it is not that I am merely trusting what the sign tells me: I have all kinds of independent grounds for believing what inner-city road-signs tell me.

An example that would be relevantly analogous to the 'Jenny' case is someone who lacks archery abilities who is being assisted by a skilled archer in firing an arrow and is thereby successful. (For example, the skilled archer helps the novice to take aim, steadies his arm, corrects her posture, and so on.) While the unskilled archer's abilities might have played *some* role in the successful outcome—such that it is *to some degree* creditable to him that he is successful—we would surely say that this success is primarily creditable to the skilled archer (or, at least, creditable to the combined efforts of the unskilled archer and the skilled archer). We certainly would not regard the success in question as being primarily creditable to the novice archer. On this basis, then, we would maintain that the unskilled archer's success does not constitute a bona fide achievement, and hence cases like this should give us no cause to reconsider our original assessment of the 'Jenny' example as one in which the agent likewise does not exhibit an achievement.

In any case, whatever the defender of the KA thesis says in response to the 'Jenny' example, remember that she must also simultaneously deal with the other problem outlined above—concerning the apparent possibility of cognitive achievements which are not cases of knowledge. Indeed, notice that it is significant that these two problems pull robust virtue epistemologists who endorse the KA thesis in two different directions. Whereas the 'Jenny' case puts pressure on them to *weaken* their robust virtue epistemology and thus allow cases of knowledge which this view would ordinarily exclude, the 'Barney' case, in contrast, puts pressure on them to *strengthen* their account in order to explain why merely exhibiting a cognitive achievement does not suffice for knowledge. This is why, when these two problems are expressed in tandem, they pose such a tricky difficulty for the robust virtue epistemologist.

It seems, then, that the KA thesis is unsustainable. Moreover, the source of the problem with the KA thesis that we have explored here is clearly the robust virtue epistemological account of knowledge (P2). Without the KA thesis, however, the robust virtue epistemologist loses the ingenious basis on which she argued for the final value of knowledge.[21]

---

[21] One might think that the alternative robust virtue-theoretic account offered by Sosa (2007) could potentially offer a way out of this problem. Rather than understanding the 'because of' relation that is

2.7. Back to the Value Problem

Does that mean that the response to the value problem offered by robust virtue epistemology must be completely abandoned? Perhaps not. On the face of it, one might think that there is a fairly straightforward way of resurrecting the KA account of the value of knowledge along these new lines. After all, while we have noted that there are cases of knowledge where the agent does not exhibit a cognitive achievement, and cases of cognitive achievement where the agent does not possess knowledge, one can nonetheless consistently argue that knowledge is the kind of epistemic standing that *tends* to go hand-in-hand with cognitive achievement. Since we have granted the prima facie plausibility of the thesis that achievements, and thus cognitive achievements, are finally valuable, the fact that knowledge at least tends to go hand-in-hand with cognitive achievement would suffice to show that knowledge at least tends to be finally valuable, even if it is sometimes not of final value. Would that be enough to answer the tertiary value problem?

In order to answer this question, we first need to form a view about just how extensive the cases of knowledge are which are not cognitive achievements. After all, although the testimonial case we have examined might initially seem quite peripheral, on reflection one might plausibly contend that quite a lot of our testimonial knowledge is gained in this fashion. Moreover, there is also

---

key to robust virtue epistemology in causal explanatory terms, Sosa instead understands it in terms of the manifestation of a power. To see how these two accounts can come apart, consider a glass that was broken as a result of someone deliberately smashing it against a wall. Ordinarily, the most salient part of the causal explanation of why the glass broke will be that someone smashed it against the wall, and in this sense it will be true to say that the glass broke because it was smashed against the wall. Note, however, that this is consistent with the claim that it was because of the glass's fragility that it broke, since here we are talking about the manifestation of a power and not offering a causal explanation. Sosa's idea is that when the robust virtue epistemology claims that knowledge is cognitive success that is because of cognitive ability, it is the 'manifestation of a power' reading that we should adopt, and not the causal explanatory reading. Although Sosa is offering a genuine alternative to Greco's reading of the robust virtue-theoretic account of knowledge, I think it should be clear that his view is no less susceptible to the problem posed here. In the Barney case, for example, it is surely even clearer that Barney's cognitive success constitutes the manifestation of his cognitive powers than that it is primarily creditable to his cognitive abilities. Indeed, Sosa recognizes this, which is why—as noted in n. 14—he argues that, contrary to intuition, environmental epistemic luck is compatible with knowledge possession. Moreover, Sosa's view will also struggle with the Jenny case, since again it is surely even clearer that Jenny's cognitive success is not the manifestation of *her* cognitive powers than that her cognitive success is not primarily creditable to her cognitive ability. This is not to say that Sosa's proposal is a complete non-starter as a type of robust virtue epistemology, since for one thing it at least avoids some of the counterintuitive consequences of Greco's view that we noted in n. 5. The point is rather that adopting such a reading of robust virtue epistemology does not offer any easy resolution of the problem in hand.

good reason to hold that there may be non-testimonial cases that have the relevant features. For example, one might claim that just as there is a substantive degree of ungrounded trust of others involved in the 'Jenny' case offered above, so there is a substantive degree of ungrounded *self*-trust involved in much of our other knowledge, such as an ungrounded trust in the reliability of our faculties. If this is right, then it may turn out that very little of our knowledge, if any, involves a cognitive achievement. The prospects for meeting the value problem with a proposal of this sort would then be dim indeed.[22]

Even if we can block this worry by arguing for a close relationship between knowledge and cognitive achievement, however, a second, and more substantive, worry remains. Recall that to say that knowledge is distinctively valuable is to say that is it more valuable, not just as a matter of degree but of kind, than that which falls short of knowledge. On this view, however, there is an epistemic standing which falls short of knowledge and which is no less valuable (indeed, which is in its nature finally valuable): cognitive achievements that are not also cases of knowledge. If that is right, then even if knowledge is the kind of thing that tends to be finally valuable, it still won't follow that knowledge is in the relevant sense distinctively valuable.

So once one rejects the idea that knowledge is a kind of achievement, the final value of achievements is no longer able to offer us a way of responding to the tertiary value problem. But given that this approach to the value problem constituted the best—indeed, the *only*—response to the value problem that seemed able in principle to support the key claim that knowledge is finally valuable, this means that the prospects for answering the value problem now appear dim indeed.

That leaves the swamping problem. Here the more modest strategy of arguing that knowledge tends to be finally valuable may gain more purchase. For recall that we noted in Chapter 1 that so long as knowledge is at least *sometimes* finally valuable then it will constitute a fundamental epistemic good. If that is right, however, then that would suffice to block the swamping argument, since that argument essentially trades on a commitment to epistemic value T-monism. Of course, as we noted earlier in this chapter, that one blocks the swamping argument by appeal to the fact that knowledge is a fundamental

---

[22] This would constitute one way of recasting the sceptical problem in value-theoretic terms. That is, the primary target of the sceptical argument would not be knowledge *simpliciter*, but rather a distinctively valuable epistemic standing. The advantage of reading the sceptic in this way is that it would clearly be irrelevant to respond to the sceptic by offering an account of knowledge on which knowledge was not distinctively valuable (indeed, this would constitute a kind of capitulation). The relevance of the problem of epistemic value to radical scepticism is discussed more fully in Chapter 4. See also Pritchard (2008d).

epistemic good leaves it open whether one is committed to a monistic or a pluralist response to that problem. But which way one jumps on this issue rests on further theoretical claims which are of secondary importance to us here.

So even though the robust virtue epistemic defence of the final value of knowledge is ultimately unsuccessful, so long as we accept the thesis that cognitive achievements are finally valuable (a claim that we will explore in more detail in Chapter 4) there may be scope to use the fact that knowledge at least tends to go hand in hand with cognitive achievements as a means of answering the swamping problem. Whether or not this is the best way to deal with the swamping problem is an issue that we will return to.

2.8. Concluding Remarks

Given what is at stake in answering the value problem—and thus the tertiary value problem—one might argue that we simply cannot leave matters at that, and that instead we must continue to seek a resolution to this problem. Indeed, it has been suggested by some that it is an adequacy condition on any theory of knowledge that it should be able to account for the distinctive value of knowledge, in the sense that if one's theory is unable to do this then this is a definitive strike against one's view.[23]

This way of thinking about the value problem and its role in the theory of knowledge is, however, surely too strong. Instead, what is presumably required is *either* that one's theory of knowledge can answer the value problem *or* that one's theory is able to provide some plausible account of why knowledge isn't really distinctively valuable after all, even though it appears to be. That is, provided one's theory of knowledge can answer the second of the two desiderata just identified, then that should suffice.

In the next chapter we will be exploring a new theory of knowledge—what I call *anti-luck virtue epistemology*—which has many of the advantages of robust virtue epistemology and none of its failings. Although this account of knowledge is unable to account for the final value of knowledge, it does enable us to gain an understanding of why knowledge may initially appear to be finally valuable. This diagnostic story regarding our intuition about the

---

[23] One finds a claim of roughly this sort expressed in a number of works. See e.g. Zagzebski (1999), Williamson (2000: ch. 1), and Kvanvig (2003: ch. 1). For a critical discussion of this assumption, see DePaul (2009). It is important to note, however, that these authors almost certainly have a different view of what it would take for knowledge to be distinctively valuable to that which has been argued for here.

distinctive value of knowledge is further reinforced in Chapter 4, where we will explore an epistemic standing—understanding, or at least a core kind of understanding anyway—which is finally valuable, and which has a close relationship to knowledge. As we will see, this discussion will lead us to rethink some of the claims about the nature and value of achievements that we have looked at in this chapter. So although the main conclusion drawn in this chapter is a negative one, from the ashes of the failure of robust virtue epistemology to adequately respond to the value problem we will be extracting some important positive epistemological conclusions.

3

Anti-Luck Virtue Epistemology

3.1. Introduction

We saw in the last chapter that the most promising account available of why knowledge, unlike that which falls short of knowledge, is finally valuable—that offered by robust virtue epistemology—is ultimately unsuccessful. We thus concluded that knowledge is not of final value after all, and hence that the tertiary value problem cannot be positively answered. The emphasis now turns from offering a solution to the value problem in its strongest (tertiary) form to explaining why a different account of the value of knowledge is desirable.

The goal of this chapter is to develop a theory of knowledge that can accommodate the intuitions that drive virtue-theoretic views but which does not succumb to the problems that they face. I call the view that I have in mind, which constitutes a new theory of knowledge, *anti-luck virtue epistemology*. As we will see, once we understand why knowledge has this structure, we will be able to diagnose where our intuition that knowledge is distinctively valuable comes from and also explain why this intuition should not be taken at face value as motivating the tertiary value problem.

3.2. *Contra* Virtue Epistemology

Let us begin by reminding ourselves where robust virtue epistemology went awry. Recall that we noted that what motivates virtue-theoretic proposals in epistemology is our strong intuition that knowledge is in some way the product of cognitive ability. Any cognitive success, even a cognitive success which is otherwise reliably produced or which would count (on some views at least) as justified, will not amount to knowledge if it is not appropriately related to the agent's cognitive abilities.

We didn't consider any examples to illustrate this point in the last chapter, but now is a good juncture to offer a suitable case. Imagine that our agent—let's call him 'Temp'—forms his beliefs about the temperature in his room by consulting a thermometer on the wall. Unbeknownst to Temp, however, the thermometer is broken and is fluctuating randomly within a given range. Nonetheless, Temp never forms a false belief about the temperature by consulting this thermometer since there is a person hidden in the room, next to the thermostat, whose job it is to ensure that whenever Temp consults the thermometer the temperature in the room corresponds to the reading on the thermometer.

Notice that it is entirely consistent with how we have set up this example that Temp's method of forming beliefs about the temperature of the room (roughly, by consulting the thermometer) is perfectly reliable, in that whenever he forms a belief in this way his belief is true. Moreover, it is also consistent with how we have set up the example that Temp's beliefs are justified. Perhaps he has no reason to think that the thermometer is broken, and has good reason for believing that it has been reliable in the past. On some views of justification, at least, this would suffice to enable his belief to be justified. Nonetheless, even though Temp's true belief formed in this way may have been reliably produced and justified, it is clearly not knowledge, and the reason for this is that his cognitive success is in no way a product of his cognitive abilities, but is rather due to a factor completely independent of his cognitive abilities (i.e. the person hidden in the room).

Adding a virtue-theoretic condition to one's theory of knowledge will deal with such cases, since one can now argue that they don't count as instances of knowledge because the virtue-theoretic condition is not met—the true belief in question, despite its other epistemic properties, is not the product of the agent's cognitive ability.

We also noted in the last chapter, however, that on the face of it adding a virtue-theoretic condition to one's theory of knowledge will not suffice by itself to deal with all cases. In particular, we pointed out that Gettier-style cases seem entirely compatible with the satisfaction of a virtue-theoretic condition on knowledge. The example we gave to illustrate this point was that of 'Roddy', who forms his true belief that there is a sheep in the field by using his highly reliable cognitive abilities, but who is subject to Gettier-style epistemic luck in that what he is looking at is not a sheep at all, but rather a sheep-shaped object which is obscuring from view a genuine sheep in the field. In this case Roddy lacks knowledge, even though his reliable cognitive abilities are generating a true belief in the target proposition.

In the light of this point, one might be tempted to opt for a modest virtue epistemology, which adds a codicil to the account of knowledge to exclude such cases and thereby make the view Gettier-proof. What was distinctive about robust virtue epistemology, however, was that it aimed to avoid the need for such a codicil by formulating the view in such a way that it could deal with Gettier-style cases after all. The way it did this was by insisting that it was not enough for knowledge that one exercised one's cognitive abilities and one was, in addition, cognitively successful. Rather, that cognitive success needed to be because of one's cognitive abilities, where this meant that it is primarily creditable to the operation of those abilities. This view had a number of advantages. For one thing, it offered an elegant account of knowledge, one that did not need to appeal to any non-virtue-theoretic component in the way that modest virtue epistemology does. Moreover, by understanding knowledge in this fashion it becomes a kind of achievement. Given the further claim that achievements are finally valuable—which we found in the last chapter to be quite plausible—this held out the promise of dealing with the value problem by demonstrating the final value of knowledge.

The problem, however, was that we found that knowledge and cognitive achievements are not the same thing. In particular, one can have knowledge while not exhibiting the corresponding cognitive achievement, and one can exhibit a cognitive achievement while failing to have knowledge. We gave the example of 'Jenny' to illustrate the former possibility. This was a case of testimonial knowledge where the agent gains this knowledge by, for the most part, trusting the word of another, and this meant that the true belief in question was not primarily creditable to her cognitive abilities (even though it was bona fide knowledge). And we gave the case of 'Barney' to illustrate the latter possibility. This is essentially the barn façade case, an example in which the agent fails to have knowledge because his belief is subject to knowledge-undermining epistemic luck but where, nonetheless (and unlike Gettier-style cases), the agent does exhibit a cognitive achievement (i.e. the agent's true belief is primarily creditable to his cognitive abilities).

Robust virtue epistemology is thus not a viable theory of knowledge, and this means that the response to the value problem that it advertises is not viable either. Still, nothing we have said so far undermines modest virtue epistemology, the view that knowledge is true belief that is the product of the agent's cognitive abilities and which, in addition, satisfies a suitably formulated 'anti-Gettier' condition. Even so, modest virtue epistemology will retain the key problem that it is an unmotivated account of knowledge. For why should knowledge have this structure such that it consists of a virtue-theoretic condition plus an apparently arbitrary anti-Gettier condition?

Moreover, we still need to be told how modest virtue epistemology can deal with cases like that involving Jenny and Barney. In the case of the former, it will be important that the virtue-theoretic condition imposes a very weak demand,

and yet if this condition is meant to capture the essence of knowledge—the anti-Gettier condition is just a codicil, remember—then that is prima facie implausible. Moreover, given the differences we have noted regarding the type of epistemic luck at issue in the Barney case when compared to standard Gettier-style cases—i.e. that it is 'environmental' epistemic luck rather than 'intervening' epistemic luck—we cannot simply take it as granted that the anti-Gettier condition imposed by modest virtue epistemology will deal with this case anyway. Indeed, insofar as we need to 'beef-up' the anti-Gettier condition in order to deal with environmental epistemic luck, then this raises the obvious question of why this condition is a mere codicil to the modest virtue epistemic proposal. Isn't this condition now playing a substantive role in this theory of knowledge?

I think that once these problems are made explicit it becomes clear that we need to step back from this debate and reconsider the motivations for the virtue-theoretic account of knowledge. Indeed, as we will see, once we undertake this re-examination of what underlies the virtue-theoretic account of knowledge we find that the right way to think about knowledge is along different lines. Virtue epistemology—in both its guises, but especially in its modest guise—comes close to gaining a correct understanding of knowledge, but ultimately fails precisely because it misunderstands the fundamental intuitions that a theory of knowledge must answer to.

3.3. Two Master Intuitions about Knowledge

I noted earlier that virtue epistemology answers to a fundamental intuition about knowledge: that knowledge is the product of one's cognitive abilities, such that when one knows one's cognitive success is, in substantial part at least, creditable to one. Call this the *ability intuition*, and call any epistemic condition that one imposes on one's theory of knowledge in order to account for this intuition an *ability condition*. Where virtue epistemology goes wrong, I will argue, is in failing to recognize that there is a second fundamental intuition about knowledge which imposes an independent constraint on one's theory of knowledge. This second master intuition is the intuition that knowledge is incompatible with luck, in the sense that if one knows then it ought not to be the case that one's true belief could easily have been false. Call this the *anti-luck intuition*, and call any epistemic condition that one imposes on one's theory of knowledge in order to account for this intuition an *anti-luck condition*.

On the face of it, one would think that these two intuitions are entirely distinct, in the sense that whatever epistemic condition one places on knowledge in order to accommodate the one intuition will not thereby accommodate the other intuition. That is, that no formulation of the ability condition could fully accommodate the anti-luck intuition and thereby obviate the need for a separate anti-luck condition, and that no formulation of the anti-luck condition could fully accommodate the ability intuition and thereby obviate the need for a separate ability condition. Let us take these points in turn.

First, one would naturally suppose that a true belief that is formed as a result of cognitive ability is not thereby immune to epistemic luck because of the possibility of Gettier-style cases (i.e. cases in which one exhibits the relevant cognitive ability and one has the target true belief, and yet one has nevertheless been 'Gettierized' such that one's true belief is epistemically lucky). More generally, that one's true belief is appropriately due to one's cognitive abilities does not seem to entail that it thereby has the required modal stability across the relevant nearby possible worlds to ensure that it is immune to knowledge-undermining epistemic luck. If that is right, however, then no formulation of the ability condition could obviate the need for an additional anti-luck condition.

Second, and conversely, it seems antecedently plausible that there could be true beliefs which meet the relevant anti-luck condition—such that the agent's true belief couldn't have easily been false—but which are not thereby formed as a result of a cognitive ability. After all, there could be all manner of reasons why one's belief tracks the truth in nearby possible worlds which have nothing to do with one's own cognitive ability (perhaps, for example, it is the facts that are changing in order to correspond with your belief rather than vice versa, as happens in the 'Temp' case). If that is right, then no formulation of the anti-luck condition could obviate the need for an additional ability condition.

In effect, however, virtue epistemologists fail to see that these two master intuitions are imposing distinct demands. In particular, they hold that the ability condition, properly formulated along virtue-theoretic lines, is, if not all that is required, then at least *pretty much* all that is required for a fully adequate account of knowledge. That is, they either hold, *qua* robust virtue epistemologists, that the virtue-theoretic ability condition—advanced, principally, in order to accommodate the ability intuition—can all by itself offer us a complete theory of knowledge. Or else they hold, *qua* modest virtue epistemologists, that a virtue-theoretic ability condition—again, advanced, principally, in order to accommodate the ability intuition—can *pretty much* offer a complete theory of knowledge by accommodating the ability intuition—all that is required is a mere codicil to handle those troublesome Gettier-style cases.

The failure of virtue-theoretic accounts of knowledge of both stripe thus reflects a failure to realize that the anti-luck intuition imposes a distinct constraint on knowledge, one that cannot be captured merely by the addition of a virtue-theoretic ability condition which is principally designed to accommodate the ability intuition. The adding of an anti-Gettier codicil to one's view simply fails to comprehend the important role that the anti-luck intuition plays in our thinking about knowledge. It is for this reason that an ability condition all by itself falls some way short of offering an adequate account of knowledge.

Now one might respond to the failure of this sort of account of knowledge by opting for the opposing radical thesis that takes the anti-luck intuition as its lead. On this view—what one might call a *robust anti-luck epistemology*—one tries to formulate an anti-luck condition on knowledge in such a demanding way that one does not need an additional ability condition in order to accommodate the other master intuition. Indeed, one could read certain modal epistemological proposals in the recent literature as proposing just such a view.[1] That is, just as robust virtue epistemologists try to accommodate the motivation for the anti-luck intuition by offering a more stringent construal of the virtue-theoretic ability condition on knowledge, so proposals along these lines offer a more stringent construal of the anti-luck condition in order to accommodate the motivation behind the ability intuition.

Such a proposal makes essentially the same mistake that robust virtue epistemology makes of failing to recognize that these two master intuitions about knowledge impose distinct constraints on one's theory of knowledge. For just as there is no formulation of the ability condition that can obviate the need for an anti-luck condition, so there is no formulation of the anti-luck condition that can obviate the need for an ability condition. After all, as noted above, it is inevitable that there will be cases in which there are true beliefs which exhibit the required modal properties to ensure that they are not lucky in the relevant sense and yet which are not formed as a result of the agent's cognitive abilities. Given the ability intuition, such cases will not count as knowledge, even though it will be the case that the agent in question could not have easily been wrong.

Indeed, we can adapt the example involving Temp that we offered above to make this point vivid. Clearly, Temp cannot gain knowledge of the temperature of the room by consulting a broken thermometer, and as noted

---

[1] To take the two most prominent examples of this tendency, see the sensitivity-based theories of knowledge offered by Dretske (e.g. 1970) and Nozick (1981). For a more general defence of the idea of a genuinely anti-luck epistemology, see Unger (1968) and Pritchard (2005; 2007a).

above, we can explain why by appeal to the ability intuition since the truth of his belief in this case is in no substantive way the product of his cognitive ability. Even so, depending on the details of the case it could nonetheless be true that Temp's belief is not subject to knowledge-undermining epistemic luck. After all, if the example is set up in the right way then it could well be the case that his true belief could not have very easily been false. Indeed, with the example suitably described it may well follow that in *all* nearby possible worlds in which Temp continues to form his belief in this way his belief is true.

Cases like Temp show that an anti-luck condition all by itself cannot offer a complete account of knowledge—that is, they demonstrate that a robust anti-luck epistemology is unsustainable. But if both robust virtue epistemology and robust anti-luck epistemology do not work, then it seems that in order to accommodate the anti-luck and the ability intuitions we will need to aim for an intermediate position between these two extremes. What we need, in short, is an *anti-luck virtue epistemology*: an account of knowledge which gives equal weight to both of the master intuitions and so incorporates both an anti-luck and an ability condition.

3.4. Anti-luck Virtue Epistemology

What is essential to anti-luck virtue epistemology is thus that it incorporates two conditions on knowledge, an anti-luck condition and an ability condition, and that it accords each condition equal weight in the sense that they are each answering to a fundamental intuition about knowledge.

Let us describe any true belief that couldn't have easily been false as *safe*.[2] The general structure of the account of knowledge offered by an anti-luck virtue epistemology can now be described as follows: knowledge is safe belief that arises out of the reliable cognitive traits that make up one's cognitive character, such that one's cognitive success is to a significant degree creditable to one's cognitive character. The safety element of the view is the anti-luck condition, while the virtue-theoretic clause is the ability condition.

To begin with, notice how the ability condition is formulated. In particular, notice that it does not demand that the cognitive success in question must be

---

[2] The general idea that knowledge entails a true belief that could not have easily been false is often referred to as the safety principle, and there are various more fine-grained formulations of this principle that have been offered in the recent literature. For our present purposes, however, we can stick with the more general formulation of safety. For some key defences of safety, see Sosa (1999; 2000) and Pritchard (2002; 2003; 2005; 2007a).

because of the agent's cognitive ability, only that it should be to a significant degree creditable to one's cognitive character, which is a weaker claim. Accordingly, there is no suggestion on this view that knowledge should be thought of on the model of achievements, and hence this proposal does not attempt to answer the tertiary value problem in the manner of robust virtue-theoretic proposals (we will come back to the issue of what anti-luck virtue epistemology does have to say about the value problem later on).

This account of knowledge is thus (on this score at least) consistent with cases of knowledge in which one's cognitive success is not *primarily* creditable to one's cognitive ability. As a result, anti-luck virtue epistemology doesn't face the problem that examples like the 'Jenny' case pose for robust virtue epistemology. After all, as we noted above, Jenny's true belief is *partly* creditable to her (this is why she is deserving of some credit for holding it), and the reason for this is that it does indeed arise out of reliable cognitive traits that make up her cognitive character. The crux is just that Jenny's cognitive success is not *primarily* creditable to her, but this need not be a bar to her possessing knowledge on this view. In epistemically friendly environments of the sort that Jenny is in—environments in which the anti-luck condition is very easily met—one can gain knowledge even though one's true belief is not primarily creditable to one. But *that*, as the 'Jenny' case indicates, is entirely in accordance with intuition.

Indeed, that we are willing to allow the exercise of relatively little cognitive ability result in the acquisition of knowledge in epistemically friendly environments lends support to the thinking behind anti-luck virtue epistemology. For consider what happens when we rerun the 'Jenny' case with our protagonist in an epistemically *un*friendly environment, one where testimonial deception is common. In such a case we would not ascribe knowledge to our hero, even when the target belief formed is true and gained from a knowledgeable and sincere source. Moreover, notice that in order for our subject to gain knowledge in this case it would be necessary for her to exhibit far more cognitive ability than is required by the corresponding hero in the standard 'Jenny' case. We would expect her, for example, to seek independent support for relying on this informant, such that she is no longer trusting this informant in the relevant sense to a substantive degree. Only then would her belief be safe and therefore satisfy the anti-luck condition. The degree of cognitive ability that is required in order to know thus varies in line with how epistemically friendly one's environment is. But this result, of course, is just what an anti-luck virtue epistemology would predict.

Anti-luck virtue epistemology also fares very well across the range of problem cases beloved by epistemologists. For example, by incorporating the anti-luck condition this proposal can deal with both the standard Gettier-style epistemic luck found in cases like that of 'Roddy' and also the more tricky environmental epistemic luck found in cases like that of 'Barney'. In all such cases, the agent's true belief could very easily have been false, and so will not count as knowledge by the lights of this proposal since the anti-luck condition is not met.[3]

Moreover, the anti-luck condition also enables anti-luck virtue epistemology to deal with so-called 'lottery' cases. The problem posed by such cases is to explain why one cannot come to know that one has a losing lottery ticket for a lottery with long odds simply by reflecting on the odds in question. The reason why this is puzzling is that one can come to know that one has lost the lottery by reading the result in a reliable newspaper, and yet it may be far more likely that the newspaper contains a misprint on this score than that one wins the lottery even despite the long odds involved.

An anti-luck condition can deal with such cases because even though the true belief in question is the result of the exercise of the agent's cognitive abilities, it nevertheless remains the case that this is a belief that could very easily have been false. For although this is a low-probability event, very little about the actual world needs to change in order for this event to obtain—in most lotteries, just a few coloured balls need to fall in a different configuration—and so there will be scenarios just like the scenario the agent is actually in in which she continues to form her belief on the same basis and yet ends up with a false belief as a result.[4]

---

[3] The anti-luck condition will also deal with Harman's (1973: 142–54) assassination case as well, at least so long as it is read in a way that the resulting belief is unsafe (see Pritchard (2005: ch. 6) for a discussion of how the assassination case is ambiguous in this respect). Cases involving misleading defeaters—which are often discussed in the same context as Gettier-style cases—can also be dealt with by this account, though not simply by appeal to the anti-luck condition. On the one hand, I argue in Pritchard (2005: ch. 5) that cases where an agent's belief satisfies the anti-luck and ability conditions but where she could so very easily have been misled by a misleading defeater (but wasn't) are entirely compatible with knowledge, and so do not pose any kind of Gettier-style challenge to one's theory of knowledge. On the other hand, cases where the agent ought to be have been aware of the misleading defeater, but wasn't—e.g. because she was inattentive to some aspect of the environment that she should have been attentive to—are dealt with by the ability condition, in that given this feature of the environment it follows that she wasn't appropriately exercising her cognitive ability (this is just a manifestation of the point made earlier that the more epistemically unfriendly the environment is, the more cognitive ability one needs to exhibit in order to know). The same point goes for cases in which the agent groundlessly disregards the misleading defeater and so continues to believe the target proposition nonetheless. Finally, it is worth noting that since the anti-luck condition is formulated in terms of safety rather than sensitivity, then it avoids the problems cases that have beset sensitivity, such as Sosa's (2000) garbage-chute case. For further discussion of the relative merits of safety and sensitivity, see Pritchard (2005: ch. 6; 2008e).

[4] There are some issues regarding the proper formulation of safety that are raised by the lottery problem, though it would take us too far afield to explore these here. For more on this point, see

Finally, the ability condition enables the proposal to deal with a range of cases like 'Temp' in which the agent has a non-lucky true belief and yet does not count as knowing because the true belief does not arise out of the cognitive abilities of the agent. Since such cases do not satisfy the ability condition, they pose no problem for a view of this sort.

Indeed, it is worth noting that the way that the ability condition deals with the Temp case also enables it to deal with cases involving necessary propositions which robust anti-luck epistemology has traditionally struggled with. Suppose one has formed one's true belief in a necessary proposition in an inappropriate way. For example, suppose that one forms a true belief in a mathematical proposition by writing out a series of calculations in one's notebook, but that one has some radically false beliefs about how to do mathematical calculations such that one is generally unreliable in these matters. Now clearly we do not want to regard this as knowledge, but the problem is that on the face of it one's belief does satisfy the anti-luck condition. After all, since the proposition believed is necessarily true, this can hardly be a true belief that could have easily been false.

The proponent of robust anti-luck epistemology might try to get around this problem by talking more generally of a doxastic output of a belief-forming method, rather than specifically of belief in the target proposition. The issue, then, would not be whether there is a nearby possible world where one believes the target proposition on the same basis as in the actual world but where one's belief is false, but rather whether there is a nearby possible world in which one employs the same belief-forming method as in the actual world and thereby

the exchange between Greco (2007c) and Pritchard (2007a). Note that anti-luck virtue epistemology is also able to deal with a related problem which is sometimes discussed—e.g. by Hawthorne (2004)—as part of the lottery problem just described. This problem arises out of the fact that one can, it seems, competently deduce from certain propositions that one appears to know that one is in possession of a losing lottery ticket, and thereby gain knowledge of this proposition in that way. For example, one might take it as obvious that one knows that one will not have sufficient funds to buy a sports-car next week. One might know, however, that one would only have such funds if one's lottery ticket were a winner. But doesn't that mean that one can competently deduce from the fact that one knows that one will not have sufficient funds to buy a sports-car next week that one's lottery ticket must be a loser, and so thereby gain knowledge of this proposition? I think the key to understanding these cases is to realize that one *doesn't* know that one will not have sufficient funds to buy a sports-car next week so long as one is in possession of a lottery ticket where one doesn't know the outcome of the lottery. This is not as counterintuitive as it may at first appear, for the whole point of buying a lottery ticket is to make scenarios that would ordinarily be far-fetched—such as having sufficient funds to buy a sports-car—modally close. Accordingly, while one can normally know that one will not have sufficient funds to buy a sports-car next week, one can't know this when one is in possession of a lottery ticket in a lottery that one does not know the outcome of, since in that case one does not satisfy the anti-luck condition: even where one truly believes the target proposition one's belief could have very easily have been false. For more on this point, see Pritchard (2007c).

comes to form a false belief as a result. Given that the target proposition is necessarily true, it would be impossible for any belief in the target proposition to be false. Even so, however, it is possible that the belief-forming process might issue in a *different* belief in a nearby possible world which is false. Employing a faulty system of mathematical calculation will almost certainly lead you to form a false belief in a mathematical proposition in some nearby possible worlds.

The problem, however, is that one can simply change the set-up of the example to reintroduce the original problem. All one needs to do, as in the Temp case, is to describe the case so that there is some factor present which always 'cancels out' one's mistakes. For example, suppose that there is a wizard in the room who is observing your calculations and whose goal it is to ensure that you end up with a correct answer. Using his magic, the wizard makes sure that any mistakes you make in your calculations get cancelled out elsewhere so that your belief-forming method always results in a true belief.

Just as in the Temp case, the problem here is that one is forming one's true belief in such a way that this belief has the required modal properties to ensure that the anti-luck condition is met. Nevertheless, this isn't knowledge, and the natural explanation of why is that the truth of the agent's belief is not appropriately connected to the agent's cognitive abilities. In particular, the truth of the agent's belief is not due even in minor part to the agent's cognitive abilities, but is rather the result of the intervention of the wizard. Adding an ability condition to one's theory of knowledge thus enables one to deal with such cases. Again, then, we find that we need both an anti-luck and an ability condition on knowledge.

Anti-luck virtue epistemology thus handles the standard range of epistemology examples very well. That anti-luck virtue epistemology is able to straightforwardly deal with these cases lends the view a great deal of prima facie support.

3.5. Interlude: Is Anti-luck Virtue Epistemology a Reductive Theory of Knowledge?

In the last chapter we examined the issue of whether robust virtue epistemology is a reductive or non-reductive account of knowledge (i.e. whether it involves a 'decomposition' of knowledge into its component parts where these parts can be specified in a knowledge-independent fashion). This issue was important there because of how we were evaluating the account's credentials at dealing with the swamping problem, where this question looms large. In particular, we noted that non-reductive accounts of knowledge which hold that knowledge is sometimes more valuable than mere true belief are naturally allied to a certain kind of monistic response to the swamping problem which treats knowledge as the sole fundamental epistemic good. In contrast, non-reductive accounts which hold that knowledge is sometimes more valuable than mere true belief are more naturally allied to a pluralist response to the swamping problem which treats knowledge as one fundamental epistemic good amongst others. Insofar as anti-luck virtue epistemology also attempts to answer the swamping problem—we shall examine what it says about this problem, and the value problem more generally as well, shortly—this issue will be important here too. Moreover, even if this issue didn't have a bearing on the swamping problem, this would still be a natural question to ask about the view.

I think the right answer to give here is the same as the answer given when we discussed robust virtue epistemology—viz., that the default reading of this view is as offering a reductive account, but that ultimately the devil will lie in the detail. That is, on the face of it there seems no obvious reason why one cannot specify the anti-luck and the ability conditions in knowledge-independent terms, and if that is right then this will constitute a reductive account of knowledge. Nonetheless, it is entirely possible that on closer inspection it could turn out that this is not in fact possible at all. In particular, one might find that one cannot specify the ability condition without making appeal to knowledge—for example, one might end up defining cognitive abilities in terms of how they are knowledge-conducive. If that turns out to be the case, then the proposal would be non-reductive.

For our present purposes, we can take a liberal view of this issue. The crux of the matter is just that knowledge has the structure set out by anti-luck virtue epistemology. Whether this structure presents us with a reductive account of knowledge is a further question, as is the issue of what bearing this question has on the response that the proponent of anti-luck virtue epistemology should offer to the swamping problem (we will set out the options on this score more fully in a moment).

3.6. Diagnosing the Structure of Knowledge

One question we might naturally ask about anti-luck virtue epistemology is why knowledge has this bipartite structure. A relevant contrast here is with robust virtue epistemology, since on this view there is a very straightforward account of why knowledge has the alleged structure which adverts to how knowledge is part of a more general phenomenon of achievements. The category of achievement is important to us, and hence it is no surprise that we have a separate subcategory of knowledge which picks out specifically cognitive achievements. This straightforward kind of story is not available to the proponent of anti-luck virtue epistemology, however. Similarly, the kind of anti-luck story told by the proponent of robust anti-luck epistemology—such that the overarching purpose of knowledge is to signal non-lucky true belief—is similarly unavailable here.

It may be helpful in this regard to undertake a thought-experiment that is suggested by Edward Craig (1990), which offers a very plausible genealogical account of our concept of knowledge. Craig tries to cast light on the nature of knowledge by considering the question of why an imaginary society which lacked this concept may feel the need to introduce it. Craig's answer is to appeal to the fact that we clearly care about being able to identify reliable informants. He thus argues that a proto-concept of knowledge would develop very quickly as a means of picking out these informants. This concept is just a proto-concept of knowledge, however, in that it is not yet similar in relevant respects to our own concept of knowledge. In particular, what is (in essence) required is that this concept, over time, should be used not just to classify actual reliable informants, but also to classify the potential reliability of informants, including oneself. This process—what Craig refers to as 'objectification'—has the effect of making the concept more demanding in its application, since it means that non-actual (but modally close) error-possibilities can now be relevant to whether or not an agent knows.

The details of Craig's view, interesting though they are, are not important for our purposes here. What is salient is rather the general features of this proposal, since they highlight a possible avenue of defence for the proponent of anti-luck virtue epistemology. In particular, what this proposal suggests is that the central importance of the concept of knowledge resides in the practical need to pick out reliable informants—informants that one can rely on.

Now one might think that this element of the view is actually contrary to the spirit of anti-luck virtue epistemology, in that it favours the virtue-theoretic account of knowledge with its focus on reliable cognitive abilities. Nevertheless, there is room for the proponent of anti-luck virtue epistemology to incorporate this motivation. The reason for this lies in an ambiguity in the very notion of a reliable informant. In one sense, it means an informant who possesses a reliable cognitive ability with regard to the target subject matter (and who is willing to sincerely communicate what she believes, something that we will take for granted in what follows). In another sense, it means an informant that one can rely on.

Now one might naturally think that this is a distinction without a difference, in that informants who possess reliable cognitive abilities in the sense just specified are thereby informants that one can rely on, and vice versa. Closer inspection, however, reveals that first appearances are deceptive on this score. In order to see this, we just need to notice that it can be appropriate to rely on an informant who is forming her true belief via an unreliable cognitive ability, and also that it can be inappropriate to rely on an informant who nevertheless is forming a true belief via a reliable cognitive ability.

First, consider an agent who possesses a reliable cognitive ability as regards a certain subject matter but who is in an environment in which there exists a misleading defeater, one which you know about, but which the agent (and prospective informant) does not, and one which, moreover, you are unable to defeat. An example might be an agent who is a reliable barn-detector but where you have been given a misleading ground for supposing that she is in barn façade county (e.g. false testimony from a good source). Such an agent is in fact a *reliable* informant about the relevant subject matter. But given that you know about the misleading defeater, and are aware that you are unable to defeat that defeater, would you be able to *rely on* this informant? Surely not.

The converse point also holds. After all, an agent might have a cognitive ability which is unreliable and yet be such that there are compensating factors known to us that mean that we can rely on this informant even though she is unreliable. Consider again, for example, the case described above of an agent with poor mathematical skills who is trying to work out a series of mathematical problems, but who is unbeknownst to him being helped by a wizard who ensures that all his beliefs formed on this basis are true. If we know that this compensating factor is in play, then we can rely on what this informant tells us even though she is not reliable about this subject matter.

So one can have an informant that one can rely on but who lacks the relevant cognitive abilities, and one can have an informant who possesses the relevant cognitive abilities but whom one cannot rely on. If we accept this distinction, and we also buy into Craig's more general idea that the core motivation for introducing the proto-concept of knowledge is to pick out reliable informants, then we are just a few steps away from giving a diagnostic rationale for anti-luck virtue epistemology. For, given this ambiguity in the idea of a reliable informant, it is natural that the concept of knowledge that evolves from the proto-concept of knowledge will generate *both* the anti-luck and the ability intuition.

That is, as the range of cases which the concept is meant to apply to widens, so the distinction will open up between informants who are reliable and informants that we can rely on, and we would expect the concept of knowledge that results to respect both sides of this distinction. In particular, examples where an agent exhibits a reliable cognitive ability but where the presence of epistemic luck means that we would not be able to rely on this agent *qua* informant would not be counted as cases of knowledge. Similarly, cases in which an agent forms a true belief in an epistemically friendly environment—such that any true belief so formed would not be subject to epistemic luck—would not be counted as cases of knowledge so long as the agent concerned failed to exhibit the relevant cognitive ability (even though we could rely on this agent *qua* informant). In short, the concept of knowledge that results will both (i) disallow cases of true belief as knowledge where the belief isn't appropriately due to a substantive degree to the relevant cognitive ability, and (ii) disallow cases of true belief as knowledge where the truth of the belief is substantively due to luck and hence unsafe.

Craig's very plausible story about the genealogy of the concept of knowledge thus lends support to anti-luck virtue epistemology after all, despite first appearances. In fact, if I am right that the goal of picking out reliable informants is ambiguous in the way just described, then, contrary to the prevailing wisdom on this score, Craig's genealogical account of the concept of knowledge actually *favours* anti-luck virtue epistemology over rival proposals.

3.7. Back to the Value Problem

But what import, ultimately, does anti-luck virtue epistemology have for the value problem? We noted in the last chapter that the best hope of accounting for the final value of knowledge lay in the robust virtue epistemic proposal to identify knowledge with cognitive achievements. This proposal, however, was shown to be untenable, and hence we concluded that a positive response to the tertiary value problem was unavailable. The best we can hope for, then, is a positive response to the primary and secondary value problems and an appropriate *diagnostic* response to the tertiary problem—i.e. an explanation of why we might naturally suppose knowledge to be distinctively valuable in the manner that the tertiary value problem demands even though it is not in fact valuable in this way. Interestingly, anti-luck virtue epistemology does seem to be in a very good position to offer a diagnostic story of this sort, and also to answer the primary and secondary value problems.

To begin with, notice that while we have denied that knowledge is finally valuable, we have granted that the separate epistemic category of cognitive achievements are distinctively valuable in the very sense at issue in the tertiary value problem. That is, they are more valuable, not merely as a matter of degree but of kind, than lesser epistemic standings, where this entails that they are finally valuable (though note that this claim will be qualified somewhat in the next chapter). This in itself gives anti-luck virtue epistemology some purchase when it comes to diagnosing the intuition that knowledge is distinctively valuable. After all, when we think of paradigm cases of knowledge we tend to think of cases where there is in addition the corresponding cognitive achievement present. In particular, when asked to describe paradigm cases of knowledge it is not, say, Jenny-style cases that spring to mind. This fact in itself goes some way towards explaining why we might initially suppose knowledge to be (distinctively, and hence) finally valuable, since if the paradigm cases of knowledge coincide with cognitive achievement, and the latter is (distinctively, and hence) finally valuable, then it is only natural to ascribe this property to knowledge more generally too.

Indeed, in the next chapter we will see that there is more that the proponent of anti-luck virtue epistemology can do on this score to diagnose where the intuition that knowledge is finally valuable comes from. In particular, there is a kind of epistemic standing—a species of understanding—which is finally valuable and which also tends to coincide with knowledge. This fact can thus help to explain why when we initially think about knowledge we tend to suppose that it is finally valuable. Moreover, it turns out that it should be no surprise that understanding of this sort is finally valuable since it is also by its nature a cognitive achievement. This is an important result, since while a number of commentators have noted the distinctive value of understanding, they have not offered an explanation of why it is finally valuable. If this species of understanding constitutes a cognitive achievement, however, then we have a straightforward explanation available to us of why it is finally valuable.

That leaves the primary and secondary formulations of the value problem. Here anti-luck virtue epistemology seems to be on strong ground when it comes to offering a positive resolution of these difficulties. After all, if the Craig-style story about the concept of knowledge is right, then we have the beginnings of a plausible answer to the secondary value problem and, thereby, the primary value problem too. For it seems that knowledge, on this view, marks out a distinctive epistemic standing which is of particular instrumental value to us. We would thus expect knowledge to be of more instrumental value than that which falls short of knowledge, even though knowledge is not finally valuable.

Finally, there is the swamping problem to deal with. Given that anti-luck virtue epistemology denies that knowledge is in its nature finally valuable, and given that a defence of the final value of knowledge would constitute the most direct way of defending the claim that knowledge is a fundamental epistemic good (and thus that true belief is not the sole fundamental epistemic good), then on the face it of it it would appear that anti-luck epistemology ought not be allied to those responses to the swamping problem—i.e. the monistic and pluralist responses—which deal with the problem by rejecting epistemic value T-monism. In this vein, one might regard anti-luck virtue epistemology as most naturally allied to the practical response to the swamping problem which maintains that knowledge is never epistemically more valuable than mere true belief, even though it is typically of greater practical value. Indeed, insofar as the practical response is viewed as a 'demystifying' response to the swamping problem, then it seems only natural that it should go hand in hand with a response to the value problem which treats the tertiary value problem as a pseudo-problem.

The matter becomes more complex, however, once one remembers that it only has to be the case that *sometimes* knowledge is of final value for it to be a fundamental epistemic good (see §1.4). And since we have so far granted the claim that cognitive achievements are finally valuable—we shall be exploring this thesis in more detail in the next chapter—it is open to the proponent of anti-luck virtue epistemology to argue that because sometimes knowledge constitutes a cognitive achievement, so sometimes it is of final value and hence knowledge is a fundamental epistemic good.

Of course, which non-practical response to the swamping problem anti-luck virtue epistemology should offer in the light of this move—whether the monistic response which treats knowledge as the sole fundamental epistemic good, or the pluralist response which allows other epistemic goods to be fundamental too—is a further matter, and will depend upon one's wider theoretical commitments (such as whether one regards one's view as a reductive theory of knowledge). We do not need to take a stand on this point here, however, since all that matters for our present concerns is that there is a response to the swamping problem available on this view.[5]

---

[5] That said, as I've noted at a number of junctures, I think that the default stance is to treat a theory of knowledge as reductive until there are grounds for regarding it otherwise. Accordingly, insofar as a reductive anti-luck virtue epistemology is more naturally allied to a pluralist response to the swamping problem, then the pluralist response is the default response to take in this regard. I explore anti-luck virtue epistemology at greater length in Pritchard (2008c).

3.8. Concluding Remarks

In this chapter we have seen that out of the ashes of robust virtue epistemology we can delineate a new account of knowledge—anti-luck virtue epistemology—which is able to avoid the problems facing both virtue-theoretic and anti-luck epistemologies. Moreover, we have also seen that while this view is unable to offer a positive response to the tertiary value problem, it is in a position to offer a diagnosis of why we might initially find the claim that knowledge is finally valuable intuitive. In essence, this diagnostic story appeals to the fact that on this view knowledge is at least sometimes a cognitive achievement, and cognitive achievements are plausibly of final value. Moreover, anti-luck virtue epistemology is in a position to offer a positive response to the secondary (and hence also the primary) value problem and also the swamping problem.

The purpose of the next chapter is to extend this diagnostic story by showing how a certain kind of understanding is finally valuable, and finally valuable precisely because, unlike knowledge, it constitutes a cognitive achievement. Along the way we will also acquire a more nuanced conception of what constitutes a cognitive achievement and a greater understanding of why achievements—or at least a certain type of achievement anyway—are of final value.

4

Understanding

4.1. Introduction

In the previous chapters we have rejected the idea that there is a theory of knowledge which can account for its final value, and hence we have concluded that there is no positive response available to the value problem in its strongest, tertiary, form. That said, we have argued for a positive conclusion about the nature of knowledge—that it is has the structure dictated by anti-luck virtue epistemology—and we have argued that two weaker value problems in the epistemic domain—the secondary (and thus also the primary) value problem and the swamping problem—can be given positive resolutions. We have also argued that anti-luck virtue epistemology is able to offer a compelling diagnosis of why we might be wrongly led into thinking that knowledge is distinctively, and hence finally, valuable. This diagnosis proceeds by appeal to the epistemic category of cognitive achievements, an epistemic standing which is closely related to knowledge but which is plausibly distinctively, and hence finally, valuable.

The aim of this chapter is to enhance this diagnostic story by demonstrating that there is a species of understanding which is closely connected to the corresponding states of knowledge and which is itself finally valuable. Moreover, it is also shown that this type of understanding is itself a kind of cognitive achievement, and hence we are in addition able to offer an explanation of why understanding of this sort is finally valuable.

4.2. The Final Value of Achievements

Before we can explore the relevance of understanding to the issues that concern us, however, we first need to revisit the very idea of an achievement, in order to get a firmer handle on why, and to what extent, achievements are finally valuable. Recall the argument offered by robust virtue epistemology in

Chapter 2 which purported to derive the final value of knowledge by appeal to a certain conception of achievement:

From Robust Virtue Epistemology to the Final Value of Knowledge

(P1) Achievements are successes that are because of ability (Achievement thesis);

(P2) knowledge is a cognitive success that is because of cognitive ability (Robust Virtue Epistemology);

(C1) so, knowledge is a cognitive achievement (KA thesis);

(P3) achievements are finally valuable (Value of Achievements thesis);

(C2) so, knowledge has final value.

In Chapter 2 our critical focus when it came to this argument was on (P2)—the robust virtue epistemological account of knowledge—and its role in generating the intermediate conclusion (C1), the KA thesis. In particular, we argued that there are cases in which agents have knowledge but don't exhibit the corresponding cognitive achievements, and also that there are cases in which agents exhibit cognitive achievements while failing to possess the corresponding knowledge. Moreover, we noted that the cases offered in this regard work just as effectively against the claim that knowledge is a cognitive success that is because of cognitive ability, and hence that the problem here does not lie with the particular conception of cognitive achievements in play (i.e. it is not as if the problem with (C1) specifically concerns (P1) rather than (P2)).

Denying (P2) is of course sufficient to block the argument, but one might nevertheless reasonably ask about the status of the other two premises that make up this argument. In Chapter 2 we said relatively little about these two premises. As regards (P3), we noted one objection which we argued was unpersuasive on closer inspection. This concerned the possibility of achievements which were, all things considered, either disvaluable or at least had very little value, such as wicked or trivial achievements. We noted that this objection didn't work because the claim that achievements have final value does not entail that all achievements are of great all-things-considered value. Instead, the claim is only that successes, *qua* achievements, have final value—i.e. it is a claim about prima facie or *pro tanto* value, and not all-things-considered value. As regards (P1) we also noted one objection—concerning the possibility of 'easy' achievements—but in this case we set this problem aside for future discussion. This is now a good juncture at which to revisit this issue. As we will see, this will also give us cause to think again about (P3) as well.

According to the 'easy achievements' objection, if one defines achievements as successes that are because of ability, then one will be forced to treat some successes as achievements which, intuitively, aren't achievements. Relatedly, these questionable cases of 'achievement' won't be plausible candidates for final value in the way that bona fide achievements are. The reason why I deferred consideration of this objection until now is because responding to it requires us to complicate our conception of achievements in ways that are only now relevant to our wider philosophical concerns. In particular, the worry posed by this objection is that the characterization of achievements as successes that are because of ability is too broad as it stands, at least if we are to simultaneously defend the claim that achievements are finally valuable.

Let's consider an example. Suppose that in normal circumstances I raise my arm. Here we clearly have a successful action on my part, in that there is something that I am aiming to do and which I do in fact do. Moreover, if circumstances really are normal then there ought to be no problem with the idea that this success was *because of* the exercise of my relevant 'arm-raising' abilities. But would we naturally call the raising of one's arm in these circumstances an achievement? Intuitively, the answer is 'no', and the reason for our reluctance to so describe this success is surely because of the ease with which it was brought about.

The reason why we do not count easy successes as real achievements is that our intuitive conception of an achievement involves either the application of a significant level of skill or at least the overcoming of a significant obstacle to the relevant success. In cases of easy successes of the sort just described, however, neither element is present. In order to see this point in more detail, notice first that where a significant level of skill is being exercised we are perfectly happy to treat any successful outcome that is thereby attained as an achievement, even if it was not a difficult feat for that agent to perform. For example, Tiger Woods may well sink a tricky put with ease, but this would still count as an achievement. There is no obstacle for him to overcome here, of course, but that there is great skill on display suffices for an achievement. Another way of putting this point is to say that while this success is easy for *him*, it is not an easy success.

Conversely, cases in which there is no great skill on display but where a significant obstacle has been overcome also qualify as bona fide achievements. Consider, for example, someone raising her arm who had suffered a serious injury and for whom such an action was extremely difficult. Here we would surely be inclined to regard this success as an achievement even though no great skill is involved in this success. The key point, however, is that a genuine obstacle is being overcome in this situation, unlike the ordinary case in which someone raises their arm.

So some successes are intuitively too easy to be in the market to count as achievements, either because they do not involve the overcoming of a significant obstacle or because they do not involve a significant degree of skill. Clearly, there are cases in the epistemic domain which illustrate this point too. Suppose that I form the true belief that the wall before me is white by looking at it in entirely normal circumstances. Here we have a cognitive success and the cognitive success is, intuitively, appropriately related to my relevant cognitive abilities in such a way that it is because of my cognitive ability. And yet it seems odd to think of such a success as an achievement on my part, given that this is a cognitive success which is neither the result of overcoming a significant obstacle to that success nor involving the exercise of significant cognitive skill.

In contrast, imagine a case which is obstacle-overcoming in the relevant sense. Perhaps, for example, there are defeaters present which indicate that there may be some deception taking place—e.g. a reliable source informs one that the lighting in the room can be apt to mislead when it comes to identifying the colour of objects in the room. Suppose now that one takes appropriate measures to defeat these defeaters. Perhaps, for example, one observes the wall with and without the aid of the lighting to determine what effect the lighting is having on the apparent colour of the wall. After completing this process, one satisfies oneself that the wall is indeed white. Would this cognitive success count as a cognitive achievement? I think so, and the natural explanation for why is that one has used one's cognitive ability in order to appropriately overcome a significant obstacle to one's cognitive success.

Similarly, there will be cases where even an easy cognitive success can count as a cognitive achievement so long as a significant degree of cognitive ability is on display. Imagine, for example, someone with acute powers of observation and deduction, such as Sherlock Holmes, observing the very same visual scene as someone with normal powers of observation and deduction, such as Holmes's sidekick Watson. Holmes may well be able to immediately observe certain features of the environment with ease that Watson could only detect with great effort and guidance. Still, Holmes's cognitive success would count as an achievement even despite the ease with which he brings this about because of the great cognitive skill that he is exhibiting.

How might the proponent of the success-because-of-ability account of achievements respond to this problem? One response could be to simply concede the point and argue that the conception of achievements in play is just a very inclusive one. That is, they might argue that all that they are trying to describe is some general sense of achievement that captures the idea of a successful exercise of agential power. Accordingly, they could simultaneously grant that there is in ordinary language a more restrictive conception of achievement which brings with it the idea that one's success involves either the exercise of great skill or the overcoming of a significant obstacle. In this spirit, let us characterize the two conceptions of achievement as follows:

> (*Weak Achievement Thesis*) Achievements are successes that are because of ability.
>
> (*Strong Achievement Thesis*) Achievements are successes that are because of ability where the success in question either involves the overcoming of a significant obstacle or the exercise of a significant level of ability.

Robust virtue epistemology is thus to be read as endorsing the weak achievement thesis rather than the more austere strong achievement thesis.

This is a perfectly legitimate move for proponents of robust virtue epistemology to make, but the problem is that while the weak achievement thesis might be an adequate account of a very inclusive sense of achievement, it is not this sense of achievement which is in play in the claim that achievements have final value. Think of the cases of easy achievements that we have just noted, such as raising one's arm in normal circumstances, or forming the belief that the wall before one is white in normal cognitive conditions. Do we have *any* intuition that such successes are finally valuable? I suggest not. In contrast, when we turn our attentions specifically towards the class of achievements demarcated by the more restrictive strong achievement thesis, the intuition of final value returns.

Now one might try to respond to this objection by making the same kind of move that we made in Chapter 2 in response to the charge that since some achievements were of little value or disvaluable it followed that they cannot be the sort of thing that has final value. There we responded by arguing that once the target thesis was properly understood—such that it merely claimed that successes *qua* achievements have final value, and hence did not maintain that achievements have a significant degree of all-things-considered value—this objection disappeared. Similarly, one might argue here that just because some achievements, construed in line with the weak achievement thesis, are lacking in final value it does not follow that there is a problem with the idea that achievements have final value on this conception.

The cases are not analogous, however, because the objection that some achievements on the weak reading lack final value does not appeal to the all-things-considered value of the achievements in question. Accordingly, there is no scope to appeal to this fact in order to rescue the claim that achievements, even on the weak conception, have final value. In order to see this, we just need to note that the easy 'achievements' in play could well be of great all-things-considered value and yet they would equally demonstrate the intended point. Perhaps, for example, there is a great practical value that accrues to raising one's arm in this context (e.g. one gets identified as the prizewinner, and so is awarded a prize that would have otherwise been missed through lack of identification). Still, there is no temptation to suppose that the mere raising of one's arm in normal circumstances, *qua* weak achievement, is of final value. The issue, then, is not that these 'achievements' are in themselves lacking in value *simpliciter*, but more specifically that they are lacking in *final* value.

With this point in mind, we should regard only achievements as understood by the strong achievement thesis as being the kind of thing that has final value. Henceforth, then, when we talk of 'achievements' we will (unless otherwise indicated) have the strong account of achievements in mind.

There are a number of advantages to understanding achievements in this way. We will explore one key advantage in a moment, which is that it enables us to get a better handle on why understanding is such a valuable epistemic state to be in. Before we do so, however, there are two further peripheral advantages to this account that are worthy of note.

First, notice that the claim that achievements are finally valuable is even more secure now that we have restricted the class of successes that count as achievements. Indeed, it is worth noting that some of the trivial achievements that we saw creating a prima facie tension for this thesis in Chapter 2 will be in any case excluded by the strong account of achievements on the basis that they are too easily gained.

Second, the strong account of achievements can also accommodate some other problem cases that might be thought to afflict the weak account of achievements. Two such cases are particularly salient in this regard, and they both have specific application to cognitive achievements.

The first concerns successes that are essentially *passive*, in that they do not involve any substantive act of will on the part of the subject. In the case of actions, it is hard to make sense of such successes as actions, since where there is no substantive act of will involved in bringing about that success it is natural to suppose that this is a mere behaviour on the part of the subject and hence not an action at all (and thus not a success that can be attributed to the agent). Think, for example, of the instinctive movements of one's body when one is asleep which take place in order to ensure that one is comfortable enough to remain asleep. Such behaviour is clearly passive in the relevant sense, but it is also intuitively not an action on the part of the subject, no matter how successful this behaviour might be at ensuring one's continued slumber.

Matters are different in the cognitive realm, however, since here it is far more plausible to suppose that there could be entirely passive cognitive successes. Indeed, one might argue that passively forming beliefs about one's environment is the norm. The problem is that where one's belief-forming is indeed passive in this sense, then it is hard to see why we would count any cognitive success that thereby results as being in the market for achievement.

There is an issue here, of course, regarding how the passivity of our belief-forming is to be understood. If one thinks that belief is in its nature truth-directed—or at least evidence-sensitive, if one takes that to be a different matter—then one might argue that in the relevant sense even our most spontaneously formed beliefs are 'directed' and hence not passive. Notice, though, that we do not need to take a stance on this issue here, for however one understands these 'passive' beliefs they are not going to pose a challenge to the strong achievement thesis. In the normal case, after all, such beliefs will be dealt with by the demand that the agent should be overcoming significant obstacles in attaining the relevant cognitive success. Moreover, although this condition need not be met in cases where significant skill is in play, it is crucial that where this further condition is met it is natural to regard the belief so formed as *not* being in the relevant sense passive. Sherlock Holmes may be able to spontaneously form quite sophisticated beliefs in response to environmental stimuli, but there is nothing passive about the exercise of this cognitive ability, despite its spontaneous application. Holmes has, after all, trained himself to acutely observe his environment, and there is nothing passive about that.

The second problem that might face the weak achievement thesis but which is avoided by the strong achievement thesis (and which is also specific to the cognitive realm) concerns cases where the target subject matter is *transparent* to the agent. For example, suppose I am suffering from a raging migraine and consequently form the true belief that I am in pain. Suppose further that I in this way gain knowledge of what I believe (this is by no means an uncontroversial supposition). Nonetheless, it seems odd to think of such a cognitive success as an achievement even though one might naturally describe it as a cognitive success that is because of one's cognitive ability.

Notice that the issue here is not simply that such cognitive success is very easy, since the problem rather relates to the fact that there could, it seems, be no such thing as an obstacle to cognitive success in this case. This is why, I take it, it is so hard to conceive of an analogue case in the realm of action, since here it is arguably always possible to think of an obstacle standing in the way of one's successful action. Now the proponent of the weak achievement thesis could respond to this problem by denying that it even makes sense to talk about knowledge in these cases, either because it makes no sense to talk of belief in this context or because it makes no sense to talk of the application of a cognitive ability. Notice, however, that the proponent of the strong achievement thesis has a very easy time accounting for these cases. For if there is indeed no obstacle present in these 'transparency' cases, and if indeed no great skill is needed to form the target belief (assuming it is a belief that is being formed), then the belief isn't even in the market to be an achievement in the first place.

There is thus a lot going for the strong achievement thesis, for not only can it handle a range of problem cases, but it also offers additional support for the idea that achievements are in their nature distinctively, and hence finally, valuable. We can now bring this account of achievements to bear on the issues regarding epistemic value that concern us. Previously we have argued that while knowledge is not, it turns out, distinctively valuable—i.e. finally valuable in a way that lesser epistemic standings are not—we can explain why we might have thought that it was by implicitly (and incorrectly) identifying knowledge with a distinct epistemic standing—that of cognitive achievement—which is distinctively valuable. We can now add a bit more precision to this claim, for it is not cognitive achievements per se that are distinctively valuable, but only cognitive achievements by the lights of the strong achievement thesis. Epistemic standings which fall short of this, including cognitive successes that only qualify as cognitive achievements by the lights of the weak achievement thesis, are lacking in final value and hence are not distinctively valuable.

As we will now see, this point is important because a particular kind of epistemic standing—understanding, or at least a species of understanding at any rate—constitutes a cognitive achievement in just this (strong) sense, and hence we are now in position to explain why this epistemic standing is of special epistemic value—i.e. why it is distinctively valuable.

4.3. Understanding

The intuition that understanding is distinctively valuable is surely even stronger than the intuition that knowledge is distinctively valuable. Indeed, insofar as knowledge and understanding come apart—we will explore whether they do, and if so, how, in a moment—then understanding seems to be preferable to knowledge. As we might be tempted to put the point, we would surely rather understand than merely know. If that is right, and assuming that knowledge and understanding do come apart, then it would be premature to conclude from the fact that knowledge is, on closer inspection, not distinctively valuable that therefore neither is understanding. Instead, we should treat these two issues as potentially separate from one another.

Before we can evaluate a claim of this sort, however, we need to be a little clearer about what we are talking about. One problem that afflicts any direct comparison between knowledge and understanding is that knowledge (of the propositional sort that we are concerned with at any rate) is concerned with propositions, whereas understanding usually isn't, at least not directly anyway. That is, the kind of knowledge we are interested in is knowledge that p, but it is rare to talk of understanding that p.

I want to take the paradigm usage of 'understands' to be in a statement like 'I understand why such-and-such is the case'. Notice that this usage is very different from a more holistic usage which applies to subject matters, as in 'I understand quantum physics', or even 'I understand my wife'. I think the holistic usage of 'understands' is related to the non-holistic, or atomistic, usage that is our focus, but the former raises problems of its own that we've not the space to cover here (though we will flag some of these problems as we go along).[1]

Regarding understanding-why—henceforth just 'understanding'—there are, interestingly, two standard views—a standard view within epistemology and a standard view *outside* of epistemology (particularly in the philosophy of science). The standard view within epistemology is that understanding is distinctively valuable but that it is *not* a species of knowledge. One finds a view of this sort in the work of such figures as Catherine Elgin (1996; 2004; 2009), Linda Zagzebski (2001), Jonathan Kvanvig (2003), and Wayne Riggs (2009), and we will examine the motivation for such a thesis in a moment.

In contrast, outside of epistemology the consensus is that understanding *is* a species of knowledge. In particular, most philosophers of science who have expressed an opinion on this matter have endorsed the claim that understanding why X is the case is equivalent to knowing why X is the case, where this is in turn equivalent to knowing that X is the case because of Y. So, for example, my understanding of why my house burned down is equivalent to my knowing why my house burned down, where this in turn is tantamount to my knowing that my house burned down because (say) of faulty wiring. One finds a view of

---

[1] For more on holistic and non-holistic conceptions of understanding, see Brogaard (2007*b*).

this general sort—expressed in varying levels of explicitness—in the work of such figures as Peter Achinstein (1983), Wesley Salmon (1989), Philip Kitcher (2002), James Woodward (2003), and Peter Lipton (2004).[2]

I will be claiming that both of these conceptions of understanding are wrong, at least strictly speaking, and that once we get clearer on the relationship between understanding and knowledge we can make some progress towards dealing with the problem of epistemic value.

Let us look first at some of the accounts of understanding offered by epistemologists. One guiding theme in this discussion is that understanding is construed along epistemically internalist lines. An extreme example of this can be found in the work of Zagzebski (2001). She argues, amongst other things, that understanding is, unlike knowledge, 'transparent' in the sense that there is no gap between seeming to understand and understanding. Relatedly, she also claims that understanding is, unlike knowledge, non-factive, in that even if one's relevant beliefs were false, one's understanding could be unaffected.[3] Finally, she holds that understanding, unlike knowledge, is immune to epistemic luck, in that if one's understanding is subject to such luck it will not thereby be undermined.

Of these claims, the first is clearly the most radical and also, I venture, the one that is most obviously false. To construe understanding in this way seems to reduce it to nothing more than some sort of minimal consistency in one's beliefs, something which might well be transparent to one (though I'm actually doubtful of this). Understanding clearly involves much more than this, however. To see this, let us focus on the non-factivity claim that Zagzebski makes. This claim is also, I will argue, false, but if understanding does imply factivity in the relevant sense, then it will be easy to show that understanding is not transparent in the way that Zagzebski suggests.

To illustrate this point, consider my understanding of why my house has burned down. Let us grant the plausible assumption that this understanding involves a coherent set of relevant beliefs concerning, for example, the faulty wiring in my house. But now suppose that these beliefs are mistaken and that, in particular, there was no faulty wiring in my house and so it played no

---

[2] Consider the following remark made by Lipton (2004: 30) and quoted in Grimm (2006: 1): 'Understanding is not some sort of super-knowledge, but simply more knowledge: knowledge of causes.' The natural way to read this passage is as suggesting that understanding why one's house burned down is just knowing why it burned down—i.e. knowing that it burned down because of (say) faulty wiring. I am grateful to Grimm (2006) for alerting me to some of these references.

[3] Riggs (2009) and Elgin (2009; cf. Elgin 1996; 2004) also argue that understanding is not factive, although their claim is ultimately much weaker than Zagzebski's since it in effect only applies to certain conceptions of understanding (and not, in particular, to the non-holistic conception of understanding in play here).

part in the fire. Would we still say that I understand why my house burned down? I think not. For sure, I *thought* I understood—indeed, it could well be that I *reasonably* (or at least *blamelessly*) thought that I understood—but the fact remains that I did not understand. Once one grants that understanding is factive in this way, however, then the transparency claim starts to look equally suspect, since there is now a distinction to be drawn between (reasonably) thinking that one understands and in fact understanding, contrary to what the transparency thesis demands.

So the transparency and non-factivity claims that Zagzebski offers are false. It is difficult to diagnose why Zagzebski made this mistake. Part of the reason may be that there is a failure to be clear about the type of understanding under consideration. After all, when it comes to the kind of holistic understanding that applies to a subject matter, this plausibly *is* compatible with at least *some* false beliefs about that subject matter, but this sort of understanding is precisely not the sort at issue. Moreover, it would seem that the analogue of Zagzebski's non-factivity claim as regards understanding when it comes to holistic understanding would be that such understanding can be possessed even though one has *no* relevant true beliefs, and that is surely implausible.[4]

More generally, however, I think that the right diagnosis of where Zagzebski's conception of understanding goes awry lies in her overstating the internalist aspect of understanding. Understanding clearly is very amenable to an account along epistemically internalist lines, in the sense that it is hard to make sense of how an agent could possess understanding and yet lack good reflectively accessible grounds in support of that understanding. Understanding thus cannot be 'opaque' to the subject in the way that knowledge, by epistemically externalist lights at least, can sometimes be. Granting this, however, does not entail that one should regard understanding as non-factive, much less transparent.

With this in mind, let us consider a second account of understanding in the epistemological literature—due to Kvanvig (2003)—which does not succumb to the mistakes made by Zagzebski's account. Zagzebski holds that both knowledge and understanding are distinctively valuable. In contrast, Kvanvig maintains that it is only understanding that is distinctively valuable, where understanding is distinct from knowing.

---

[4] It should be noted that there are some good arguments offered by Elgin (2009) in this respect regarding the growth of understanding within false scientific theories, and the use of idealizations in scientific thinking, which might seem to suggest a conception of holistic understanding which is entirely non-factive. It would take us too far afield to consider these arguments here, however, and Zagzebski clearly doesn't have considerations like this in mind when she offers her conception of (non-holistic) understanding. For my own part, I think that even here we should say that genuine understanding entails a system of beliefs which is broadly correct, at least as regards the beliefs that are fundamental to that system. For more on this point, see Pritchard (forthcoming *c*: §5).

Unlike Zagzebski, Kvanvig does not hold that understanding is transparent or non-factive. He does, however, treat the notion along internalist lines which, as we have just noted, is entirely plausible. The way in which he distinguishes knowledge from understanding is primarily through two further claims. The first is that understanding, unlike knowledge, admits of degrees. The second is that understanding, unlike knowledge, is immune to epistemic luck, a thesis which we saw Zagzebski putting forward a moment ago.

The import of the first claim is, I think, moot. After all, even if this is true, it needn't follow that there are cases of knowledge which aren't corresponding cases of understanding, or that there are cases of understanding which aren't corresponding cases of knowledge. The weight of the distinction between knowledge and understanding on this view thus falls on the second claim, which merits further consideration.

This thesis is meant to reflect, I take it, the internalist dimension to understanding. That is, the idea is that just as one's justification, internalistically conceived, is not undermined by epistemic luck (just the sufficiency of that justification, with true belief, for knowledge), so one's understanding is not undermined either. Closer inspection of this claim reveals that the relationship between understanding and epistemic luck is, however, more complex than Kvanvig and Zagzebski suppose.

4.4. Understanding and Epistemic Luck

The example that Kvanvig offers to illustrate his claim that understanding, unlike knowledge, is compatible with (knowledge-undermining) epistemic luck is that of someone who, by reading a book on the Comanche tribe, gains a series of beliefs about the Comanche and, thereby, a 'historical understanding of the Comanche dominance of the southern plains of North America from the late seventeenth until the late nineteenth century' (Kvanvig 2003: 197).[5] We are told that the relevant class of beliefs contains no falsehood, and that the agent can answer all the relevant questions correctly in this regard (thereby illustrating that the putative knowledge possessed is not 'opaque'). However, Kvanvig argues that although in such a case one would expect the agent to have knowledge of the relevant beliefs, this is not essential—it could well

[5] Understanding of this very general claim might start to look dangerously close to holistic understanding of a subject matter, rather than the non-holistic understanding that we are interested in here. In what follows, I will set this concern to one side and simply read it as non-holistic understanding.

be, as he points out, that the true beliefs in question have been 'gettierized', perhaps because the information that the agent has is only 'accidentally true' (ibid.).

I think that a case like this is ambiguous in a crucial respect, but we can get a better handle on what is going on here by taking a simpler case and then returning to consider this more complex example in the light of our intuitions as regards the simpler case.

Consider again the example of understanding why one's house burned down. Suppose first that we have a standard Gettier-style case in which something 'intervenes' between the agent's belief and fact—on the model of the 'Roddy' example considered in Chapter 2—in order to ensure that one's true belief is only true as a matter of luck, and so is unsafe. For example, imagine that, upon finding one's house in flames, one approaches someone who looks as if she is the fire officer in charge and one asks her what the reason for the fire is. Suppose one is told by this person that the reason why one's house is aflame is faulty wiring, and that this coheres with one's wider set of beliefs. But suppose now that the person one asked in this regard is not in fact the fire officer in charge but instead someone who is simply dressed in a fire officer's uniform and who is on her way to a fancy-dress party. Still, one did indeed gain a true belief in this regard. So, even though the epistemic luck in question prevents one from having knowledge of the relevant propositions, does one lose one's understanding? Seemingly, one does, for ask yourself the question now of whether you understand why your house burnt down. Surely the answer to this question is a straightforward 'no'. One cannot gain an understanding of why one's house burnt down by consulting someone who, unbeknownst to you, is not a real fire officer but instead merely someone in fancy dress.

So does this mean that Kvanvig is just wrong in thinking that understanding is immune to epistemic luck? Not entirely, since, as we have noted in Chapter 2 (see §2.5), there is a kind of epistemic luck—what we referred to as *environmental* epistemic luck, and which we noted was found in the barn façade case—which is knowledge-undermining but which is not of the sort that appears in standard Gettier-style cases where the luck 'intervenes' between belief and fact. In cases of environmental luck the luckiness of one's true belief is entirely due to the fact that one is in an epistemically unfriendly environment (e.g. an environment in which barn façades are common, although what one is looking at is indeed a genuine barn).

With this distinction between two kinds of knowledge-undermining epistemic luck in mind, consider a variant on the case just described where the kind of epistemic luck that is at issue is specifically the environmental epistemic luck found in the barn façade case. For example, imagine that the apparent fire officer that one asks about the cause of the fire is indeed a genuine fire officer, but that one could nevertheless have been easily wrong in forming one's belief in this way because there are other people in the vicinity dressed as fire officers — all going to the same fancy-dress party, say — whom one could very easily have asked and who would have given one a false answer (while failing to indicate that they were not real fire officers).

In such a case, as we saw in Chapter 2, one's cognitive success would be because of one's cognitive abilities, and so would constitute a cognitive achievement, and yet the environmental epistemic luck at issue would prevent it from counting as knowledge. The critical question for us, however, is whether this is a case of understanding. I want to argue that it is, and thus that Kvanvig is right on at least this score: environmental epistemic luck, unlike standard Gettier-style epistemic luck, *is* compatible with understanding. After all, the agent concerned has all the true beliefs required for understanding why his house burned down, and also acquired this understanding in the right fashion. It is thus hard to see why the mere presence of environmental epistemic luck should deprive the agent of understanding.

With this distinction between two types of epistemic luck in mind — one, the standard Gettier-style epistemic luck, which is inconsistent with understanding, and a second, the environmental epistemic luck, which is consistent with understanding — we can return to evaluate Kvanvig's 'Comanche' case. Whether or not the agent retains her understanding in this case will depend on the type of epistemic luck at issue.

So, for example, suppose that the agent forms her beliefs about the Comanches by reading an apparently scholarly book which is in fact nothing of the sort. Let us say, for instance, that the author of this book simply took lots of rumours and unchecked stories about the Comanche and presented them, along with some inventive guesswork, as established fact. But suppose further that, despite this lack of attention to scholarship, the author did get matters entirely right. This would thus be a standard Gettier-style case in which our agent gains lots of true beliefs about the Comanches: she has good reason to think that her beliefs about the Comanche are true, and they are true, but it is just a matter of luck that they are true given that the source of these beliefs is so unreliable. Can one gain an understanding of the Comanche tribe in this way? In particular, can one gain a historical understanding of why the Comanche were so dominant in the southern plains of North America from the late seventeenth until the late nineteenth century in this fashion? I want to suggest that one cannot, any more than one can gain an understanding of why one's house burnt down by gaining a true belief about what caused the fire from someone pretending to be a fire officer.

Matters are different, however, if we redescribe the case as specifically involving environmental epistemic luck, rather than standard Gettier-style epistemic luck. Suppose, for example, that the book that the agent consults is indeed appropriately scholarly—and thus reliable—when it comes to this subject matter, and that the agent accordingly gains lots of true beliefs about the Comanche. Nevertheless, luck enters the picture because of how all the other books on this topic—which are also superficially just as scholarly—are very unreliable, and one could very easily have consulted one of these books. Does epistemic luck of this sort undermine one's understanding in the way that it would undermine one's knowledge? I don't think that it does, since one did indeed find out the relevant facts in the right kind of way. Just as one can gain an understanding of why one's house burnt down by speaking to the fire officer—even though one could just have easily been misled by someone who isn't the fire officer—so one can gain an understanding of the Comanche by reading a reliable book even though one could have very easily consulted an unreliable book.[6]

So while Kvanvig and others are right to think that understanding is compatible with a certain type of knowledge-undermining epistemic luck, they are wrong to think that it is compatible with all types of knowledge-undermining epistemic luck. Their mistake is to fail to distinguish between two crucial ways in which epistemic luck can be knowledge-undermining. That understanding is compatible with one type of knowledge-undermining epistemic luck suffices, however, to show that knowledge is distinct from understanding, since it entails that one can have understanding without the associated knowledge.

4.5. Understanding and Cognitive Achievement

One consequence of this point is that the standard view of understanding outside of epistemology, such that understanding is a species of knowledge,

[6] While noticing that Kvanvig's claim that understanding is compatible with epistemic luck is not quite right, Grimm (2006) fails to recognize that the mistake here is simply to equate environmental epistemic luck with Gettier-style epistemic luck. As a result, he concludes that understanding is just as incompatible with epistemic luck as knowledge is, and thus that knowledge is a species of understanding after all.

is false. Indeed, this is not the only respect in which this conception of understanding is mistaken. Recall that on this conception of understanding, to understand why X is the case is equivalent to knowing why X is the case, which is in turn equivalent to knowing that X is the case because of Y. As we have seen, however, cases involving environmental epistemic luck illustrate that I can understand why my house burned down even while failing to know why it burned down (indeed, even while failing to know that it burned down because of faulty wiring).

There is also a second respect in which this conception of understanding is mistaken, since it is possible to know why one's house has burned down (and indeed know that it burned down because of faulty wiring), even though one does not understand why one's house burned down. We can illustrate this point via an example of testimonial knowledge cast along the general lines of the 'Jenny' case considered in Chapter 2.

Suppose that I understand why my house burned down, know why it burned down, and also know that it burned down because of faulty wiring. Imagine further that my young son asks me why his house burned down and I tell him. He has no conception of how faulty wiring might cause a fire, so we could hardly imagine that merely knowing this much suffices to afford him understanding of why his house burned down. Nevertheless, he surely does know that his house burned down because of faulty wiring, and thus also knows why his house burned down. Indeed, we can imagine a teacher asking my son if he knows why his house burned down and him telling the teacher the reason. It asked by a second teacher if my son knew why his house burned down, we could then imagine the first teacher saying that he did. So, it seems, one can not only have understanding without the corresponding knowledge, but also knowledge without the corresponding understanding.[7]

Just as the 'Jenny' case offered in Chapter 2 demonstrated that sometimes one might have knowledge without exhibiting the corresponding cognitive achievement, so the same moral can be drawn here. My son might know why his house burned down, but this knowledge does not constitute a cognitive achievement on his part (even by the lights of the weak achievement thesis) because of how the truth of his belief is not sufficiently creditable to his cognitive ability. Interestingly, however, we have just seen that while knowledge and cognitive achievement come apart on this score, understanding and cognitive achievement do not. My son's knowledge does not constitute a cognitive

---

[7] For more on the relationship between understanding and knowing-why, see Pritchard (2008c).

achievement, but then neither does it constitute genuine understanding on his part.[8]

Indeed, there is good reason to think that all understanding involves cognitive achievement. More specifically, there is good reason to hold that all understanding involves cognitive achievement even by the lights of the more restrictive strong achievement thesis. Recall that the moral of the barn façade case described in Chapter 2 was that one could exhibit a cognitive achievement and yet lack knowledge, because of how knowledge, unlike cognitive achievement, is incompatible with environmental epistemic luck. The same applies to understanding. When one couples this observation to the fact that the cases in which an agent has knowledge while not exhibiting a cognitive achievement are cases in which the agent lacks the relevant understanding, then one can see that there is a strong prima facie case for thinking that all understanding involves a cognitive achievement.

Indeed, I think this thesis is highly plausible. Its plausibility relates to the fact that understanding seems to be essentially an epistemically internalist notion, in the sense that if one has understanding then it should not be opaque to one that that one has this understanding—in particular, one should have good reflectively accessible grounds in support of the relevant beliefs that undergird that understanding. But given that this is a requirement of understanding, it is unsurprising that one can construct a 'Jenny'-style testimonial case in which an agent has knowledge but not understanding, since such cases work precisely by using examples of agents who, while having knowledge, lack good reflectively accessible grounds in favour of their beliefs.

That understanding is both factive and resistant to standard Gettier-style epistemic luck also demonstrates, however, that we should be wary of construing understanding along purely internalist lines. One's reflectively accessible grounds in favour of one's belief might well survive the falsity of what one believes and also be compatible with standard Gettier-style luck, but as we have seen, the same is not true of understanding. Just as genuine cognitive achievements do not depend exclusively on the cognitive efforts of the agent, but also on the relevant cognitive success and the right connection obtaining between cognitive ability and cognitive success, so genuine understanding makes the same 'external' demands.

Finally, notice that the kind of cognitive achievement in play when one has understanding seems to explicitly be of the sort at issue in the strong achievement thesis. Typically, after all, one gains understanding by undertaking an

---

[8] I argue in Pritchard (2008c) that this point has some important implications for the epistemology of testimony. See also Pritchard (2008a).

obstacle-overcoming effort to piece together the relevant pieces of information. Moreover, where understanding is gained with ease, this will be because of the fact that one is bringing to bear significant cognitive ability. Perhaps, for example, in coming across one's house in flames one is immediately able to gain an understanding of why this event is occurring because one is able to observe some crucial feature of the event taking place before one which—along, say, with the relevant background information that one possesses—definitively indicates how this event came about in such a way as to afford one the relevant understanding. But here the spontaneity of the understanding is entirely due to the exercise of significant cognitive ability, and hence poses no challenge to the idea that understanding specifically involves cognitive achievement along the lines set out by the strong achievement thesis.

4.6. Back to the Value Problem

The import of this point about understanding being a form of cognitive achievement in keeping with the strong achievement thesis is that it gives us a way of validating our intuition that understating is distinctively—and therefore finally—valuable. Indeed, as noted above, it is often claimed in epistemology that understanding is distinctively valuable without any explanation being offered of why this is so. Instead, there is a mere appeal to intuition on this score. By tying our account of understanding to a conception of cognitive achievement, an epistemic standing which has been shown to be itself of distinctive value, we are able to go much further in this regard and offer a concrete explanation of why this epistemic standing is valuable in this way.

Moreover, given that understanding of the sort that we have discussed here will tend to go hand-in-hand with the corresponding states of knowledge—e.g. typically, when one understands why X is the case then one will know that X is the case because of Y—the distinctive value of understanding further supports the diagnostic story about why we tend to suppose that knowledge is distinctively valuable that was offered at the end of Chapter 3. For if there is an epistemic standing that tends to go hand-in-hand with knowledge and which is distinctively valuable, then it is hardly all that surprising that we might initially regard knowledge as itself distinctively valuable, prior to a closer inspection.

This also means, of course, that one will be unable to run a swamping problem for this epistemic standing. This is because the final value of understanding ensures that it is a fundamental epistemic good, and hence its epistemic value cannot be swamped by the value of the cognitive success that is involved in acquiring that understanding.

4.7. Two Potential Implications of the Distinctive Value of Understanding Thesis

This claim that it is understanding, *qua* cognitive achievement, which is distinctively valuable, and not knowledge, potentially has some important ramifications for our understanding of a number of central issues in epistemology. I will close by outlining two such potential ramifications.

The first concerns the problem of *radical scepticism*. Typically, the radical sceptical problem is understood as being designed to deprive us of knowledge. If knowledge is not distinctively valuable in the way that many suppose, however, then this raises the obvious question of whether the difficulty posed by scepticism is best interpreted in this fashion. That is, why not treat the sceptic as trying to deprive us of an epistemic standing that is distinctively valuable, such as either cognitive achievement (on the strong conception) more generally or understanding more specifically?

The import of this point is that it would no longer be enough to respond to the sceptic by simply showing that one has the widespread knowledge that the sceptical problem, traditionally conceived, aims to deprive us of. Instead, given that one can possess that knowledge even while lacking a distinctively valuable epistemic standing, one would have to argue for the more specific thesis that the distinctively valuable epistemic standing in question is widely attained. Moreover, at least where we are focusing on understanding here, then there are good prima facie grounds for supposing that this task is going to be more difficult.

On the one hand, understanding has a strong internalist element to it, in that when one has understanding that understanding is backed by good reflectively accessible grounds. And yet it is often noted that radical scepticism poses a far stronger threat to epistemic internalist accounts of knowledge than to epistemic externalist accounts.[9] On the other hand, however, it is not as if understanding is a pure internalist notion, as a classical internalist account of the justification is often characterized. That is, as we have noted above, in order to possess understanding various external conditions must be realized

---

[9] This is a point that I explore in detail in Pritchard (2005: Part I).

as well, not least of which is that one's belief in the target proposition must be true. Had understanding been a purely internalist notion then one option might have been to insist that it is not touched by sceptical arguments at all, in that there is no difference in epistemic standing in this regard between oneself and one's radically deceived (e.g. envatted) counterpart.[10] Clearly this option is unavailable to an anti-sceptical defender of understanding.

On the face of it, then, the realization that understanding, unlike knowledge, is distinctively valuable gives us good reasons both for recasting the sceptical problem as being directed against understanding rather than knowledge, and also for thinking that such a sceptical challenge will be far harder to resolve than its knowledge-directed counterpart.[11]

The second potential ramification of this thesis regarding the distinctive value of understanding that I want to mention concerns how we should conceive of the *goal of enquiry*. Various conceptions of the goal of enquiry have been offered, including truth, justified belief, explanatory adequate belief, coherent belief, and knowledge. I want to suggest that the story told here regarding the distinctive value of understanding should give us pause to wonder whether we should instead regard understanding as the goal of enquiry.

In order to see why there may be some mileage in this suggestion, compare how understanding fares against the most robust epistemic standing just listed as a potential goal of enquiry—viz., knowledge. Now ask yourself whether an enquiry that resulted in knowledge but not in the corresponding understanding would be deemed a successful enquiry (and thus a 'closed' enquiry, at least as regards the original question under investigation). I suggest not.

Imagine, for example, that one's enquiry leads one to a reliable informant who passes on the answer that you were looking for. One could thereby gain knowledge of this answer. But suppose now that this answer, which you don't doubt is correct (you know the informant is reliable and sincere, and so on), simply makes no sense to you. That is, while you grant that it is correct, you cannot make sense of *why* it is correct. In such a case one would lack understanding in the relevant sense. But then wouldn't one as a result continue enquiring in order to gain such an understanding?

Consider the example of someone coming home and finding her house ablaze. This would naturally prompt our hero to begin an enquiry into the reason why her house is burning down. Merely gaining knowledge from a reliable source that the cause was faulty wiring will, however,

---

[10] This is the so-called 'new evil genius' intuition about justification, first introduced by Lehrer and Cohen (1983).

[11] I explore this recasting of the sceptical problem in more detail in Pritchard (2008d).

not settle this enquiry if she has no conception of how faulty wiring could do this. Instead, we would expect her, *qua* responsible enquirer, to continue enquiring until she has gained an understanding of why her house burned down. Her enquiry has not yet reached its goal.[12]

Given the centrality of the sceptical debate and the question of the goal of enquiry to epistemological theorizing, there is thus a strong prima facie case for holding that the thesis we have argued for here regarding the distinctive value of understanding has important ramifications for contemporary epistemology.[13]

4.8. Concluding Remarks

I will conclude by summarizing the main claims that I have argued for. First, I argued for a certain account of the value problem, such that it demands, in its strongest (tertiary) form, that one be able to show that knowledge is distinctively valuable, in the sense that it is more valuable not merely as a matter of degree but of kind than that which falls short of knowledge. I argued

---

[12]   This way of thinking about the goal of enquiry prompts some very interesting further questions. For example, we have noted that understanding, unlike knowledge, is compatible with environmental epistemic luck. Does that mean that we would deem an enquiry as settled even where the understanding gained by the enquirer was subject to environmental luck? On the face of it, one would think not. On closer inspection, however, this does not seem quite so implausible. After all, discovering that one's understanding is subject to environmental luck would not make one reopen the enquiry. Think, for example, of the case in which one gains an understanding of why one's house burned down by listening to the testimony of a genuine fire officer in an environment in which one could have very easily been deceived by a fake fire officer. Crucially, however, discovering that one's belief is subject to environmental luck in this way would in fact *confirm* the pedigree of one's epistemic source, and hence it would be very odd to take this as a reason for further enquiry in this regard.

A related issue is whether there can be cognitive achievements in the strong sense that are not thereby understandings. I'm inclined to think that there are, but not in the context of an enquiry. That is, I would argue that for an enquiry to generate a cognitive achievement in the strong sense is for it to thereby generate understanding. I discuss what ramifications the distinctive value of understanding has for the way we should think of the goal of enquiry in more detail in Pritchard (2008c).

[13]   Another possible ramification of this account of the distinctive value of understanding—developed by Hills (2008) in response to the account of understanding that I offer in Pritchard (forthcoming c)—is that it may offer a way of neutralizing some of the counterintuitive implications of the idea that there could be ethical experts. In essence, the thought is that while one could gain ethical knowledge merely by listening to the testimony of an ethical expert, one could not gain ethical understanding in this way, and yet it is the latter that one should be seeking in this regard. In a similar way, one might be able to appeal to this account of understanding in order to explain why it is in general, and all other things being equal, preferable to find things out for oneself rather than by merely trusting the (reliable) word of another. After all, while trust in others can issue one with knowledge, it cannot issue one with understanding, and yet it is understanding that is the distinctively valuable epistemic standing.

that answering the value problem, so conceived, requires one to show that knowledge has final value.

Second, I considered, and rejected, what I took to be the best possible defence of the distinctive, and thus final, value of knowledge, which is due to robust virtue epistemology. In particular, I argued that contrary to this proposal knowledge is not to be identified with cognitive achievement. Thus, even if cognitive achievements are distinctively valuable, this won't suffice to ensure that knowledge is distinctively valuable. I concluded that a positive response to the value problem in its tertiary form was not going to be possible, and hence that we must instead seek a diagnostic story regarding why we might have supposed knowledge to be distinctively valuable in this way even though it in fact isn't.

Third, in light of the failure of the robust virtue epistemic proposal, I argued for a new theory of knowledge—anti-luck virtue epistemology—which has many of the advantages of other views (like robust virtue epistemology) and none of their failings. Moreover, I showed how anti-luck virtue epistemology is in a position to answer the value problem in its weaker (primary and secondary) forms and also offer a compelling diagnosis of why we might wrongly suppose knowledge to be distinctively valuable.

Fourth, I argued for a certain account of understanding and demonstrated that this epistemic standing, so construed, was in its nature a cognitive achievement. Accordingly, I argued that while knowledge is not distinctively valuable, understanding is.

Along the way we have also explored what bearing the swamping problem has for the debate about the value of epistemic standings. As we saw early on, this problem is not as closely related to the value problem for knowledge as many suppose.

We began our enquiry into the value of knowledge by noting that part of what drives the intuition that knowledge is distinctively valuable is that if it is not valuable in this way then it is simply odd that much of our epistemological theorizing has tended to focus on this epistemic standing to the exclusion of others. When we made this observation we were engaged in the project of seeking a way to *validate* this largely tacit meta-epistemological presupposition, but as we have progressed on our journey through this topic we have found that a certain degree of *revisionism* is in fact necessary in this regard.

Taking the revisionist line can often be a depressing and defensive activity, as when a forest ranger destroys a section of forest in order to preserve the trees as yet left untouched by the oncoming conflagration. As we have seen, however, the recognition that knowledge is lacking in distinctive value brings with it a new way of thinking, not just about the value of epistemic standings, but also about the structure of knowledge and its place in epistemological enquiry. To pursue the metaphor, revisionism of this sort is more akin to a farmer burning off the chaff in the field in order to prepare the land for a new and more fruitful crop in the years to come.[14]

[14] Much of the material that makes up my contribution to this book has been presented at various venues over the last few years. These venues include the Royal Institute of Philosophy in London as part of the 'Epistemology' lecture series in October 2006; the 'Basic Knowledge' conference at the University of St Andrews in November 2006; the *Dialectica* annual conference in Geneva in December 2006; a conference on 'Epistemology' at the University of Leuven in February 2007; a Pacific APA invited symposium on 'Epistemic Value' in San Francisco in April 2007; the Newcastle Philosophy Society annual conference in August 2007; the Joint Session of the Mind Association and the Aristotelian Society in July 2008; a workshop 'The Value of Knowledge' at the University of Stirling in October 2008; and departmental talks during 2006, 2007, and 2008 at the Universities of Edinburgh, Geneva, Leeds, Lund, Sheffield, St Andrews, Sussex, and UNAM, Mexico City. Thanks to Sharar Ali, Kelly Becker, Martijn Blaauw, Jesus Zamora Bonilla, Brit Brogaard, Campbell Brown, Ross Cameron, Matthew Chrisman, Andy Clark, John Divers, Igor Douven, Julien Dutant, Pascal Engel, Paul Faulkner, Miguel Fernandez, Gordon Finlayson, Lizzie Fricker, Peter Graham, John Greco, Patrick Greenough, Dominic Gregory, Lars Gundersen, Bob Hale, Lottie Hanson, John Hawthorne, Allan Hazlett, Chris Hookway, Robert Hopkins, Jennifer Hornsby, Carrie Jenkins, Jesper Kallestrup, Matthew Kieran, Jon Kvanvig, Bob Lockie, Anne Meylan, Andy McGonigal, Michael Morris, Antony O'Hear, Erik Olsson, Steve Petersen, Diana Raffman, Murali Ramachandran, Mike Ridge, Bruce Russell, Jenny Saul, Sarah Sawyer, Barry Smith, Jason Stanley, Bob Stern, Helen Steward, Kathleen Stock, John Turri, Margarita Valdes, Robbie Williams, Tim Williamson, René van Woudenberg, and Crispin Wright. Special thanks to Adam Carter, Georgi Gardiner, Adrian Haddock, Chris Kelp, Alan Millar, Wayne Riggs, and Ernie Sosa. My research in this area has benefited from an AHRC Research Leave award and a Philip Leverhulme Prize.

II

KNOWLEDGE
AND RECOGNITION

Alan Millar

PART II

ANALYTICAL TABLE
OF CONTENTS

Chapter 5. Knowledge in Recent Epistemology: Some Problems

5.1. Introduction

The traditional framework and the traditional analytical project. Opposition to the traditional framework. The centrality to enquiry of aiming at knowledge. The importance of knowledge for how we inform others. Making sense of why knowledge matters as a central task of epistemology.

5.2. The Traditional Analytical Project and the Central Tension

There is a central tension between the assumption that *knowledge* admits of reductive analysis along traditional lines and the roles that knowledge and thinking about knowledge plays in our lives. While an analysis of knowledge should reflect the logical role of the concept, the prospects for providing a reductive analysis that meets this desideratum are dim.

5.3. Knowledge, Evidence, and Reasons

Two clusters of problems for the traditional framework: the problem of making sense of how strong evidence must be if it is to be adequate for justification that satisfies the justification requirement for knowledge; the problem of making sense of the justification requirement for some modes of knowledge. In connection with the first problem we need to make sense of how evidence adequate for knowledge can be conclusive in order to do justice to the connection between knowing and responsibly taking the matter to be settled. This theme is taken up in Chapter 7. Perceptual knowledge raises problems in the second cluster that are addressed in Chapter 6.

5.4. Concepts versus Phenomena

Why the emphasis thus far on concepts might seem misplaced. Why there is a place for conceptual enquiry in epistemology. This enquiry need not aim at reductive conceptual analysis.

5.5. The Way Ahead

The aim of Part II is to show that there can be substantive epistemology even if knowledge does not yield to reductive analysis. The approach adopted will help us to make sense of why so much knowledge is readily available to us.

Chapter 6: Perceptual Knowledge and Recognitional Abilities

6.1. Introduction

Perceptual knowledge as a paradigm of knowing. Perception often enables us to acquire knowledge but also, in most circumstances, enables us responsibly to take the matter to be settled and vouch for the truth. Though perceptual knowledge is phenomenologically immediate it can have rich content extending beyond the superficial properties of things that go to make up their appearance. This is thanks to our having perceptual-recognitional abilities.

6.2. Perceptual-Recognitional Abilities

Perceptual-recognitional abilities depend on things having distinctive appearances. The notion of the exercise of such an ability is a success notion. Fallibility is accommodated because we do not exercise an ability every time we aspire to. A perspective on barn examples: the subject does not know in the fake-barn scenario because there barns lack a distinctive visual appearance and one cannot tell of structures that they are barns from their visual appearance. That is compatible with being able to tell back home where barns have a distinctive appearance.

6.3. Broad and Narrow Competence

As conceived here, recognitional abilities are broadly individuated—they are abilities with respect to some favourable environment. This contrasts with a view on which the subject in barn cases manifests the same competence in the fake-barn scenario as he manifests in his home territory.

6.4. Avoiding Reduction

The view that broad competence can be explained in terms of narrow competence does not reflect our understanding of the abilities displayed in perceptual recognition. The conceptual level at which we encounter perceptual knowledge is that of knowing that something is so through seeing or otherwise perceiving it to be so. The view presented here respects the actual order of understanding.

6.5. Perceptual Knowledge and Justified Belief

How does perceptual knowledge relate to justified belief? In cases of knowing that p through seeing that p, it is the fact that we see that p that is our reason and provides our justification for believing. Such facts are made available through our having higher-order recognitional abilities that are responsive to the same experiences that trigger the corresponding first-order recognitional abilities.

6.6. Closure and Doxastic Responsibility

Implications of the proposed account for zebra cases. A problem of doxastic responsibility: what is the status of the understandings of the workings of the world that inform our perceptual-recognitional abilities? We need to resist the idea that in order to be able responsibly to exploit an understanding, and in order to count as having a recognitional ability informed by that understanding, the elements of that understanding must be independently supported. This theme is taken up in Chapter 7.

Chapter 7: Knowledge from Indicators

7.1. Introduction

Recent epistemology commonly works with a weak conception of evidence adequate for knowledge. We need to make sense of how evidence can clinch it that something is so, not just render it probable that it is so, as when the tracks on the path clinch it that deer have recently passed.

7.2. Knowledge from Indicators

The cases under consideration are one in which the occurrence of some phenomenon indicates that something is so. Indication is factive and has a modal dimension. *The standard model* for such cases assumes that we require evidence for a covering generalization. That would create problems for the view that evidence can be clinching and is open to independent objection.

7.3. Recognitional Abilities Again

We can have a basic perceptual-recognitional ability that enables us, for instance, to tell what our car's fuel gauge reads, and a further recognitional ability that enables us to recognize the significance of this reading with respect to the fuel level in the tank. The similarities between basic perceptual recognition and recognition of the indicative significance of indicators are striking. Both depend on favourable environments. Neither is 'blind'. Both are akin to practical skills. Neither depends on having evidence for covering generalizations. The role of experience in honing recognitional abilities contrasts with the role of experience in furnishing us with evidence.

7.4. Detached Standing Knowledge

Detached standing knowledge is standing knowledge of facts where we have lost touch with the sources of information for those facts. It is not, in the clear sense, knowledge based on evidence. It consists in an ability to recall a known fact—an ability that has been honed by encounters with knowledge-incorporating sources. How such knowledge yields justified belief.

7.5. Back to Knowledge from Indicators

The understandings that inform our recognitional abilities can include our detached standing knowledge. But we cannot account for those understandings just in terms of such knowledge. Generalizations covering the connection between indicator phenomena and what they indicate can figure in our understandings. They can be indeterminate and might even be false without detriment to the recognitional abilities that they inform. The status of these generalizations derives from their role in constituting the ability in question.

7.6. Taking Stock

Problems concerning knowledge are largely about how we gain so much from what seems so little. The accounts of various modes of knowledge considered so far are aimed at addressing those problems in a manner that enables us to see how knowledge puts us in a position to take a matter to be settled and to vouch for the truth.

Chapter 8: The Social Transmission of Knowledge

8.1. Why Knowledge Matters

An explanation is given of why it should be that *knowledge* is the goal of enquiry in terms of the idea that an interest in the truth as to whether or not something is so is an interest in reflectively knowing that it is so—knowing with knowledge of how, or at least that, one knows. Only such knowledge puts us in a position to take the matter to be settled, to terminate enquiry and to vouch for the truth of the matter. Why it is a mistake to think of the value of knowledge in terms of the value of merely true belief.

8.2. Approaching the Epistemology of Testimony

The focus is on *straightforward* cases of gaining knowledge from testimony in which knowledge is gained on the say so of the informant. The problem we need to address is how to make sense of the discriminative capacities of recipients given that they do not engage in deliberation, weigh up evidence, and the like. The account proposed here makes recognitional abilities central and invokes a conception of practices that is applied to communicative practice and especially to the speech-act of telling. Our grasp of the practice of telling enables us to discriminative tellings from other sayings.

8.3. Telling and Informing

My telling you that *p* is an act of saying to you that *p* by which I give you to understand that I am informing you that *p* and thus speaking from knowledge that *p*. Not all acts of saying something are acts of telling. The discrimination of tellings is made possible by recognitional abilities.

8.4. Acquiring True Beliefs and Acquiring Knowledge through Being Told

There is a rule governing telling to the effect that you do not tell people something unless you are by that act informing them of that thing and thus speaking from knowledge. Participating in the practice incurs a commitment to following this and any other rules. Felicitous telling is telling in keeping with its governing rules. The practice explains why it is that by relying on testimony we shall so often gain true beliefs. But it does not explain how we gain knowledge from testimony. For that we need to explain how we can often identify informants as being trustworthy, that is, competent and sincere, on the matter in hand. The account presented here exploits the conception of recognitional abilities developed in Chapters 6 and 7.

8.5. Access to Facts about Knowledge

Central to the approach taken in these chapters has been the rejection of conceptual-reductionist accounts of knowledge. Instead of trying to provide necessary and sufficient conditions for knowledge in terms that do not implicate the concept, I have focused on central kinds of knowledge aiming all along to do justice to how those kinds of knowledge figure in our thinking. On the proposed approach, knowledge is not an elusive and complex condition. There are familiar and commonly acknowledged ways of telling, including the subject-matter-specific recognitional abilities that have figured so prominently. Our general conception of knowledge is, in large measure, a conception of what can be gained by such means.

5

Knowledge in Recent Epistemology: Some Problems

5.1. Introduction

There is an influential framework—the traditional framework—according to which knowledge is belief that satisfies certain conditions, including truth. Many theorists have pursued the traditional analytic project—the attempt to find an analysis of knowledge within this framework. The aim of the analysis is to provide necessary and sufficient conditions for the truth of statements of the form 'S knows that p' in terms that spell out what needs to be added to belief to make knowledge. The analysis sought is often conceived as conceptual in that it would be an analysis of the concept of knowledge and reductive in that it would analyse knowledge in terms that do not implicate the concept of knowledge. Even when the problem of how to give a complete conceptual analysis of *knowledge* along these lines is not the focus of enquiry, and even when the reductive aspiration is abandoned, the traditional framework continues to shape research. It can do so, for instance, via the assumption that the notion of justified belief is more basic than that of knowledge and must be explicable independently of the concept of knowledge. Opposition to the traditional framework comes from at least two camps. On the one hand, there are theorists who think that knowledge is central to enquiry, and that the concept of knowledge is a key concept for epistemology, but who offer radical critiques of the traditional project, targeting the very idea that knowledge admits of analysis along traditional lines (McDowell 1982; 1994, 1995; Williamson 1995; 2000). On the other hand, there are theorists who doubt that knowledge is such an important concept for either epistemology or enquiry (Kaplan 1985; Wright 1991: 88) or who take it to be at least an open question whether the activities of enquiring and deliberating are bound to presuppose that concepts like those of knowledge and justified belief are central to those activities (Hookway 2003). Given the state of play, it is easy to lose sight of the intimate relation between enquiry and the search for knowledge. Even if an enquiry starts off in an open-ended way as enquiry about something, it will soon have to transform itself into enquiry whether or not this or that is so. The natural way to express the goal of such focused enquiry is in terms of finding out, that is, coming to know, whether this or that is so. I believe that we should take this at face value. It shows that the search for knowledge is central to our concerns, since we are all interested in enquiry, if only at relatively unsophisticated levels.[1]

Enquiries can go on indefinitely, but many that bear on our practical affairs conclude successfully. What is needed for success is not just that knowledge has in fact been acquired but also that investigators cease enquiring *because* they know that they now have the knowledge they seek. So there is a reflective element to the successful completion of an enquiry. There is, similarly, a reflective element to another activity that shows knowledge to be central to our concerns—informing others. When we inform others that something is so we give it to be understood that we know that it is so. We can felicitously do so, and be a good informant on the matter, only if in fact we do know that it is so. So since being a good informant is likely to be crucial for our social interactions, having relevant knowledge is crucial too. As with bringing focused enquiry to successful completion, it matters for felicitous informing not just whether or not we have the relevant knowledge but also that we know whether or not we have it. If we know we don't know we shall need to modulate what we say to others accordingly. A theory of knowledge should reflect these considerations and help us to make sense of them. This is the central thought that shapes the discussion in these four chapters. I believe that the traditional framework makes the value of knowledge—value we recognize in relation to enquiring and informing—hard to understand. Yet it is not clear how theorizing about knowledge should proceed if not in the terms of that framework. The aim of the chapters is to make some headway in this territory and thereby achieve a better understanding of the nature and value of knowledge.

---

[1] I consider why it is natural that enquiry should take this form in Chapter 8.

5.2. The Traditional Analytical Project and the Central Tension

There are problems internal to the traditional analytical project. Here are some:

(1) Attempts to provide a traditional analysis of knowledge appear not to have been successful. Each analysis seems to be vulnerable to counterexamples. So there are at least inductive grounds for wondering whether it is likely that any analysis will succeed (Williamson 1995; 2000).

(2) There are grounds for doubting that any traditional analysis could succeed if it analysed knowledge as true belief plus something else the obtaining of which does not guarantee the truth of the belief. For a priori it looks as if any such account will be vulnerable to Gettier cases. There will be a logical space for cases in which the truth requirement is met, and the further requirements, but relative to how the belief was formed it seems accidental that the subject forms a *true* belief (Zagzebski 1999; Williamson 2000: ch. 3).

(3) It is a mistake to suppose that all concepts of which we have mastery admit of reductive conceptual analysis in terms of necessary and sufficient conditions. So there is a question as to why we should suppose that the concept of knowledge admits of such analysis. Perhaps we grasp the concept through grasping certain central modes of knowledge, and apply the general concept to instances of those modes and to cases sufficiently like them.

There is room for traditional theorists to attempt to defuse each one of these problems. Nonetheless, the fact is that the nature of knowledge, conceived as something that can be explicated by reductive conceptual analysis, has proved to be extraordinarily elusive. In this chapter I argue that there is a tension between the assumption that *knowledge* admits of reductive conceptual analysis along traditional lines and the roles that knowledge and thinking about knowledge play in our lives. I shall call this *the central tension*. The chapters that follow are steps towards an alternative way of thinking about knowledge and its value.

Knowledge on many matters is not an aspiration that is hard to achieve. For those who are suitably equipped it is often readily acquired. For instance, by simply looking in my filing cabinet I can come to know that a copy of an article I want to read is in a folder there. Those who acquire knowledge by such straightforward means will usually be in a position to know that they have done so, through knowing how they know. Having found the copy, I would know that I came to know where it was by looking in the filing cabinet and finding it by its title. Facts about what others know are also often readily available. We often know that others know this or that because they tell us. Sometimes, from their orientation and behaviour, we can tell what they have seen or heard to be so and thus know to be so. We might notice, for instance, that someone else has noticed, and thus knows, that so-and-so has entered the room.

As already emphasized, our ability to access facts about knowledge matters for successful enquiry and for felicitous informing. It is, therefore, vital for guiding action and for our social interactions. Think of the difference between knowing that the gas on the cooking hob is turned off because one has just checked and believing that it is off because one knows that by and large one switches it off automatically when one has stopped using the hob. In the first of those situations, but not in the second, I could responsibly take it to be settled that the gas is off and thus responsibly vouch for it being off. Someone wishing to be assured on the matter would not be assured on finding out that the reason for my thinking the gas is off is that usually I turn it off after using the hob. In this example something of importance is at stake, but the distinction between knowing and being in some lesser state can matter in low-stakes cases too. Vouching for something's being so gives our hearers to understand that we know. If they take this at face value they will now take themselves to know. If we were routinely to vouch for what we do not know, we would risk letting down those we seek to inform and causing them inconvenience or disappointment. Smooth relations with others depend on this sort of thing not happening too often.

The upshot of these considerations is that knowledge can play the role that it does because knowledge is often achievable, often obtained, and facts as to what we, or others, know are often accessible to us. Traditional theorizing makes this hard to understand. This is what I called the central tension. There are really two aspects to the tension. The first is that our actual thinking about knowledge is not as would be expected if knowledge admitted of a reductive analysis in terms of belief plus further conditions. The second is that when we try to characterize our actual thinking about knowledge—the modes of thought about knowledge that come naturally to us—it becomes less and less plausible that the concept of knowledge that we deploy admits of a reductive analysis in terms of belief plus further conditions. My principle aim in these chapters is to take steps towards a constructive account of knowledge, as we understand it. The account will seek to explain certain modes of knowledge in terms of abilities exercised in acquiring knowledge in those modes. Since these abilities are characterized as ways of telling that something is so, thus as ways of knowing, the account will not be reductive, but it will, I hope, be informative. In this chapter I discuss the central tension.

The following is a plausible methodological assumption:

(A) An adequate analysis of the concept of knowledge should reflect the logical role of the concept in our thinking.

We need to bear in mind that traditional analyses are meant to spell out conditions sufficient and necessary for the correct, in the sense of true, application of the concept of knowledge *that we deploy in practice* [2] It is the logical role of that concept in which we are interested—what that concept contributes to the content of the thoughts, judgements, beliefs, and the like which bring it into play. If we are to become clear about that role it can only be by reflection on the commitments incurred by applying the concept and on why people count or fail to count as knowing in this or that circumstance. There is an understanding of these matters of which those who possess the concept have a more or less adequate grasp. To recover the role of the concept we have to tap into that understanding, hence the prominent role given to examples of knowledge and of what falls short of knowledge—examples that are meant to reflect our ordinary understanding of what knowledge is.

Our actual thought and talk about knowledge is no doubt messy. There is no reason to suppose that all considered applications of the concept of knowledge, even by those who have a good grasp of it, are correct. We should not assume that everything that strikes us as obvious in this area is true. Nor should we even assume in advance of enquiry that there is a clear and coherent understanding that informs our thinking. But there might be some order in the mess. I take it to be a methodological presupposition of any recognizably philosophical enquiry into the concept of knowledge or any other concept, that such order might be discernible by attention to the factors to which we

---

[2] This is how the analytical project was originally conceived and is still conceived by many now. With the upsurge of naturalism, and the concomitant suspicion of the very idea of analytic/conceptual truth, there are theorists now who disavow interest in analysis so conceived and view analysis in terms of providing a plausible characterization of the phenomenon of knowledge, irrespective of what is to be said about the ordinary concept of knowledge. See further in §5.4.

are sensitive in deploying those concepts. This is not something that traditional theorists need resist. Indeed, it seems to be a presupposition of the traditional analytical project, at least if conceived as a project of conceptual analysis.

The thinking surrounding (A) is that those who possess the concept of knowledge have a more or less adequate understanding of what knowledge is and that the logical role of the concept is recoverable from reflection on this understanding. If this is right, and I think it is, then it is a condition of the adequacy of any account of *knowledge* that it should reflect this understanding. This quickly takes us to:

> (B) The prospects for providing a reductive conceptual analysis that satisfies condition (A) are dim.

If an analysis of the concept were adequate then it would capture the understanding of *knowledge* that informs our thinking. And if that were so then competent applications of the concept would be sensitive to whether or not the conditions given by the analysis are satisfied. Well-grounded attributions of knowledge would be based on well-grounded judgements to the effect that the conditions obtain. The problem is that it is doubtful that those with a mastery of the concept do in fact display the required sensitivity. There are two factors of relevance at this point.

(a) Those who have mastery of the concept of knowledge need not possess the concepts that figure in the conditions provided by traditional analyses and so would not be in a position to take into account whether the conditions given in the analysis are satisfied. A concept like that of a *reliable belief-forming process* does not routinely figure in the thinking of those who deploy the concept of knowledge. It is not even clear that the concept of justified belief that figures in reductive theorizing reflects how we actually think about justification in practice or can plausibly serve the purposes of an analysis. That is in part because we tend to think of justification for believing as depending on our having reasons supplied by what we know.[3] But it is also in part because the notion of justified belief that figures in traditional analysis and in descriptions of Gettier cases is so very weak. It has everything to do with a kind of reasonableness that renders one blameless in thinking that something is so, but little to do with the kind of well-groundedness that settles that something is so and on that account entitles one to take it to be so. Consider a variant of a familiar perceptual Gettier case. As I approach the open front door of my friend Bill's house, looking, as it seems, through the door I form a belief that Bill is standing in the entrance hall just behind the door. In fact, I am looking

---

[3] For related thinking, see Unger (1975) and Williamson (2000: ch. 9).

at a life-size photograph of Bill, so for a few moments it is just as if Bill is positioned where I take him to be against the background I take to be there. In fact, he is so positioned against just such a background. My belief is true and, for the short time I hold it, is reasonable. It is reasonable because from what I see it is just as if Bill is where I take him to be and there is no evident reason for me to think otherwise on my first sight of the doorway. But there is a sense of 'entitled' on which I am not entitled to take it that Bill is there. If am entitled to something then I have secured a title to it. Under the circumstances of the case, I am no more entitled to take it that Bill is there than I would be entitled to receive a sum of money simply on the grounds that I reasonably believe myself to have inherited it, having been told so, falsely, by someone I have no reason to distrust. To be entitled to receive the money on account of having inherited it, I must actually have inherited it. To be entitled to take it that Bill is there in response to the visual experiences I had I would need to have seen Bill and recognized him to be Bill. In the absence of such perceptual-cognitive contact with Bill, and with the fact that he is there, my belief that he is there is not well grounded and thus not one to which I am entitled. Perhaps in cases in which we do know things from what we see to be so it will always be that we reasonably take these things to be so in the weak sense that is tied to blamelessness. But it is a further question whether knowledge can be analysed in terms of reasonable true belief plus some further anti-Gettier condition. An adequate account of knowledge should explain how one who knows that p has a well-grounded belief that p and thus has a reason to believe that p that provides such grounding. One is not guaranteed to have such a belief in view of possessing a reasonable belief. In the perceptual Gettier case just considered I have a reasonable true belief that Bill is there, but I lack the reason I would have if knew that Bill was there in the way I take myself to. For if I knew that Bill was there by seeing him, then *that I see that he is there* would be a reason—and a reason I have—for believing that he is there. Since I do not see that Bill is there I have no such reason.[4] A second reason for being sceptical about the prospects for analysing knowledge in terms of reasonable belief plus further conditions is that reasonableness, conceived as here, will not enable us to understand how, when we know that something is so, the matter can be settled. When I look at the life-sized photograph of Bill it is not settled that he is there. This emerges as soon as I see that it is a life-sized photograph at which I am looking and not Bill. It might be thought that the weakness of the notion of reasonableness could be offset in perceptual cases by requiring

---

[4] How reasons of this sort can illuminate perceptual knowledge and justification is considered in the next chapter. I touch on related matters in §5.3 below.

there to be a causal-explanatory link between what we perceive and what we take to be so, or requiring that what we believe should be the upshot of a belief-forming process that reliably yields true beliefs. Even if such conditions have a role in an adequate account of knowledge, their incorporation does not address the issue of how, when we know perceptually that such-and-such, the matter can properly be taken to be settled. (The notions of reasonableness and of entitlement will surface more than once in subsequent discussion.)[5]

(b) It is far from clear that the concepts that do figure in our thinking about knowledge are good prospects for conceptual analysis independently of the concept of knowledge. When you know that a pig is there on seeing the pig it is natural to think of you as deploying a way of telling that a pig is there, in particular, telling that a pig is there by looking and seeing one to be there. Similarly, if I know that water in my electric kettle has come to the boil having just heard the kettle switch off, I tell that it has come to the boil from hearing it switch off. A way of telling is just a way of coming to know. We explain why you know in the particular case in terms of your having and deploying a way of coming to know that kind of thing. We have common-sense, readily understood, ways of specifying such ways of telling—*telling by looking that a pig is there, telling from hearing the kettle switch off that the water in it has come to the boil*. I shall argue in Chapter 6 that we should be sceptical about the prospects of providing an analysis of *way of telling* in terms that do not implicate the concept of knowledge. Yet the explanation of the knowledge in the particular case is informative. Some other way of telling might have been employed, so it is informative to know that this way of telling is what did the trick on the given occasion.

If the concept of knowledge we deploy in practice admitted of a traditional analysis, then we should not expect it to have been so difficult to provide an adequate analysis that commands widespread acceptance. I am not assuming here that those who possess a concept are bound to have a perspicuous view of its character. People may count as possessing a concept though they have a partial or even an erroneous grasp of it.[6] Children may have some grasp

---

[5]   The term 'entitlement' is sometimes used a species of warrant that is not provided by a (conceptually) accessible reason, as in Burge (2003). Wright (2004) uses 'entitlement' for 'a type of rational warrant whose possession does not require the existence of evidence—in the broad sense, encompassing both *a priori* and empirical considerations—for the truth of the warranted proposition' (174–5). Peacocke (2004) and McDowell (2009a) both use 'entitled' of, among other things, beliefs based on experience. I use 'entitled' so that it may apply to cases in which beliefs that are justified in the sense of well-grounded. They may be grounded in evidence or proof or in perception. It is then an open question whether there are entitlements additional to those conferred by what one perceives or by evidence or proof that one possesses.

[6]   For some relevant discussion, see Millar (2004: 162–5), drawing upon Burge (1979).

of the concept of an uncle, through having learned to recognize this or that person as their uncle, while having a dim conception of what it takes for one person to be the uncle of another. Even so, somebody with a full grasp of the concept should not find it too difficult on reflection to make this explicit. It is puzzling that, after so much philosophical effort, the conditions for knowing, conceived as conditions spelled out by a traditional conceptual analysis, have eluded us despite the fact that these conditions should reflect an understanding of knowledge that informs our thinking.

By way of response to the foregoing it might be said, first, that some concepts are so complex that it takes immense effort to provide an adequate analysis of them, and second that I am not giving enough weight to the fact that there is a gap between mastering a concept and being able to provide a perspicuous view of its character. Arguably, philosophical enquiry into the character of interesting concepts like *knowledge, explanation, belief, intention, reasons for actions*, and *free will* is called for precisely because with respect to those concepts the gap between possession and perspicuous view is hard to leap over.[7] Hume (*Treatise of Human Nature*, Bk. I, Part III, § VII) was wrong about the psychological nature of belief—beliefs are not, as he thought, a species of idea if ideas are, as he thought, a species of experience. Yet Hume was no doubt able to deploy the concept of belief for non-philosophical purposes as well as anyone. The suggested upshot is that it is no surprise that those who are well able to deploy the concept of knowledge in their non-philosophical thinking should find it hard to analyse it. This response does not, I think, come to grips with the problem. To repeat, it is not in dispute that there is a gap between having the ability to deploy a concept and being able to provide a perspicuous representation of its character. If that were not so we would not be debating these matters. But the gap that creates the problem is not just *that* gap. It is the gap which the traditionalist must suppose there is between mastering a concept that we routinely deploy *that admits of reductive conceptual analysis* and being able to provide the relevant analysis. The problem is to see how such a gap should so stubbornly resist being bridged if it were true that in our deployment of the concept of knowledge we are more or less sensitive to whether the conditions given by the analysis are satisfied.

Still, it may be argued that the problem can be solved with the help of a more subtle way of thinking about the relation between the analysis of concepts and mastery of those concepts. Analyses, it might be said, may deploy concepts that need not be within the repertoires even of those whose mastery of the concept is as good as it could be. Consider a case study. In

---

[7] Cf. Wittgenstein (1958: Part I, 122).

a classic discussion of perceptual knowledge Alvin Goldman (1976) offers an analysis of the knowledge that is explicitly designed to 'explicate the concept of knowledge' (1976: 771). The analysis makes use of the notion of a relevant alternative. The idea was that if, for instance, I know that the object over there is a dog then it must be that there is no relevant alternative to the object's being a dog. In this case a relevant alternative would be, roughly speaking, a possible state of affairs in which there is no dog but which is such that, had it obtained instead, I would have responded just as I do in the actual situation, believing, in that event falsely, that the object is a dog. However, as Goldman observed, this will not do; I would not be rendered unable to know perceptually that an object is a dog simply on the grounds that I mistake wolves for certain types of dog, say, German shepherds. I may be well able to tell perceptually that an object before me is a dachshund and thus a dog, even if, had it been a wolf, I would still have believed it to be a dog. To address the problem Goldman introduces the idea that a relevant alternative must be a *perceptual equivalent*. Again roughly speaking, '[a] *perceptual equivalent* of an actual state of affairs is a possible state of affairs that would produce the same, or a sufficiently similar, perceptual experience' (1976: 779–80). The state of affairs in which the object is a wolf is not a relevant alternative—not one that prevents me knowing that the object is a dog in the way I do—since its obtaining would not have resulted in my having experiences of the sort that I actually have on looking at the dachshund and in response to which I judge it to be a dog. Goldman introduces further technical concepts to refine the notion of a perceptual equivalent, including that of a distance-orientation-environment (DOE) relation. Such a relation captures the distance and orientation of the perceived object from the subject and prevailing environmental conditions that determine the character of the subject's experience. The point of introducing this notion is to fix the character of subject's experience in given circumstances with a view to providing a more precise definition of a perceptual equivalent,[8] which can in turn be plugged into an analysis of non-inferential perceptual knowledge. The details do not matter for present purposes. The analysis well illustrates the complexities to which attempts to provide a conceptual analysis of *knowledge* can lead. What more specifically interests me is what

---

[8] The definition is as follows. 'If object *b* has the maximal set of properties J [one that exhaustively characterizes *b* at *t*] and is in DOE relation R to S at *t*, if S has some percept P at *t* that is perceptually caused by *b*'s having J and being in R to S at *t* and if P non-inferentially causes S to believe (or sustains S in believing) of object *b* that it has property F, then $<c, K, R^*>$ is *a perceptual equivalent of* $<b, J, R>$ *for S at t relative to property F* if and only if (1) if at *t* object *c* had K and were in R^* to S, then this would perceptually cause S to have some percept P^* at *t*, (2) P^* would cause S non-inferentially to believe (or sustain S in believing) of object *c* that it has F, and (3) P^* would not differ from P in any respect that is relevant to S's F-belief' (Goldman 1976: 783).

might be said to defend such analyses in the face of my concerns about the relation between analyses and concept-mastery. Here is one possible line of thought:

> It is entirely legitimate to take seriously an analysis of perceptual knowledge that brings such notions as perceptual equivalents and DOE relations into play. For instance, it is clearly relevant to whether I know by looking at it that a certain object is a dog that the object should be positioned and illuminated so that I can see it clearly enough. This is at least part of what the notion of a DOE relation is meant to capture. So, notwithstanding that most people who have a perfectly adequate grasp of the concept of knowledge have no grasp of the concept of a DOE relation, what the concept picks out is a bunch of factors to which applications of the concept of knowing through visual perception are sensitive.

Considerations along these lines might well figure in the thinking of those who propose complex conditions for knowledge in general, or some particular form of knowledge, using technical notions. Their drift is that analyses of the sort under consideration surely can tell us something about knowledge notwithstanding that they deploy 'technical' concepts. I believe that this response can be defused by acknowledging that such accounts might direct our attention to factors that are relevant to whether a subject knows, while denying that they provide an adequate reductive conceptual analysis.

Suppose that I see that, and thus know that, my friend has spotted his dog running back to him from some bushes. It is clearly relevant to my doing so that the dog is in my friend's line of sight and that the prevailing conditions of light enable him to see the dog. Had I observed that there was something obstructing my friend's view so that he could not see the dog, I would not have known or believed that he had spotted it. There is no question that to see the dog my friend must be suitably oriented towards it, and that environmental conditions must be suitable. Nor is it in question that for me to tell that he sees and recognizes his dog I must be in some way sensitive to these factors. However, it does not follow that for this purpose I must register *at the level of judgement* that some specific DOE relation obtains or that to make a well-founded attribution of perceptual knowledge of the relevant sort I must have a general grasp of which such relations make for visual-perceptual knowledge. Two considerations are salient. First, it seems plausible that we have a capacity to recognize in particular circumstances that a subject is or is not in a position to see and recognize something. On the imagined occasion, given my view of my friend in relation to the dog, and of the prevailing environmental conditions, I can recognize that the dog is visible from where he is. In a different circumstance I might recognize that the dog is not visible from where he is because it is behind a bush that interposes between him and the dog. It does not follow that I have a general understanding of the DOE relations that facilitate or inhibit seeing and recognition that could serve the purposes of a reductive analysis of perceptual knowledge. This takes us to the second consideration. It is plausible that the nearest we come to deploying a conception of a DOE relation is via the notion of things being such that an object can (or cannot) be seen by a subject. Indeed, where the issue is whether someone knows something about an object from seeing it, we work with the notion of things being such that a subject can see an object *and recognize it* to be of some kind, say. The first consideration tells against the prospect of a reductive analysis simply because such an analysis will not reflect the conceptual resources at our disposal. Well-founded attributions to subjects of perceptual knowledge about an object, made from observation of those subjects, are indeed sensitive to how they are orientated vis-à-vis the object in question, but they do not rest on judgements about specific DOE relations. The second consideration also tells against reductive conceptual analysis because it casts doubt on whether the analysis would be non-circular. That someone is so oriented and situated that he can recognize his dog is a matter of that person's being so placed that he can tell by seeing, and in that way know, that his dog is there. Arguably, such grasp as we have of what makes conditions suitable is dependent on our grasp of what it takes to know by seeing that the dog in question is returning.

It is not in dispute that accounts such as Goldman's highlight important factors that are relevant to whether people know through visual perception or even that they can shed light on the logical role of concepts like that of knowing through seeing. What is in dispute is the character of our sensitivity to those factors, and the bearing of this on the prospects of reductive conceptual analysis.[9]

The idea that it can be crucial to mastering a concept that one should be sensitive to certain factors, even though this sensitivity is not a matter of being prepared to take account of those factors at the level of judgement, is important for understanding perceptual knowledge and its scope. In applying the concept of a cow in response to what we see, we are sensitive to the relevant appearance. It does not follow that when applying the concept in this way we take account of whether or not the features that make up the

---

[9] Goldman (1992*b*) is sympathetic to an exemplar approach to concept representation. Applying such an approach to the concept of knowledge avoids commitment to analyses of knowledge in terms of necessary and sufficient conditions in the usual style.

appearance of a cow are present, if that means registering propositionally, at the level of judgement, that this or that feature is present. As with perceptual recognition more generally, the information conveyed by any description of features that we'd be likely to give underdetermines what we respond to when looking. We tell from the appearance of the thing perceived, but it would be a mistake to suppose that this is a matter of inferring from assumptions that detail the relevant features. There is such a thing as being sensitive to a visual *Gestalt*, for instance, even though that sensitivity does not take the form of taking account (at the level of judgement) of whether features that contribute to this *Gestalt* are present. Similar considerations apply to other sensory modalities. Think of recognizing music to be the music of a particular composer. Some who can reliably identify musical performances as of works by Mahler without being able to recognize the particular piece would be hard put to do more than gesture at descriptions of the features that reveal that they are by Mahler. Sophisticated lovers of music have a conceptual repertoire that enables them to provide fuller descriptions, but the understanding that goes with their specialized concepts is still recognitional. The descriptions can be grasped only via acquaintance with works that have the features that the descriptions pick out.

These considerations, which concern the application of concepts that are applied through perceptually recognizing something to be some sort, have a bearing on how we are able to apply the concept of knowledge through perceiving. The scope of our perceptual knowledge is much broader than is generally supposed. Thanks to the sophisticated character of the recognitional abilities that we can acquire, we can take in perceptually rich facts, including facts as to what others know perceptually. This means that there is the prospect of accounting for how certain factors can bear on whether someone knows something through perception even if those factors are not routinely registered at the level of judgement by those attributing or withholding attribution of knowledge. Analyses such as Goldman's have been genuinely illuminating because they have drawn attention to such factors, not because they give plausible reductive conceptual analyses.

I have been focusing on considerations that make the prospects for an adequate analysis of knowledge along traditional lines look dim. They are considerations that provide reason to doubt whether any reductive conceptual analysis is likely to reflect the understanding of knowledge that informs our actual thinking. The more subtle and complex analyses become, the less plausible it is that they reflect our actual thinking and the more difficult it becomes to understand why we are as good as we are at telling when we and others know this or that.

5.3. Knowledge, Evidence, and Reasons

Other problems for the traditional framework come into view when we focus on issues concerning justified belief. Of particular interest are two clusters of problems for traditional theories that make justification a necessary condition for knowledge. The first concerns knowledge based on evidence. The problems in this cluster arise because it is not clear how much evidential support is required in order to have justification for believing something that is strong enough to satisfy any justification requirement for knowledge. The problems in the second cluster arise because there are modes of knowledge with respect to which it is not clear how any justification requirement is satisfied. The most obvious example is perceptual knowledge.

I should stress that I mean to contrast perceptual knowledge with *knowledge based on evidence*. Perceptual knowledge supplies us with evidence, but there is a clear sense in which it is not itself evidence-based.[10] In this clear sense evidence-based knowledge is of the form *knowing that* p *on the basis of evidence to the effect that* q, r, s. When I know that my coffee cup is nearly empty in virtue of seeing it to be so, my seeing it to be so is a form of knowing it to be so but that knowledge is not evidence-based in the clear sense just explained. I recognize that my cup is half-full, rather than make a judgement that it is half-full based on something else, for instance, that I recall having drunk half of the coffee.[11]

Focusing, then, on the first cluster of problems, it seems important to acknowledge that empirical evidence for a proposition can be strong even though it is compatible with the falsity of the proposition. In view of this, it is natural to suppose that the justification requirement that is widely held to apply to knowledge may be satisfied on the basis of evidence that warrants a high degree of confidence that p, yet does not entail $<p>$. This gives rise to two problems. The first concerns how to reconcile the proposed way of thinking of knowledge based on evidence with the plausible assumption that knowing something can enable the matter to be settled so that one can responsibly

[10] Here I respect J. L. Austin's remarks about seeing the pig versus having evidence of the pig's being around the place (Austin 1962: 115).

[11] This is in keeping with Williamson (2000). The point that seeing-that is a form of knowing is sometimes doubted. This might be because it is conflated with seeing-as. If I see something as an F the concept of an F comes into play but need not be applied to the object seen. (One might not actually believe the thing to be an F.) I take it that *seeing that* X is an F is a matter of seeing X and, by means of thus seeing X, recognizing, and so coming to know, X to be an F. However, much of what I have to say about perceptual knowledge could be reformulated without the assumption that seeing-that is itself a form of knowledge.

terminate enquiry.[12] If my evidence that p does no more than warrant my having a high degree of confidence that p, but does not entail $<p>$, then how can it enable it to be settled that p? The second problem is that among evidence that warrants at best a high degree of confidence that p, but does not entail $<p>$, there seems to be no principled way of distinguishing between strength of evidence that is adequate for knowledge and strength of evidence that is not adequate for knowledge so long as we think of degree of support as being on a sliding scale. This being so, it is hard to explain, with respect to knowledge based on evidence, why the distinction between what we know and what we don't know should matter in the way it does. Why in particular should we bother, as we do, about the distinction between evidence adequate for knowing and evidence that warrants having a high degree of confidence yet falls short of being adequate for knowing?

It is one thing to identify this problem and another to work out how to account for evidence adequate for knowledge. A crucial part of any promising treatment of evidence-based knowledge will be recognizing that we are not faced with an exhaustive choice between conceiving of evidence for $<p>$ adequate for knowledge as entailing $<p>$ and conceiving of it as warranting some hard-to-specify degree of confidence that p linked to degree of evidential support. It seems plausible that if evidence for $<p>$ is adequate for knowledge that p then it must clinch it—settle it—that p. That is to say, it must in a certain sense be *conclusive*.[13] It can be conclusive short of entailing $<p>$ by being such that in the circumstances there would be this evidence only if p. That there are these tracks on the muddy path can in this sense be conclusive evidence that deer have recently passed: the presence of the tracks indicates that deer have recently passed in a sense that entails that there would be these tracks only if deer had recently passed.[14] I pursue this line of thought in Chapter 7.

---

[12] That I can responsibly treat a matter as being settled is compatible with continuing sensitivity to counterevidence, by which I mean being so alert that were such evidence to emerge one would give it due attention. To treat the matter as being settled is to treat it as not calling for further enquiry.

[13] Fred Dretske (1971) argued that for knowledge there must be reasons for belief that are conclusive. John McDowell has protested against accounts of knowledge of other minds that envisage 'ascribing knowledge on the strength of something compatible with the falsity of what is supposedly known' (1982; 372), though he does not, I think, explain how we should think of knowledge based on evidence if such ascriptions are proscribed. Charles Travis (2005) has commended a view on which knowledge requires proof—not necessarily mathematical proof but, nonetheless, something far stronger than merely evidence making what is known highly probable.

[14] There are readings of 'The streets would not be wet unless it had rained' and of 'The streets would be wet only if it had rained' on which they are not equivalent. For relevant discussion see Sosa (2003). I believe there also readings on which they are equivalent, but I shall stick with subjunctives of the latter type when characterizing the relation between conclusive evidence and that for which it is conclusive evidence.

The problems in the second cluster arise because there are modes of knowledge with respect to which it is not clear how any justification requirement is satisfied. Suppose that I know that Mary has arrived because I see and recognize her. Under the terms of the traditional analytical project this breaks down into true belief plus the satisfaction of further conditions. Assuming that one of those conditions is that I should be justified in believing that Mary has arrived, the question arises as to how this condition is satisfied in the present case. A natural way to think of justification is in terms of the possession of an adequate reason for believing that Mary has arrived. And a natural way to think of what it is to possess a reason to believe something is in terms of standing in some relation to a (distinct) consideration in view of which one is justified in believing that thing. Thus, seeing that her car is in the driveway I may believe that my wife has already arrived home. My reason for believing is that her car is in the driveway. It is a reason that is constituted by the consideration that her car is in the driveway though, of course, it would not be *my reason* unless I believed this consideration. By contrast, in the case in which I believe that Mary has arrived I do not seem to believe for some reason that is connected to her arrival in anything like the way that the consideration in play in the example of my wife connects with her having already arrived at home. The consideration that my wife's car is at home articulates evidence that my wife has already arrived—evidence that is the basis for my belief that she has. By contrast, it simply strikes me on looking that Mary has arrived; I do not take her to be there on the basis of evidence that she is there, not at any rate if the role of evidence is conceived on the model of the example concerning my wife. So how should we account for the justification of the implicated belief in cases of perceptual knowledge like this?

A number of responses are suggested by recent epistemological tradition:

(a) We could give up the idea that knowledge requires justified belief and adopt some kind of reliabilist conception of knowledge.

(b) We could reject the idea that justification is tied to reasons, while adopting a reliabilist account of justified belief (as in Goldman 1979), thus retaining the link between knowledge and justified belief.

(c) We could propose a conception of justification that makes it possible for beliefs to be justified directly on the basis of experiences, at least in the absence of countervailing reasons.[15]

---

[15] Accounts of this general form have been popular for years. Pryor (2002) is a recent influential source. For criticism, see Neta (2004). A further option recommended to me by Matthew Chrisman would be to represent justified belief as a procedural matter—being able to justify your belief if asked.

Responses (a) and (b) are not especially promising. There are familiar problems for reliabilist accounts of knowledge and justified belief. If these are offered as conceptual analyses then they inherit the general problems of reductive analyses.[16] Response (c) also faces problems. It can be developed in two ways. To preserve the link between justified belief and the possession of reasons the conception of reasons might be extended to embrace reasons that are not propositionally constituted. Experiences themselves, rather than considerations about experiences, are taken to be reasons (as in Millar 1991). Or the link between justified belief and the possession of reasons might be severed while preserving the idea that experiences provide justification (as in Pryor 2002). In either development experiences tend to be conceived in non-committal terms. Looking at a rose, for instance, you might have an experience such that it looks to you just as if a rose is before you. Having such an experience is understood to be compatible with there being no rose before you. So if you are justified in believing that a rose is before you it is on the basis of an experience that it is possible that one should have even if no rose were there. We have here, again, the problem of explaining how we can draw out of this way of thinking an account of a standing that is stronger than mere reasonableness. There is, so far as I can see, little if any prospect of doing justice to the idea that we can have well-grounded empirical beliefs if we do not acknowledge that the reasons that perceptual knowledge puts in our way depend on our being in cognitive contact with the world through seeing or otherwise perceiving this and that to be so. Seeing yesterday that Bill was in town puts us in a different position in relation to believing that Bill was then in town than merely having had an experience such that it looked just as if Bill was in town. It furnishes us with knowledge that Bill was in town and knowledge that one saw that Bill was in town. The latter is our access to a clinching reason to believe that Bill was then in town. (See further §6.5.) Having had an experience such that it looked just as if we was in town can account for the reasonableness of believing that Bill was in town: it was just as if we saw that he was and so just as if we had a clinching reason for thinking he was there. But it can hardly confer the entitlement to believe that is conferred by seeing that he was in town. Perhaps this in itself is not in dispute. It is,

---

While I agree that having a justified belief involves being in a position to justify one's belief, it seems to me that there remains a question as to what it is about one's current state that enables one to offer justification. On the option I favour this is understood in terms of possession of a reason to believe.

[16] I have in mind particularly the Generality Problem, which concerns how to single out the disposition or process relevant to whether a given belief counts as justified or as knowledge. I acknowledge that there are responses to this and other problems. I am sceptical that we have a grip on the relevant dispositions or processes other than by abstraction from familiar ways of telling. See §6.4.

after all, common sense. The problem comes when one tries to delve below the level of seeing that Bill was in town so that the well-groundedness that it confers is supposed to be derivative from experiences that can never do more than confer reasonableness. It has seemed necessary to do the delving because of worries about how our being in factive states like seeings-that can be accessible to us. But these worries, it seems to me, are relatively untroubling in comparison with the problem of trying to work well-groundedness out of experiences that are not conceived as perceivings-that. To make sense of this we need a positive account of perceptual knowledge that puts perceivings-that centre stage.

There is a further problem for the way of thinking under consideration posed by the distance between the theorist's representation of what makes for justified belief in perceptual cases and our natural ways of thinking about justified belief in those cases. It is not perspicuous how experiences can be reasons or, if they are not reasons, how they are supposed to justify beliefs.[17] Reasons as we ordinarily think of them are constituted by considerations. When we have such reasons we accept the considerations that constitute them. When we think or act for such reasons we do so in view of those reasons. I do not mean by this that we necessarily deliberate or think about them. But they are *in view* in the sense that they are available to be cited by way of justifying what we believe or rendering what we do intelligible.[18] Were it not for the fact that there has seemed to be an issue about what justification we have for belief in cases of perceptual knowledge, there would be little incentive to postulate reasons that do not routinely figure in our actual thinking about perceptual knowledge.

Fortunately, there is an account of perceptual knowledge that is not reductionist about knowledge in general, or about perceivings-that, and which explicates such knowledge in terms of perceptual recognitional abilities. Central to the account is that perceptual-recognitional abilities are externalistically individuated. One can tell that something is a barn from the way it looks only with respect to environments in which barns have a distinctive appearance or appearances. (For more on this, see §§6.2 and 6.7.) From within the traditional framework it can hardly be denied that we can tell by looking that an object has such-and-such features, or is of this or that kind, and that in doing so we thereby come to know. So there is pressure from this direction to accommodate perceptual-recognitional abilities by giving an analytical account

---

[17] I appreciated the problem in Millar (1991) and addressed it. I now think that the story I told took us too far away from the ordinary way of thinking to which I allude in what immediately follows.

[18] The latter does not always involve justification in any ordinary sense. See Millar (2004: ch. 2).

of them in terms of competences conceived as individuated independently of the environment. My own view is that this approach has things the wrong way around. Any grasp we have of what such competences are is conceptually dependent on our grasp of the kind of externalistically individuated abilities that figure in my account.

Within the suggested framework there is no need for a recherché conception of a reason to account for how reasons are tied to perceptual knowledge. The fact that we see that something is so can supply us with a reason to think it so.[19] But instead of accounting for knowledge in terms of the possession of appropriate reasons, I propose to explain the possession of reasons in terms of the acquisition of knowledge.

5.4. Concepts versus Phenomena

I have been concentrating attention on a brand of conceptual-analytical epistemology that remains influential. From the standpoint of some theorists my focus on this brand might seem misplaced. Even granted that enquiry into the concept of knowledge should take the form of a reductive analysis, there are ways of thinking about analysis on which it is no objection to an analysis that the analysans makes use of concepts that do not figure in our ordinary thinking about knowledge. In keeping with this, it might be suggested that our conception of analysis should be guided by the form that analyses take in the work of those who offer us analyses. There is no question that philosophers often do use concepts that need not figure in the thinking of those who have command of the concept of knowledge.[20] Moreover, there is a long-standing issue about how analyses can be anything other than trivial if the expression that expresses the analysans has the same meaning as the expression that expresses the concept to be analysed.[21] In the light of this it might be supposed that interesting philosophical analyses tell us something we did not know already—something about what falls under the concept analysed.

---

[19] Earlier treatments of perceptual-recognitional abilities can be found in Millar (2007a; 2007b; 2008a; and 2008b). I am inspired by the centrality given to factive states in the work of John McDowell (1982; 1994; 1995), Timothy Williamson (2000), Barry Stroud (2004), and Quassim Cassam (2007), but seek to embed some of their insights in a framework that makes it easier to see how the reasons provided by the factive states can be readily available to us and that makes recognition a key concept in an adequate epistemology.

[20] This has been emphasized by Michael DePaul (2009).

[21] See Langford (1942) on the paradox of analysis.

I have no brief to defend reductive conceptual analysis in philosophy. Suppose, for the sake of argument, that we are in that business and attempting to analyse an existing concept. Suppose further that one thinks that the *analysans* of an analysis may deploy concepts not necessarily grasped by those who have as good a mastery of the concept as one could have. Then, it seems to me, there is little point in thinking of this enterprise as reductive conceptual analysis as opposed to a theoretical investigation of the nature of what falls under the concept. An analysis of an existing concept that merits the description 'conceptual' must tell us something about the logical role of that concept—how it figures in our thinking and the constraints that it imposes on our thinking. My objection to reductive conceptual analyses of the concept of knowledge in terms of belief plus further conditions is that what they imply about the logical role of the concept is false. In deploying the concept we are not guided by an understanding that knowledge is what any reductive analysis tells us that it is. In particular, in ascribing knowledge that something is so to someone we do not incur a commitment to supposing that this person satisfies the conditions of any traditional analysis.

I have already acknowledged (in discussing Goldman's 1976 account of perceptual knowledge in §5.2 above) that concepts that do not figure in our pre-theoretical thinking about knowledge may legitimately figure in accounts of knowledge even when they do not serve the purposes of a reductive analysis. I have conceded too that they might shed light on the logical role of the concept by revealing factors to which applications of a concept are sensitive. My critical target is reductive conceptual analysis that deploys concepts that do not figure in our pre-theoretical thinking, not any attempt to shed light on the logical role of a concept using concepts that do not figure in our pre-theoretical thinking. As to the worry about the informativeness of analysis, I am not sure that it would be a sound objection to a reductive conceptual analysis that it is not very informative. But that might suggest that the genuinely informative philosophical accounts should not be conceived as reductive conceptual analyses.

Not all epistemologists who think of knowledge as a species of belief conceive of epistemology as conceptual analysis. Indeed, they may think that epistemology should not be conceived as conceptual enquiry at all. In a study examining methodological issues, Hilary Kornblith suggests that 'the subject matter of epistemology is knowledge itself, not our concept of knowledge' (2002: 1). This seems to me to be a misleading contrast. It is encouraged by the idea that whereas conceptual enquiry is *a priori* enquiry, which aspires to discover *a priori* knowable conceptual truths, enquiry into phenomena is empirical and thus not conceptual. It is moot whether this is the right way to think of conceptual enquiry. It was implicit in the discussion of §5.2 above that philosophical enquiry into concepts is answerable to considerations about how people deploy the concepts in question. That is why discussion has such a central role in philosophy: it serves to test claims about the character of interesting concepts by inviting participants to reflect on whether those claims are in keeping with the understanding that they link with those concepts and thus the sensitivities they display in deploying them. (It is a methodological presupposition of such investigation that there are shared understandings linked with concepts, though in principle discussion could reveal that the word that is taken to express a concept is equivocal or that the supposed concept is too fluid to pin down.) I am inclined to agree with Kornblith that epistemology should not be conceived as purely *a priori* because no such position does justice to the fact that philosophical claims are answerable to facts concerning judgement-formation. But that leaves unscathed the idea that philosophy has an important role for enquiry into the character of concepts. Rightly understood, enquiry into the concept of knowledge aspires to reach conclusions about the phenomenon of knowledge. It has the prospect of success because phenomena have what might be called a *conceptual shape*.

When we get it right, the stuff that we actually call water is (largely) made up of H_2O. But that does not tell us that water is a natural kind, because it is compatible with the hypothesis that water is any stuff that has the superficial, readily detectable properties we associate with water, irrespective of whether it is H_2O. If that hypothesis is false, it is not shown to be so by empirical investigation into the molecular composition of samples of the water from our taps and elsewhere. That enquiry does not tell us why we should not apply the concept of water to any stuff that has the superficial, readily detectable properties, irrespective of its composition. If the standard philosopher's story about water is right, then the hypothesis in question is false because water is a substance and it is possible that something should have superficial properties by which we pick out this substance and yet not be this substance. But it takes a form of conceptual enquiry to show that this story is right. It needs to be shown that our concept of water not only de facto picks out something in the category of substance, because the stuff we actually call water is a substance, but that nothing counts as water unless it is the same substance as that substance. That requires enquiry into the concept that is in play in our actual thinking about water and the thinking that was available to people before they knew the molecular composition of water. Similarly, showing that brittleness is a dispositional property requires investigation of our concept of being brittle. It is not investigation of molecular composition that enables us to see that brittleness is dispositional, but reflection on the fact that whether something counts as being brittle depends on how, absent freakish circumstances, it would behave when struck hard. It is understanding what the concept demands of something to which it applies that tells us that brittleness is of its nature dispositional.

Enquiry into the concept of knowledge can take the form of enquiry into the conceptual shape of knowledge. It is commonly thought that knowledge has the conceptual shape of a composite, an ingredient of which is belief. This is something that Kornblith accepts, though he differs from those I have called traditionalists in not taking epistemology to be to any significant extent in the business of conceptual analysis. But it may be that knowledge does not have this conceptual shape at all, even if knowledge entails true belief.[22] This is a view that I shall take seriously in what follows.

5.5. The Way Ahead

My hope is that the picture emerging in the ensuing discussion will not only show us that there can be substantive epistemology even if *knowledge* does not admit of a reductive conceptual analysis, and is not best conceived as belief plus the satisfaction of further conditions. I shall be as much concerned to offer an account of how knowledge on many matters is readily available, and how facts as to what we, and others, know can be readily available. Much of the discussion will be about forms of knowledge, rather than directly about the value of knowledge, but the results are, I believe, crucial for an understanding of how knowledge can be of value in the way that it is in advancing enquiry and in enabling us to be good informants.

A number of challenges will have to be met. First, if I am right in thinking that knowledge enables matters to be settled then a theory of knowledge must explain how this can be. The challenge will be most acute in relation to evidence-based knowledge, since it must explain how empirical evidence can be conclusive. It has loomed large in my efforts to account for various modes of knowledge in Chapters 7 and 8. Second, the alternative on offer should not face problems analogous to those of the traditional framework. I have acknowledged that there is a gap between possessing a concept and having a clear view of its character, while claiming that the traditional framework has a special problem because it commits us to a particular way of representing our grasp of the concept of knowledge that is problematic. A plausible alternative should not be just as problematic. In particular, it must reflect an understanding

---

[22] On this see Williamson (2000: chs. 1–3).

of knowledge that plausibly informs our thinking and there must be some explanation of why the alternative has eluded us, despite the fact that this understanding informs our thinking.

In Chapter 6 I outline a conception of perceptual knowledge in which perceptual-recognitional abilities are central. In Chapter 7 I apply the notion of a recognitional ability in a treatment of knowledge from indicators. I have in mind, for instance, knowledge that sheep are nearby from the sound of bleating. In Chapter 8 I discuss testimony, directly address issues concerning the value of knowledge, and show how the theoretical picture I have painted helps us to explain the importance we place on knowing.

6

Perceptual Knowledge
and Recognitional Abilities

6.1. Introduction

Perceptual knowledge includes knowledge we have of current states of our surroundings through seeing, hearing, touching, smelling, or tasting something. Such knowledge is recognitional in that it involves the recognition of something you perceive as being of some kind (e.g. an apple) or as having a certain property (e.g. being tall), or as being some individual (e.g. Bill). Recognition here is to be contrasted with the formation of a belief based on evidence. It is a direct response to perceiving some object, events, scene, or whatever.

It is convenient to take perceptual knowledge also to comprise knowledge that is acquired perceptually in past encounters and sustained by remembering the relevant encounters. Suppose I know perceptually that my colleague is around the Department because I hear her speaking to someone in the corridor and recognize her voice. Subsequently, I might retain in memory that she was there then because I remember having heard her in the corridor. My current knowledge that she was around earlier has a claim to be called perceptual because it remains grounded in what I heard earlier. It is grounded in this way not just in that I originally came to know that she was around through having earlier heard her, but because the earlier encounter, through being retained in memory, explains the manner in which I now know that she was around: I know that she was around because I heard her earlier and remember doing so.

Perceptual knowing is a paradigm of knowing. It is clear, not only that perception enables us to acquire knowledge, but also that, in at least most circumstances in which we know something perceptually, we can responsibly take the matter to be settled. In the example given earlier I could responsibly take it to be settled that my colleague is around while I hear her, and, so long as I remember having heard her, I could responsibly take it to be settled that she was around earlier. Being in the latter position I could responsibly vouch

for her having been around. My position would be different if the only reason
for thinking she is around is that she usually is at that time. That would not
clinch it, and I would not take it to do so, since routines can too easily be
disrupted. Considerations such as these reflect common-sense thinking about
perceptual knowledge and are among the data for which a theory of perceptual
knowledge should account.

It seems fairly clear that an adequate theory of perceptual knowledge should,
in addition, accommodate the following:

> (1) Perceptual knowledge is phenomenologically immediate: when we
> know that p in virtue of seeing that p we do not infer that p from
> prior assumptions. Rather, because of what we see—our seeing this
> or that object, event, or whatever—it simply strikes us that p. This
> is why it is so natural to speak of recognition in connection with
> perceptual knowledge.

> (2) Nonetheless, perceptual knowledge can have rich content. For
> instance, I can know that Bill is sitting over there, because I see
> that *he* is there, not just that something is there with such-and-such
> superficial features that give it the appearance of Bill. The same applies
> to cases of perceptually knowing that something is of such-and-such
> a kind. I can take in perceptually that this flower is a rose, not just
> that it has the various features that give it the look of a rose.[1]

Strongly empiricist instincts might lead one to balk at (2). Someone visually
indistinguishable from Bill might look just as Bill looks as he sits over there. So
it might seem as if what I know by sight is less than that *Bill* is there—some
fact as to the presence of an object with such-and-such superficial features. On
such a view it need not be assumed that I need to conclude that Bill is there
by reasoning from a prior assumption about features. The idea might be that,
although I simultaneously acquire the belief that an object with such-and-such
features is there, and that Bill is there, the latter belief is sustained by the
former. All else equal, were I to doubt that an object with the relevant features
is there, I would be likely to doubt that it is Bill who is there, and any doubt
that arose as to whether Bill was there would be likely to be resisted so long
as I continued to believe that an object with such-and-such features is there.
Even so, such a view distorts the phenomenology of perceptual knowledge.
The view has it that when we know something through perceiving it to be so
there is available to us certain reasons for believing the thing we know that are

---

[1] For discussion of the scope of perceptual knowledge, see Millar (2001). The view that there can
be recognitional capacities for natural kinds is defended by Jessica Brown (1998).

provided by the superficial features of what we perceive. The problem is that it is open to question whether in practice we routinely exploit such reasons when we acquire perceptual knowledge.

Note first that it seems possible that we should have the ability to recognize Bill as Bill through looking at him, yet lack the resources to see, and thus judge, that the person we are looking at has the features that go to make up his visual appearance. There is no reason a priori to suppose that facility at recognizing people goes with facility at registering a person's features at the level of judgement.[2] But the more fundamental objection is that even if we have the ability to think about the visible features of Bill, and are capable of attending to these in thought, what we register of these features at the level of judgement falls far short of articulating that to which we respond when recognizing Bill by sight. Any judgement as to salient features leaves it underdetermined how the features coalesce to make up the *Gestalt* of a face, or a distinctive gait. That is why those reading novels with descriptions of people are liable to conjure up very different images of the people described. No matter how vivid and detailed the description, it can merely provide pointers to how a person might look and so imagination fills the gap, but in different ways in different people. The same phenomenon of underdetermination is at work when someone tries to direct our minds to a particular person by means of a description of that person's salient features. In the usual course of events communications like this succeed because the description triggers recollection of what this person looks like—recollection made possible by past visual acquaintance with him or her. The description does not capture an adequate reason to think that the person is *whoever*; it nonetheless enables those with suitable past experience to know who is being referred to. Very similar considerations apply to the recognition of things as being instances of natural kinds or kinds of artefact. We learn to identify flowers, shrubs, birds, and fish from the way they look. We learn to identify buses, postboxes, telephone kiosks, and kettles from the way they look. Our responses are geared to the visual appearance of the thing, not to a list of features that we register at the level of judgement. We respond to a *Gestalt* rather than to features that we take to be present. Much the same applies to other sensory modalities. Think of recognizing the distinctive voice of an acquaintance, the smell of burnt toast, or the taste of beer.

The key claim here is that perceptual recognition of something as a specified individual, or as an instance of a kind, or as having some rich (non-superficial) property, is not a matter of taking in facts pertaining to superficial properties

---

[2] Indeed, there are reasons to the contrary. See Rosch (1978) for evidence that the concepts we first acquire are not concepts of features but sortal concepts of objects.

and making a judgement on the basis of those facts. That is as much as to say that perceptual knowledge, even when of rich facts, really is recognitional. In response it might be suggested that in the situations under consideration we take in the fact that the object in question appears a certain way, even if we lack the resources to conceptualize the features that go into its appearing that way. But while most of us have the resources to form beliefs and judgements as to the appearances of things, there is no reason to think that perceptual knowledge must implicate such judgements. For one thing, it does not seem necessary that subjects capable of perceptual knowledge should have the conceptual resources to think of appearances as such. For another, it is plausible that our capacity to recognize appearances as such depends on our capacity to recognize things as being of this or that kind or as being this or that individual or as having this or that property. We learn, for instance, to recognize roses by sight and can from that obtain a grasp of the look of a rose.

No one is likely to dispute that in judging something to be red from what we see we do so from the way it looks. To regard such a judgement as evidence-based would be to assimilate it, wrongly, to cases in which we judge one thing on the basis of another, as when we judge that our car's fuel tank is half-full from a reading of the fuel gauge. In the latter case we take in a fact at the level of judgement—that the fuel gauge reads half-full. This fact provides us with a reason to think that the tank is half full. In view of this fact, and exploiting our understanding of its significance, we judge that the tank is half-full. In the normal course of events we would be in a position to explain and justify our judgement by citing the fact about the fuel gauge. (This sort of case is examined more fully in Chapter 7.) There is nothing quite like this when we tell that a surface is red from the way it looks. In such a case the content of the fact we take in—that *this* surface is red—is the content of what we judge in response to what we see. I am suggesting that similar considerations apply when we have perceptual knowledge with rich content, as when we recognize something to be of some kind (e.g. a rose or a telephone). Often when we effect such recognition we are able to mention some distinctive feature of what we recognize. For instance, I might explain how I tell that a certain bird is a goldfinch 'from its red head'. But it would be a mistake for me to take the fact that the bird has a red head as the reason for my thinking that it is a goldfinch. As Austin observes, that would imply wrongly 'that all I have noted, or needed to note, about it is that its head is red (nothing special or peculiar about the shade, shape, &c. of the patch)' (1946: 85). We should not be surprised at the gesturing character of the explanation that points to the bird's red head. It reflects the fact that our ability to tell is genuinely recognitional, being a response to the *Gestalt* presented by the bird.

It is thanks to our perceptual-recognitional abilities that perceptual knowledge can have rich content: *that* is Bill; *that* bird is a goldfinch; *that* appliance is a fridge; *these* cells (seen through a microscope) are abnormal. The aim of this chapter is to shed some light on the structure of those abilities and on how they relate to the acquisition of knowledge and justified belief.

6.2. Perceptual-Recognitional Abilities

If we are to make headway in understanding the abilities that enable us to acquire perceptual knowledge we need to go well beyond consideration of conditions suitable for perceiving middle-sized objects via some sensory modality. We need to look at highly specific perceptual-recognitional abilities. The ability to recognize that a variety of potato plant is Kerr's Pink from the look of the leaves requires not only that one's visual system should be in good working order, and that the conditions of light and the location of the plant vis-à-vis the observer should be suitable for seeing the visible features of the plant. Nor is it enough to add to these conditions that the observer possesses the concept of the Kerr's Pink plant. The observer needs to have learned visually to recognize this variety of potato plant, that is, learned to tell by looking at plants at a certain stage of development that they are of that variety.

The language we use to describe perceptual-recognitional abilities is often less specific than is required to capture the character of the ability described. If we describe someone as able to recognize orchids from the way they look, we probably do not mean to commit ourselves to supposing that with respect to any orchid viewed in conditions suitable for visual recognition this person would tell that it is an orchid. There might be varieties of orchid that the person would not recognize as orchids. We need to distinguish between having an ability to tell *whether or not* something is an orchid, from its appearance, and the more limited ability to tell of things in a certain range that they are orchids from their appearance. Having the former ability is such that, always or nearly always, when one sees something one can tell from its appearance that it is an orchid or tell from its appearance that it is not an orchid.[3] Having the more limited ability is compatible with not being able to do this.

In its broadest sense, an appearance of things of a certain kind is just a way that things of that kind can appear (look, feel, sound, smell, or taste).

---

[3] In saying 'one can tell' I shall take it for granted that the ability is relative to conditions suitable for a clear view of the appearance of the thing seen.

Appearances as conceived here are thus worldly appearances, not psychological states or sense-data, conceived as inner objects of awareness. In what follows I shall largely confine my attention to visual appearances, though I believe it would be instructive to consider more fully the very idea of an appearance in relation to other sensory modalities.

To be able to recognize Fs by sight, and thus from ways they look, it is necessary that there should be some appearance that is *distinctive* of Fs in that with a high degree of reliability the possession of that appearance by things indicates that they are Fs.[4] When an appearance of something is distinctive of Fs, not easily could something have this appearance and not be an F.

Appearances of things of some kind can vary along two different dimensions. (a) They can vary in ways that are dependent on conditions of viewing (including points of view and conditions of light). A garment that is orange in colour looks orange in a range of 'standard' viewing conditions but might not under certain kinds of street lighting. Variation of this sort is compatible with constancy of visual characteristic—in the case of the garment, constancy of colour. (b) Appearances of things of some kind can also vary in ways that reflect variations in visible characteristics. Cars of different models are all cars but differ in visual characteristics and accordingly in visual appearance.

There is a certain indeterminacy attached to talk of visual appearances. In speaking of the appearance of the Matterhorn you might mean the appearance it exhibits in postcards made from photographs taken from some standard point of view on a sunny day with clear blue sky, or its appearance from some different point of view in different conditions of weather and light, or you might mean vaguely to pick out various ways the Matterhorn can look in a variety of conditions and be recognizable as the Matterhorn. This simply reflects the fact that appearances can be more or less determinately specified. There is no need for precision for my purposes. I shall often speak of telling that something is such-and-such from its appearance, taking it to be understood from the context roughly what sort of appearance that I have in mind.

As understood here, the notion of *the exercise of a perceptual-recognitional ability* is a *success notion*. I do not exercise the ability to φ unless I φ. If I were mistakenly to judge a performance of music to be by Haydn when it is by Mozart then I would not have exercised the ability to tell by listening to a performance of music that it is by Haydn. (How could I when I did not tell that it was by Haydn?) Yet possession of an ability to tell of something that it is such-and-such is compatible with sometimes judging wrongly when one means so to tell. For instance, I might be able accurately to read a clinical

---

[4] An appearance of something indicates that it is an F only if it is an F. See further in §7.2.

thermometer yet through tiredness or distraction mistakenly judge that such a thermometer displays a reading of 98.5 degrees when in fact it reads 97.5 degrees. A mistake of this sort is in a clear sense a failure of performance on my part: I have the ability but do not exercise it because I look without due care.

There are interesting cases in which failure to judge correctly, or failure to know even if one does judge correctly, is due to lacking the required ability, though one presupposes that one has it. I have in mind fake-barn examples. Here is a version (after Goldman 1976, which credits Carl Ginet). In the countryside with which he is familiar Barney can tell of structures having a certain visual appearance or range of such appearances that they are barns from the way they look. More specifically, he can do this from points of view at roadsides that are close enough to the structures to enable their shape and style to be visible. Barney has a perceptual-recognitional ability. Given sight from the relevant point of view of structures with an appearance in the right range, he can tell by looking that they are barns, without further inspection in or around those structures. In this way—that is, through the exercise of this ability—he has often come to know that this or that structure is a barn from the way it looks. Now imagine Barney in a different environment, which superficially looks much like his familiar home territory, but in which a good proportion of the structures that have an appearance in the relevant range are fake barns—façades that present the appearance to the sort of point of view from which Barney, hitherto, has been able to tell by sight that certain structures are barns. He is unaware of the presence of the fake barns and in response to what he perceives judges structures to be barns just as he would back home. If Barney judges that something is a barn from the way it looks in this territory he will often be wrong. And even when he judges correctly, he does not know that the structure he is looking at is a barn.

There is a simple and natural explanation of why Barney does not know even when he judges correctly. To be able to tell by looking from roadside points of view that a structure is a barn there must be appearances presented to those points of view that are distinctive of barns. In fake-barn territory the appearances in the relevant range are not distinctive of barns. Back in Barney's familiar territory things are different. When he is there Barney has no need to distinguish barns from fake barns because there the appearances from which he judges structures to be barns are distinctive of barns.

When Barney judges falsely in fake-barn territory he fails to exercise an ability to tell of certain structures that they are barns from the way they look. Indeed, he does not have an ability to tell of structures around there that they are barns from the way they look. Of course, when he is there he does something that he also does back home—judge of structures that look like barns that they are barns—and in doing so he will sometimes judge correctly. But that does not amount to his being able to tell of structures that they are barns from the way they look.

An important feature of this account is that, while it treats *exercising a perceptual-recognitional ability* as a success notion, it is able to accommodate our fallibility. We are fallible because we do not exercise a recognitional ability whenever we aspire to do so. Barney fails to exercise the required ability in fake-barn territory because he lacks the ability to tell of structures there, from the way they look, that they are barns. Back in his home territory he might through carelessness mistakenly judge something to be a barn and thereby fail to exercise the ability to tell of structures there that they are barns from the way they look. There can also be cases in which a failure to exercise a recognitional ability is due to bad luck rather than carelessness or the like. Suppose that I am at a well-organized flower show and some joker flouts security arrangements and substitutes for a real orchid an artificial orchid, which looks exactly like a real one from points of view that would normally suffice for visual identification. By my account of distinctiveness, on the assumption that such substitutes are very rare, the appearance possessed by orchids and substitutes alike could still be distinctive of orchids, even with respect to this environment, since it is still true that in this environment having the appearance in question is a highly reliable indicator of being an orchid. The situation is one in which, even with respect to this environment, I could have the ability to tell of certain plants that they are orchids from their visual appearance, but I would not exercise that ability if I were to judge from its appearance that the artificial orchid is an orchid. (After all, in so judging I would not have come to know that it was an orchid.) My failure to judge correctly would be due to bad luck—an unusual intervention in an otherwise favourable environment. This does not mean that if I were to exercise the ability with respect to this environment I would be lucky. It means that whether I exercise the ability and acquire knowledge depends on the absence of bad luck. (Not being stymied by bad luck is not the same as being lucky.) Of course, if there were enough artificial orchids the appearance in question would not be distinctive of orchids. Between a number of instances that are compatible with distinctiveness and a number that are not there will be cases in which there is no fact of the matter as to whether or not the subject has the ability.[5]

---

[5] Have I done justice to the fallibility of abilities? Isn't my ability to throw a dart into the 25 ring something I exercise when I miss but nearly hit within the ring? The ability here is not strictly speaking an ability to throw the dart into the 25 ring but, roughly, an ability to do that a certain proportion of the times on which I try over a series of throws. I exercise the ability when over a series of throws I achieve roughly the proportion in question. I develop this at more length in Millar (2009).

6.3. Broad and Narrow Competence

There is another direction in which one might be driven by fake-barn considerations: one might think it odd that when Barney judges correctly in the fake barn scenario he does not know, yet in his home territory when he judges correctly he often does know. I envisage two sources for this sense of oddness.

The first source is the idea that if there is a place—a real place—where there are plenty of fake barns, then the appearance on which Barney relies in his home territory might not be truly distinctive of barns. If we think of distinctiveness with respect to some wide domain embracing fake-barn territory and Barney's home territory, then it might be that the visual appearance or appearances in question—those that elicit the judgement that a structure is a barn—are not distinctive of barns since too many structures in the domain that have one or other of the appearances in question are not barns. From this one might conclude that Barney does not know in either territory. However, on the account I offer one can gain perceptual knowledge of the presence of Fs in some domain from their appearance provided that the appearance is *within that domain* distinctive of Fs. Something similar applies to other sorts of ability. When we claim that someone can run a mile in five minutes, we don't mean *can run a mile in five minutes no matter what the conditions and circumstances.* But nor do we have a determinate conception of the conditions that are propitious for the exercise of the ability. We attribute such abilities without refined qualifications when we are operating in a social milieu in which there is a shared background picture on which events consisting in running a mile occur at tracks used for just this purpose or along certain roads used for the purpose. If we attribute the ability to run a mile in five minutes we would not on that account alone incur a commitment to thinking that the person in question could perform this feat high in the Andes where the air is thin. Similarly, attributing to Barney the ability to recognize barns as barns by sight incurs no commitment to thinking that Barney can pull off this feat anywhere you like. It is entirely in keeping with our common-sense understanding of how people tell this or that from a thing's appearance—the way it looks, feels, sounds, tastes, or smells—that the ways of telling they deploy—the abilities they exercise—require favourable environments for their exercise. Just which environments are required might never be made explicit and might be impossible to specify with any precision. That is rarely an obstacle either to our ability to acquire perceptual knowledge or to our ability correctly to attribute perceptual knowledge. We operate within environments that are relevantly favourable, and we don't unknowingly move from favourable to unfavourable environments or deal with subjects who, unknown to us, are moving from favourable to unfavourable environments. Of course, much of our perceptual recognition is from appearances that are distinctive in a way that, to all intents and purposes, if not with respect to the universe, is unlimited. But we don't need to assume unrestricted distinctiveness (to all intents and purposes) in order to make sense of perceptual knowledge.

The second source of the sense of oddness about the asymmetrical treatment of the two barn scenarios depends on two assumptions: (i) that whether Barney knows in either environment depends on the competence that he manifests in judging from what he sees that a barn is before him; and (ii) that Barney manifests the same competence in both circumstances. Underpinning (ii) might be the idea that in both environments Barney is prepared to judge of something he sees that it is a barn when it presents a certain range of appearances and that since this is so he manifests the same competence in both environments. Against this background, the difficulty that might seem to loom is that it is hard to explain why a correct judgement made by Barney falls short of knowledge in fake-barn territory but not on his home turf when the competence manifested is the same in both cases, and he gets it right in both cases through manifesting that competence.

It is moot whether the preparedness that on this line of thought is taken to be a competence is truly a competence. A competence is an ability, and there seems to be nothing about the mere fact that one has this preparedness that marks it as an ability. But let us not quibble about words. If it is a competence it is competence narrowly conceived—*narrow competence*—since it is individuated independently of the environment in which the subject is placed. Narrow competence is to the fore in a recent discussion of cognitive competence by Ernest Sosa. For Sosa, a performance is apt if it is accurate and sufficiently due to the adroitness of the performer (2007: 28, 79). Since adroitness is competence, Sosa also says that aptness requires a manifestation of competence. He applies this way of thinking to a kaleidoscope example. Imagine that I am looking at a red surface. It looks red and from its appearance I judge it to be red. Though my judgement is correct, unknown to me the ambient light is controlled by a trickster who can fix it that the surface will look to be of some colour when it is not. It just happens that it is red and looks red when I make my judgement. Sosa thinks that this judgement is a manifestation of competence:

The kaleidoscope perceiver does seem to exercise his competent color vision in its appropriate conditions. These include his open-eyed alertness, the well-lit medium, the proximity and size of the unoccluded surface, etc. Plausibly he gets it right, in believing the seen surface to be red, through the exercise of a perceptual competence in its appropriate conditions.   (2007: 99–100)

Sosa conceives of competence in general terms as 'a disposition, one with a basis resident in the competent agent, one that would in appropriately normal conditions ensure (or make highly likely) the success of any relevant performance issued by it' (ibid. 29). A competence might be present even if the conditions are not 'appropriately normal'. It is implied that a competence can be *manifested* when conditions are not appropriately normal; it is just that too often in such conditions manifestations of competence will be inaccurate.[6]

My immediate interest in these ideas lies in highlighting the contrasting treatment of fake-barn scenarios and kaleidoscope scenarios that is available when one thinks of the perceptual knowledge as being acquired through the exercise of perceptual-recognitional abilities and conceives of these abilities as abilities *with respect to a favourable environment*. Such abilities undoubtedly constitute competences broadly conceived—*broad competences*—since they are competences with respect to an environment or type of environment.

Assuming that the kaleidoscope scenario is one in which the trickster regularly switches the lighting conditions so that often things look to have such-and-such a colour when they do not have that colour, the colour-appearances in this environment are not distinctive of the corresponding colours. (Looking red, for instance is not distinctive of being red since it is not a reliable indicator of being red.) Since this is so, we should not expect that anyone should be able to tell what colour a thing is from the way it looks. I am relying here on a common-sense assumption about what it takes to be able to tell that something has a certain property from its visual appearance. The assumption is that you cannot tell that something is G from its visual appearance—the way it looks—unless that appearance is distinctive of things that are G. I do not dispute that in the circumstance in which the subject in the kaleidoscope case judges correctly the conditions are appropriate for seeing the true colour of the surface in question. This, I think, is what motivates Sosa's claim, quoted above, that the subject exercises 'a perceptual competence in

---

[6] With respect to the kaleidoscope scenario, Sosa is sensitive to the difficulty in claiming that I know that the surface is red. He thinks nonetheless that there is a sense in which I do know, explained in terms of aptness, and traces reluctance to judge that I know to the absence of *reflective knowledge* that the surface is red. For reflective knowledge that the surface is red I would need to manifest not only the competence to judge the surface to be red from the way it looks. In addition, I would need to manifest competence in judging that my judgement to that effect is apt. I cannot do that in the kaleidoscope scenario, according to Sosa (2007: 102), since I am not in a position to judge that the conditions of light are appropriate for viewing colour.

the appropriate conditions'. But being able to see the true colour of the surface is not the same as being able to tell which colour that surface has.

A natural suggestion at this point is that where perceptual knowledge is concerned, broad competence—the kind of competence that enables one to tell that something is a rose from its appearance—is just narrow competence embedded in a favourable environment. I turn to this in the next section. Before that I would like to address a line of thought advanced by Duncan Pritchard.

Pritchard aims to undermine the idea that knowledge may be equated with cognitive achievement, that is, success due to cognitive ability (this volume, §2.5). To this end he argues that there are cases in which a subject has cognitive success due to cognitive ability (thus achievement) but which are not cases of knowledge. He takes the fake-barn scenario, in which Barney correctly believes that the structure he is looking is a barn, to be just such an example. By his account this is not a case of knowledge but it is a case of success due to ability because Barney acquires a true belief because of his cognitive ability. Pritchard does not say what the ability is an ability to do. He does claim that, by contrast with Gettier cases (as originally conceived), Barney 'does not make any cognitive error in forming his belief in the way he does' (this volume, pp. 35–6). Clearly, what Pritchard counts as a cognitive ability is not a recognitional ability in my sense. I do not find it at all natural to suppose that cognitive success is something less than the acquisition of knowledge, but I have no quarrel with the idea that, under Pritchard's conceptions of cognitive success and cognitive ability, knowledge is not success because of cognitive ability. The issue that needs to be addressed is whether the considerations advanced by him pose any problem for the manner in which I take cognitive abilities to be individuated.

There are two distinguishable strands in Pritchard's argument against deploying the idea that cognitive abilities are relative to environments with a view to undermining his claim that there can be cognitive achievement without cognitive knowledge. One is to argue that, since the manifestation of abilities is not in general undermined by environmental luck, it would be odd if Barney turned out not to manifest the relevant cognitive abilities because of environmental luck. We are to imagine that on some occasion, a piano-player is able to play the piano—to manifest an ability to play the piano—but could easily not have been because she could easily have been under water. She is, say, in a chamber that might easily have been full of water, preventing her from playing. So it is lucky that she is able to play. This luck is what Pritchard calls environmental luck. He invites us to think that it would be odd to treat the fake-barn scenario differently, that is, odd to suppose that Barney does not exercise the relevant cognitive ability when, subject to environmental luck, he makes a correct judgement. However, *if* the ability Barney would need to have and exercise to gain knowledge is a perceptual-recognitional ability there is a clear difference between this case and the case of the pianist. Since environmental luck prevents Barney from having knowledge, it also prevents him for having, and thus exercising, a perceptual-recognitional ability, for that ability consists in an ability to gain a certain kind of knowledge. There is a clear explanation of why Barney does not manifest the relevant ability: he is unable to tell—that is, come to know—of structures in this environment that they are barns from their visual appearance to the relevant points of view. It is no surprise that the pianist exercises her ability to play the piano while subject to environmental luck, because in the circumstances all that it takes for her to play the piano is present. But nor is it a surprise that Barney does not exercise an ability to tell of structures that they are barns from the way they look. How could he tell such a thing in a place where barns do not have a distinctive appearance?[7] This takes us to the other strand in Pritchard's argument. As he views the matter, invoking environment-relative abilities to make sense of the idea that Barney does not manifest achievement in the fake-barn scenario, when he correctly judges that the structure he is looking at is a barn, would commit us to an implausibly fine-grained conception of the relevant abilities (this volume, p. 37). I am not sure exactly what the worry is here. Pritchard does not deny that abilities require suitable conditions for their exercise. It is true that our attributions of abilities, for instance, the ability to ride a bicycle, do not routinely stand proxy for some more specific attribution tying the ability to some particular environment or type of environment. Still, we do sometimes explicitly characterize abilities as being abilities with respect to a type of environment, as when we say of a novice sailor that he can handle only small sailing-boats in fairly calm waters. Specifying the type of environment here is integral to specifying the kind of ability. I do not need, in any case, to assume that our attributions of abilities routinely stand proxy for attributions that include some determinate specification of a type of environment. There is no need for our attributions to have this character, since they are generally made within a context in which there is a shared picture of the world embodying

---

[7] There are archer cases in which the weirdness of the environment is incompatible not just with the archer's success being due to his ability but with the archer's having the ability. In a freakish environment, in which there is regular interference from forces that divert arrows, archers would lack the ability to hit targets as we ordinarily think of it. Possessing that ability depends on it being the case that, by and large, if one were to aim at a target one would hit it. That condition is not met in a case in which an archer hits the target but only because he is by sheer luck not being affected by the interfering forces.

some rather indeterminate presuppositions as to conditions favourable to the exercise of the ability in question and as to the obtaining of those conditions, at least at some places and times. (You can ride a bicycle in lots of conditions but you can't ride a bicycle in the face of a hurricane.) We are perfectly capable of being more precise if the need arises. The fake-barn scenario creates just such a need. It highlights that visual-recognitional abilities depend on the environment's being favourable in that things recognized as being, say, of some kind must have a visual appearance such that, with a high degree of reliability, having that appearance goes with being of that kind. It calls for us to say that Barney lacks an ability to tell of structures in fake-barn territory that they are barns from the way they look from the relevant point of view. Far from being eccentric, this conception reflects a mode of characterizing our abilities that is in keeping with common-sense thinking about how we acquire perceptual knowledge.[8]

6.4. Avoiding Reduction

Here I pick up the issue of whether we might account for broad competence in terms of narrow competence. It is important at this juncture to recall the character of the present project. In Chapter 5 I criticized reductive analytical theories of knowledge for being insufficiently attentive to the nature of our understanding of knowledge as this is reflected in the constraints on the deployment of the concept of knowledge to which we are sensitive. From this perspective it matters if an account purports to be an analysis of the concept of knowledge while setting out conditions for knowledge that those with a mastery of the concept do not routinely acknowledge as conditions for knowledge. Obviously, it also matters if an account fails to make contact with the factors that we do acknowledge as being relevant to whether or not someone knows.

We happily count people as knowing that something is an F when they see an F, and they may be presumed to have what it takes to tell of something they see that it is an F from the way it looks. Similar considerations apply to other sensory modalities. The conceptual level at which we encounter the perceptual knowledge that we have, or that others have, is that of *knowing that* p *through seeing or otherwise perceiving that* p, *by means of an ability to tell*

---

[8] I explore contrasts between my conception of recognitional abilities and virtue-theoretic conceptions of cognitive abilities, and discuss issues concerning the individuation of abilities, in Millar (2009).

that such a thing is so from the look or other appearance of what is perceived. The
assumption that an illuminating account of knowledge must be at the level
of concepts that do not implicate the concept of knowledge motivates the
idea that we must delve below this conceptual level. Given this general
approach, there is an incentive to think of the competence manifested in
the acquisition of perceptual knowledge in terms that do not implicate the
concept of knowledge. It can easily seem that such an account is, in any case,
available. There is the idea that the competence manifested in the acquisition
of perceptual knowledge should be characterized at the level of propensities
to form judgements in response to appropriate sensory experiences. Since the
experience Barney has as he looks at a barn is one he might have even if
no barn were there, working at this level makes it look as if we can do the
business without invoking knowing-that through perceiving-that, and without
invoking ways of telling as understood here. This, I think, is an illusion.

There is little doubt that we have, or can readily acquire, some grasp of what
it is to be prepared to judge whether something is a rose from its appearance,
when the appearance is in a certain range. Nor can there be much doubt that
we can form a conception of what it is to be prepared to judge that something
is, say, a rose in response to experiences such that it is just as if a rose is before
one, where these experiences are conceived in such a way that they can be
had irrespective of whether anything before one is a rose or even looks like
a rose. The issue is whether we should think of our understanding of what it
is to be able to tell that something is a rose from the way it looks as being
built up from an understanding of such judgement-forming propensities. For
unless it is so built up there is no prospect of showing that ways of telling,
as I conceive of them, and as I think common sense conceives of them,
are conceptually reducible to such judgement-forming propensities situated in
a favourable environment. There is good reason to think that the order of
understanding is the reverse of what conceptual reduction requires.

In this connection, it is striking that our grasp of what it is for appearances
to be in the right range for making judgements to the effect that a rose is
before one is in terms of what it is to see roses or visual representations of
roses (photographs, illustrations). The intended range has to be *appearances that
are distinctive of roses.* Our grasp of the range is in the form of knowing how
to generate informative specifications of appearances in the range: pick out
a rose, or a visual representation or depiction of a rose; specify the look of
what you see, or see represented or depicted, as a way that roses can look.
We can, of course, conceive of things that look like roses but are not roses.
But our conception of how *they* look is just a conception of how *roses* look.
(A well-made artificial rose might serve the needs of informing someone of

the appearances of roses but it can do so only because it looks just like a real rose.)

These considerations about appearances have implications for our conception of experiences in response to which we are liable to judge, absent countervailing considerations, that a rose is before us. It is in terms of our conception of what roses look like, and thus of what it is to see a rose, that we think of experiences in the relevant range. We can make sense of having such experiences when no rose is present, but still we think of *these* experiences as being just like the ones we have when we see a rose.[9]

Perhaps it is possible at some theoretical level to characterize the appearances, and experiences, in response to which we judge roses to be present in terms that are independent of our ordinary understanding of what it is like to see a rose. That is not to the point for present purposes, since such a characterisation would have no role in a plausible account of the understanding of knowledge that informs our thinking about knowledge and no role in the epistemology of everyday attributions of knowledge. What does inform our thinking about perceptual knowledge is an understanding of what it is to see or otherwise perceive that something is so—an understanding that implicates specific conceptions of ways of telling from the appearances of things. There is no doubt that we have these conceptions and that in practice we readily apply them. Having heard the sound of the fire alarm, I am in a position to know how I know that the alarm has gone off. That is because I know that one can tell from that sound that the fire alarm has gone off. We are often in a position to tell that others know things. For instance, looking for someone in a crowd, I might spot him before he sees me and then see from his reaction that he has seen and recognized me and therefore knows that I am right here. I know that he can recognize me because I know him well enough. Sometimes we know what others know because they are identifiable as having expertise in certain areas. Expert gardeners know how to recognize a wide variety of plants and shrubs from their appearance. Expert ornithologists know how to identify a wide variety of birds from their appearance. We would be in a hopeless position if we had to make extensive checks on everyone who professes to have expertise of some sort. Our ability to identify people as having expertise, and thus as being in command of a range of ways of telling, depends in part on there being distinctive socially recognized marks of expertise. Someone on a television programme about trees and shrubs might display the marks of an expert in these matters. Someone turning up at your house unannounced,

---

[9] Disjunctivists make analogous claims about the order of understanding. See e.g. Child (1994: 143–6).

professing to know all about trees and shrubs, and offering to prune your trees, might not. The nature of the social environment is crucial for whether we can tell that others are equipped to know whether this or that is so. An environment in which we cannot tell the genuine experts on some subject matter from the charlatans would not be one with respect to which we could readily tell whether someone has the know-how that enables us to have well-grounded confidence that they speak from knowledge on that subject matter. I shall explore these matters more fully in connection with testimony. My present concern is simply to draw attention to how natural it is to think of our understanding of knowledge as being linked to ways of telling and to the fact that often we can readily tell that others are in command of these ways of telling.

On the style of thinking to which I am opposed it is by means of having a grip on appropriate judgement-forming propensities that we have a grip on what ways of telling are. I am sceptical about this style of thinking just because it seems plausible that the order of our understanding is from knowledge-implicating notions, like those of our various perceptual-recognitional abilities, to notions of judgement-forming propensities rather than the reverse. On the alternative picture presented here, any conception we have of the propensities is by abstraction from ways of telling and generalization to cases in which it is merely as if one has a way of telling. Viewed from this perspective, it is a mistake is to think that it is by means of having a grip on sensory experiences such that it looks to us as if an F is there that we have a grip on what is to see that an F is there. (Do we even come by the notions from which our concept of seeing is supposed to be built up before we learn about philosophical theories of perception and perceptual knowledge?) The alternative picture is that any conception we have of the experiences is by abstraction from cases of seeing that an F is there and generalization to cases in which it merely looks to us as if an F is there.[10] It is tempting to say that the mistake is of a general type—that of mistakenly treating what is in fact an abstraction as if it were an ingredient. My point is more modest. It is simply that we have no independent conceptual grip on what some theorists treat as ingredients. The lesson applied to the case in hand is that we should not represent our understanding of perceivings-that

---

[10] Disjunctivists would agree. It is a further question whether this gives them all that they want. According to Child's summary (1994: 144), the view is that there is no state of affairs in common to success cases—seeing that an F is there—and subjectively indistinguishable failure cases in which it merely looks to one as if an F is there. A different way of putting what I take to be much the same point would be to say that there is no psychological state in common between such pairs of cases. The point about abstraction does not itself deliver this result. It is a point about the order of understanding, not about the metaphysics of the states in question.

and associated ways of telling as if it incorporated an independently understood conception of the posited ingredients.

6.5. Perceptual Knowledge and Justified Belief

I have insisted that perceptual knowledge should be viewed as being genuinely recognitional and not as being implicitly evidence-based. There are theorists who think otherwise. Consider the case in which I am looking at a zebra in an enclosure at a zoo. Many theorists think it compelling that if I know that the animal is a zebra via perception then this is in part due to my having evidence that it is. The evidence might be conceived in one of two ways: as worldly evidence provided by the zebra's looking a certain way, or as evidence provided by my having a visual experience such that it looks to me just as if a zebra is before me.

In Chapter 5 and earlier in this chapter I observed that in judging on the basis of visual perception that a thing is an instance of a specified kind, we respond directly to the *Gestalt* that it presents—to the way it looks. Most of us have the resources to think about the way a zebra looks *as* the way a zebra looks. Looking at a zebra, we would no doubt take in both that what we are looking at is a zebra and that it has the look of a zebra. That said, there is no reason to think it necessary to have command of the concept of the look of a zebra in order to be able to recognize zebras. Where command of the latter concept is lacking, recognition is obviously not explicable in terms of judgement based on evidence to the effect that what one is looking at has the look of a zebra. But nor is there any real pressure to think of perceptual knowledge in these terms. Learning to tell that something is a zebra from the way it looks is a matter of acquiring a technique for judgement. Cases in which you don't judge correctly would need explanation. They would be ones in which you are distracted, careless, or confused or ones in which some odd trick is being played—like cleverly disguising a mule to look like a zebra. Whether or not you *take in* that something you are looking at has the look of a zebra, when you judge it to be a zebra, is beside the point. What matters is that you respond appropriately to what are in fact zebras and have the distinctive look of zebras. So, even if most of us do take in that zebras we are looking at look like zebras, our doing so is not necessary in order to explain how we know that they are zebras.

The second evidentialist view, on which the evidence is constituted by the subject's experiences, raises additional problems of its own, not least of which is that we do not routinely think of our experiences in that way. Plausibly, if experiences did constitute evidence giving us reason to believe things, such that we believed those things for those reasons, we would routinely treat having those experiences as providing us with reasons. It is not at all clear that this is so since, as noted in the previous section, our routine discourse about perception is at the level of perceiving objects and perceiving something to be so.

Some theorists find the views that I am challenging hard to resist if one is to make sense of the intimate connection between knowing that p and being justified in believing that p. If even perceptual knowledge is evidence-based then there is a way of explaining how perceptual knowledge links up with justified belief. In the zebra case we could say that the justification is provided by evidence comprising the way the animal looks or the visual experiences I have as I look at it. That evidence can provide me with a reason to think that the animal is a zebra. This in turn can explain why it could be no less reasonable for me to believe that it is a zebra in the bad case when it is a cleverly disguised mule, looking just like a zebra, than in the good case when it is a zebra.[11] These apparent theoretical advantages raise the question whether the framework provided by the account of perceptual-recognitional abilities that I am presenting here can account for the intimate connection between knowledge and justified belief in perceptual cases.

According to the account, the acquisition of knowledge that the animal is a zebra is the exercise of an ability to tell that an animal is a zebra from its appearance. As I have already stressed, I have the ability only with respect to environments in which zebras have a distinctive visual appearance. Of course, I need to have acquired the relevant ability. I have done that largely through being taught from illustrations, photographs, and films of zebras. Test me on recognizing zebras as zebras and I'd do well.

Note that in normal circumstances I do not exercise my recognitional ability blindly, with no understanding or knowledge of what I am doing. First, it is part of my picture of the world that zebras can be encountered near where I live only in zoos and safari parks, and that these are well-organized places in which enclosures with animals are suitably labelled. It is also part of that picture that it is possible to tell that animals are zebras from the way they look, and that I am myself in command of that way of telling. It not a mystery to me that I find myself judging that an animal in the zoo is a zebra from the way it looks,

---

[11] Both of these considerations have recently been advanced by way of objection to McDowell's disjunctivism by Earl Conee (2007: 32–3). A similar line of thought is advanced by Dylan Dodd (2007: 639) to mark a contrast with the view of perceptual knowledge suggested in Williamson (2000).

because this fits with a conception that I have of myself and of the environment I inhabit. I could draw on this conception to explain how you can tell that an animal is a zebra or to explain how I know of some animal that it is a zebra on a particular occasion. Second, episodes in which I come to know that an animal I am looking at is a zebra are, barring rare, dire confusion, or rare and bizarre deception, episodes in which the fact that I see that the animal is a zebra is available to me as a reason to believe that it is a zebra and to continue to believe that it was thereafter.[12] The intimate connection between perceptual knowledge and justified belief is accommodated by acknowledging that the fact that I see that the animal is a zebra can constitute a reason I have to take it to be one. But instead of explaining the knowledge as, so to speak, built up from justified belief, we treat the knowledge as what enables one to be justified in believing. Knowing that the animal is a zebra through seeing that it is enables me to be justified in believing that it is. There is a question as to what makes this justifying reason available to me.

Recognitional abilities come into the picture at this as point too. Just as I have acquired a first-order ability to tell that something is a zebra from the way it looks, so I have also acquired a higher-order ability to tell that I see that an animal is a zebra when I do. The latter ability is dependent on the former and is as much tied to the relevant favourable environment as it is. If zebras did not have a distinctive visual appearance then it would no more be possible to tell that one has seen that a zebra is before one than it would be to tell by sight that a zebra is before one. Note that we do not need to invoke any sort of inner sense to account for the higher-order ability. The ability is responsive to the very same experiences to which the corresponding first-order ability is responsive. The upshot is that, thanks to the higher-order ability, the very episode of seeing that the animal is a zebra that discloses that the animal is a zebra also discloses itself.

What, then, are we to make of the idea that I could just as reasonably believe that the animal is a zebra in the bad case in which it is a cleverly disguised mule as in the good case when it is indeed a zebra? If no indication is available to me in the bad case that it is a bad case then it is just as if I see that, and on that account know that, the animal is a zebra. That is why in this situation my belief that the animal is a zebra is reasonable in the weak sense identified in Chapter 5. I hold it in a situation in which it is just as if I know it to be true. It does not follow from this that there is no difference to the grounding of my belief in the two cases. In the good case there is a reason

---

[12] There is a kinship here with views advanced by John McDowell (1994; 1995). My own view has developed through an attempt to work out what I take to be right in McDowell's picture.

for me to believe that the animal is a zebra—I see that it is. Since I believe for that reason, my belief is well grounded and the nature of its grounding not only makes it reasonable to hold it but also entitles me to hold it. (Recall my remarks about entitlement in Chapter 5, pp. 102–4.) In the bad case, I blamelessly take there to be a reason to believe that the animal is a zebra since, as it seems to me, I see that it is. But there is no such reason and no corresponding entitlement.

I am in effect working here with two quite different notions that might be expressed in terms of being justified. One is what I have been calling 'reasonableness'. This is the kind of reasonableness that is picked out by the notion of justification as that is standardly applied to Gettier cases by epistemologists. With respect to reasonableness, the good and bad cases are on a par. The other is the notion of well-groundedness that clinches it that something is so and suffices for entitlement to hold it to be so.[13] With respect to this sort of well-groundedness the good and bad cases are not on a par. The idea of reasonableness here is an abstraction from cases of such well-groundedness generalized to cases in which well-groundedness is absent. From this perspective it is a major error to suppose that our understanding of the knowledge in the good case is to be explained as built up from an understanding of what makes the belief reasonable. This is another case in which it is important not to reverse the natural order of understanding.

6.6. Closure and Doxastic Responsibility

Zebra cases have been used to highlight a problem for the principle that knowledge is closed under known entailment.[14] The point can be made as follows:

> According to the closure principle, if I know that p and that $<p>$ entails $<q>$ then I am in a position to know that q. But it seems that I can know that this animal I am looking at is a zebra, know that $<$This animal is a zebra$>$ entails $<$This animal is not a cleverly disguised mule$>$ yet not be in a position to know that the animal is not a cleverly disguised mule.

---

[13] An interesting question, which I shall not pursue, is whether there can be entitlement to believe based on a justification that is less than clinching. I am inclined to think not, while acknowledging that we can be entitled to believe that something is highly probable in the light of evidence that is not clinching.

[14] Dretske (1970; 2005). See also Vogel (1990).

Crucial to the problem is the assumption that if I know that the animal is a zebra from the way it looks my reason for thinking that it is a zebra does not justify my thinking that it is not a cleverly disguised mule. A way of putting the point is to say that one's reason for believing that the animal is a zebra does not transmit to the belief that it is not a cleverly disguised mule.[15] Why might one think this to be so? Here is one line of thought:

> The reason I have for thinking that the animal is a zebra is that it looks like a zebra. But that it looks like a zebra is no reason to think that it is not a cleverly disguised mule since if it were a cleverly disguised mule it would look much the same.

Given this reasoning, however, there would be a problem not just about the justification provided via perception for thinking that the animal is not a cleverly disguised mule, but also about the justification for thinking it is a zebra. For if having the look of a zebra does not justify my thinking that the animal is not a cleverly disguised mule, there is surely a question as to how it can justify me in thinking that it is a zebra.[16]

On my picture, telling from its appearance that the animal is a zebra need not be a matter of having a reason to believe that it is a zebra, which is constituted by its having this appearance. It is a matter of visually recognizing it to be a zebra, thus exercising an ability to do just that. If one has knowingly effected such recognition, and knows that being a zebra precludes something from being a cleverly disguised mule, one is a position to know that the animal is not a cleverly disguised mule.

I am recommending that in this case we should think of the appearance as something from which a person equipped with the appropriate recognitional ability can tell that the animal is a zebra. If am to count as having such an ability, it must be that the appearance in question is distinctive of zebras: except in rare cases, if something had the appearance of a zebra it would be a zebra and thus not a mule disguised as a zebra. But reasons naturally come into the picture. What justifies my thinking that the animal in the enclosure is not a cleverly disguised mule is that I have seen that it is a zebra. In view of the fact that I have seen that it is a zebra, I am entitled to believe that it is a zebra.

---

[15] See Davies (2004), Wright (2002; 2004), Dretske (2005), and Hawthorne (2005).

[16] Dretske has a way of answering this question: it's true that it would not have the appearance of a zebra unless it were a zebra, and so true that there is a conclusive reason to think it a zebra, but false that it would not have this appearance unless it were not a cleverly disguised mule, and so false that there is a conclusive reason to think it is not a cleverly disguised mule. However, this view depends on a reading of the second counterfactual that is neither mandatory nor the most natural way of reading it in relation to the context. There is a sense in which in the circumstances the animal would not have the appearance it does unless it were not a cleverly disguised mule.

There is no mystery to the idea that whether I have the needed ability with respect to zebras depends on how things actually are. It turns on the truism that unless there were a visual appearance that is distinctive of zebras I could not tell that something is a zebra from the way it looks. But when there is a visual appearance that is distinctive of zebras one can learn to tell that something is a zebra from the way it looks. Of course, if I did not see that the animal is a zebra—if it were a cleverly disguised mule—then I would not be entitled to believe that it is not a cleverly disguised mule. Seeing that it is a zebra makes all the difference—the difference between a belief that I am entitled to hold because of how it is grounded, and a belief that I am not entitled to hold, but which might nonetheless be reasonable.

The stance I am defending raises interesting questions about doxastic responsibility. It is no part of the barn story that Barney, ensconced in his home environment, need have taken steps to satisfy himself that he is not in fake-barn territory in order to be in a position to know, or be justified in thinking, that a structure is a barn from how it looks. It is no part of the zebra story that I need to take steps to satisfy myself that they don't have mules disguised as zebras in the zoo if I am to know that the animal in the enclosure is a zebra from the way it looks. But what if the issue arises for Barney as to how he can tell without further ado that the structure is not a fake barn? Can he responsibly believe that it is a barn? And what if the issue arises for me as to how I can tell without further ado that the animal is not a cleverly disguised mule? Can I responsibly believe that it is a zebra?

Sticking with the zebra case, it is striking that, except in a rather special kind of environment, raising the issue of whether the animal is a cleverly disguised mule would be entirely frivolous. It would be no less frivolous if raised while looking in a zebra enclosure at Edinburgh Zoo than it would if the context were the savannah of southern Africa where zebra roam freely. Indeed, it would be positively irresponsible to take the issue seriously if a child were to ask one in either context which animal *that* is, pointing at the zebra. At least part of the reason for this is that whether or not my judgements about zebras are responsible depends on the picture or understanding of zoos and how they work against the background of which I make my judgements. It is unavoidable that my thinking about zebras, including my responses to unusual questions, like the question whether the animal in the enclosure might be a disguised mule, should exploit this understanding, and it would be irresponsible, if it were possible, to attempt to withdraw from that understanding or hold it in abeyance without good reason to think it contains false elements relevant to the matter in hand. Of course, it would be a different matter if such good reasons were supplied. One cannot responsibly exploit elements of an understanding in the face of good reasons that show them to be false or cast serious doubt upon them.

Problems in this area arise if one supposes that in order to be able to exploit an understanding, and in order to count as having a recognitional ability informed by that understanding, the elements of that understanding must be independently supported. That way leads to an epistemological dead end, since the suggested condition need not and could not be met. Empirical knowledge is possible only because the environments in which we try to acquire it exhibit uniformities that we take for granted. Included among such uniformities are those to the effect that having such-and-such an appearance is distinctive of being of such-and-such a kind. That our environments exhibit those uniformities is likely to be, by and large, compatible with the course of our experience, but that is a long way off from our having established that the uniformities obtain. Nonetheless, we operate with understandings on which they are presumed to obtain. There is good reason to try to achieve a perspective on those understandings that is psychologically and epistemologically realistic. A step towards such a perspective is to think of them as equipment in relation to our powers of knowledge-acquisition and to think of their elements as deriving their status from that role rather than as depending on evidential support. I shall revisit related matters in the next chapter.

7

Knowledge from Indicators

7.1. Introduction

A striking feature of current and recent epistemology is that it operates with weak conceptions of evidence adequate for knowledge. It is widely assumed that knowledge can be based on evidence that makes the thing known only highly probable. This is understandable. The following line of thought provides a rationale:

> We sometimes know things on the basis of evidence. When this is so the knowledge implicates a belief that is justified on the basis of evidence. But except in cases in which the content of the belief is entailed by a description of the evidence, the evidential support will render the belief probable to some degree, while being compatible with its falsity. If this were not so our empirical knowledge would be very much narrower in scope than we generally take it to be.

Reflection on particular cases can serve to reinforce such thinking. Here are some cases that are alive in the literature.

> *Parked Car*: You parked your car in a sidestreet a few hours ago and clearly remember where you left it. We are invited to think that, absent countervailing considerations, it would be natural to say that you know where your car is now parked (Vogel 1990: 15).

> *Bank*: On some Friday afternoon you want to deposit money in your bank. Noticing that the queues in the bank are long, you decide to postpone depositing the money until the next day. We are invited to think that absent countervailing considerations, it would be natural for you or others to suppose that you know that the bank will be open the next day on the grounds that it was open two weeks ago on a Saturday (DeRose 1992: 913).

Disappointed Traveller: You would like to go on safari in Africa next year but you have modest financial resources that would not suffice to fund the project. This circumstance is unlikely to change by the time you would wish to go. We are invited to think that, absent countervailing considerations, it would be natural to say that you know you will not have enough money for the safari, even though you play the lottery and your grounds do not rule out the possibility that you win a sum of money that would enable you to take the trip (Hawthorne 2004: 1).

Each of these examples is meant to be a case in which there is evidence that something is so that is adequate for knowledge. They can of course be filled out in different ways. I suspect that many theorists suppose that on any filling out on which it is plausible that the subject knows we shall have to think of the available evidence as doing no more than give a high degree of support to, and thus render highly probable, the proposition that is supposed to be known.[1] In support of this it might be suggested that if we do not take such a line we shall be unable to explain how we know a very great deal that we take ourselves to know on the basis of evidence.

We have here a picture of evidence adequate for knowledge to which I drew attention in Chapter 5 (§5.3). On this picture it is anyone's guess where the dividing-line between evidence adequate for knowledge and evidence inadequate for knowledge should be drawn. It is correspondingly difficult to understand why we should care about the difference, yet we do care if we care about whether we can responsibly terminate enquiry or whether we can be responsible informants. (If we aim to be responsible informants we shall not vouch for something unless we take it to be settled that it is true, since it would be misleading to do so. This theme is picked up in Chapter 8.) Now, if evidence can be adequate for knowledge when it merely renders a proposition highly probable then it is hard to make sense of how it can be that when we know something on the basis of evidence, the evidence settles or clinches it. On the face of it, though, evidence can sometimes establish—clinch it, settle it—that something is so. The wetness of outdoor surfaces can clinch it that it has been raining. The presence of a certain smell can clinch it that toast has been burnt. The sound of bleating can clinch it that sheep are nearby. The position of a mains switch can clinch it that the power is off. A display on a watch can clinch it that the time is, or is very close to, twelve noon. These cases strikingly contrast with the cases displayed above. There might be circumstances in which the fact that the

---

[1] When I speak of high probability I shall mean probability falling short of certainty.

bank was open on a Saturday two weeks ago would clinch it that the bank is open on the following Saturday. (Perhaps there are places where the banks have not changed their opening hours in the last thirty years and will not for the foreseeable future.) But the example as described does not give us enough to make it plausible that the specified evidence is clinching evidence. Accordingly, it does not give us enough to make it plausible that the subject knows. Analogous considerations apply in the other cases. Leaving your car in a place, unless it is a secure place or the car is immobilized, does not clinch it that it will remain there until you collect it. If you play a fair lottery with big prizes nothing would clinch it that you will not have enough money to go on African safari next year. This is not because of any general difficulty about knowledge of the future. Evidence for future happenings *can* be clinching. That the rotor blades of a helicopter in flight have just disintegrated clinches it that the helicopter will fall to the ground. That someone becomes inescapably engulfed by fire clinches it that the person will die from burns or suffocation.

The way we respond to cases in which a matter is clinched contrasts with how we respond to cases in which it is not. Where banking is a highly competitive business, and bankers have shaken off the good old conservatism of the past, who knows when banks are going to increase their opening hours to attract business or reduce opening hours to save on staff costs? In such an environment it would be entirely natural for the subject to concede, even when nothing much is at stake, that he does not know that the bank is open on the following Saturday even though it was open on a Saturday a few weeks ago. Against this it might be suggested, first, that at least when the stakes are low most of us would be prepared to say that the bank will be open on the following Saturday on the basis in question and, second, that in so saying we would give it to be understood that we know and could naturally be taken to know. I think if we grant both of these points we are assuming that our banking environment is not the competitive and fluid one I was envisaging. If it is in fact a more stable environment then the evidence in question might well clinch it that the bank will be open. Exactly analogous considerations apply to car-park cases. Finding it natural to think of the subject as knowing in a given case is explicable by our taking the environment to be favourable to knowing in that case, in virtue of it being possible for the evidence to be clinching. It does not lend decisive support to a weak conception of evidence adequate for knowing.

I suspect that many reading the foregoing will feel pulled in different directions. On the one hand, there does seem a difference between taking it that deer have recently passed by because local deer have a regular, though not invariable, habit of doing so a little earlier in the day, and taking it that they have passed by because of the tracks on the path. This difference corresponds to the difference between evidence that merely renders probable and evidence that clinches. On the other hand, one might be tempted to say that this distinction is blurred because there is always some possibility, however remote, that the supposedly clinching evidence should obtain and deer not have passed.

To respond to this tension we need to be clearer on what it takes for evidence to be clinching. Consider some unlikely, but eminently possible, circumstance in which the tracks on the path are caused by a disturbed philosophy student skilfully wielding a set of deer's feet and bent on causing difficulties for one of his teachers whom he believes to be insufficiently moved by scepticism. The temptation just noticed arises from thinking that in this case the gamekeeper, who is unaware of these proceedings, has the very same evidence that he would have had if the prints were deer tracks –tracks left by the passage of deer. Now, whether or not the prints are deer tracks, as opposed to deer-track forgeries, is certainly relevant to whether the gamekeeper knows that deer have recently passed on the basis of the prints, so it would be odd if the evidential value of there being those prints were independent of whether or not they are deer tracks. To make this more vivid, consider a different case. It matters to the forensic scientist that the fibre on the clothing of the suspect should actually derive from contact with the victim if the fibre is to be evidence of contact with the victim. So if the defence lawyer makes a case that the fibre might easily have come from elsewhere she will in effect be making a case that the fibre is not evidence of the suspect's contact with the victim. We certainly have such a notion of evidence, and it is evidence in this sense that is relevant to the epistemology of indicator cases. Evidence that something is so in this sense (clinching evidence) indicates (factively) that it is so. It is not just that the phenomenon constituting the evidence suggests that the thing is so; its significance is that the thing is so.[2] This bears on the tension that this paragraph is addressing. The distinction between clinching evidence and evidence that merely renders highly probable seemed to be undermined by its being possible that there should be evidence that on my account would clinch it that deer have recently passed by but which might obtain even if deer had not passed by. That way of thinking depends on the assumption that the same evidence is available in both the ordinary and the deceptive

---

[2] My puzzlement about central ideas in Travis (2005), along lines set out in Millar (2005), provoked the development of the views defended in this chapter. Travis makes use of a notion of factive meaning that is at least a close kin to my notion of indication.

situation. I am suggesting that this assumption is false.[3] It is understandable that theorists should have thought otherwise. The gamekeeper's judgement that deer have recently passed in the deceptive situation might be no less reasonable than the corresponding judgement in the ordinary situation. But, as we saw in connection with the fake-barn scenario, the fact that a judgement is reasonable does not entail that one is entitled to make it. For knowledge we need the judgement to be grounded in evidence that clinches it that its content is true.

What matters for clinching evidence that p is that in the circumstances there would be the evidence-constituting phenomenon only if p. There is a sense in which an evidence-constituting phenomenon in relation to the proposition that p would be evidence that p only if the circumstances were such that there would be this phenomenon only if p. In such circumstance there would be evidence constituted by the phenomenon only if p. There could, of course, be other circumstances in which there is the same phenomenon yet it is not the case that p.

To show this general approach to be plausible it is obviously not enough to draw attention to a natural way of thinking about clinching evidence. A metaphysics of clinching evidence, such that e is clinching evidence that p only if p, clearly does not give us an understanding of how a person must stand to that evidence to be in a position to treat it as clinching evidence. I take some steps towards this in the sections of this chapter that follow.

Before proceeding I should stress a couple of points. (i) I have no intention of undermining the idea that there can be evidence that merely renders something probable to a greater or lesser degree and that falls short of being clinching. Evidence can support a claim in virtue of the fact that it is unlikely that the evidence would obtain if the claim were false. (ii) Although it is important for our enquiries and our dealings with others that we can readily distinguish between clinching evidence and evidence that merely renders something highly probable, we often have to act in the absence of clinching evidence. Life has to go on. There isn't time, and we often lack the means, to establish the truth of everything on which we are prepared to act. We would be hopelessly restricted if we did not take risks and badly debilitated if we held back from action to check everything we take for granted. But in many situations, for instance, when stakes are high, we do not settle for less than knowledge if knowledge can be had. I want to know that the mains power is off before touching a bare

---

[3] There are close similarities here with McDowell's (1982) treatment of what he calls the argument from illusion.

electrical wire that is connected to the mains. For that I need more than the fact that someone else is pretty sure, or even justified in being pretty sure, that it is off.[4] I need someone to have checked that the mains switch is set at the off-position.

In the previous chapter I focused on perceptual knowledge because it clearly has the characteristics that knowledge has to have if it is to play the role in our lives that it does. It puts us in a position in which a matter is settled and properly taken to be settled. In this chapter I outline a position on which it becomes intelligible that knowledge from indicator phenomena satisfies those conditions. In the next chapter the results will be applied to knowledge from testimony.

7.2. Knowledge from Indicators

By way of sketching an epistemology for indicator cases I shall invoke once again a conception of recognitional abilities and associated ways of telling.

It is possible to tell that a car's fuel tank is half-full by looking at the reading on the fuel gauge. When we do this the basis of our knowledge is provided by an indicator. In this case the indicator is the reading on the gauge, which indicates the approximate quantity of fuel in the tank. As I said above, indication is to be understood as factive: the reading on the gauge indicates that the tank is half-full only if the tank *is* half-full. There is also a modal dimension to indication: the reading indicates that the tank is half-full only if the reading would be as it is only if the tank were half-full. In the case in hand, indication is grounded in a causal relation: the quantity of fuel in the tank is what causes the gauge to read half-full. When knowledge is acquired by applying the relevant way of telling we have the following elements in the situation:

(1) The fuel gauge reads half-full.

---

[4] Attributer contextualists (DeRose 1992) invite us to think that if in a bank scenario the stakes are high (you'd be penalized heavily if you didn't deposit the money on the Saturday) it would not be true that you know that the bank would be open on the Saturday. It seems to me that you would not know in either the low-stakes case or the high-stakes case on the basis of the evidence described. What is certainly true is that in the high-stakes case it would be foolish to postpone depositing, but in the low-stakes case tolerating the risk that the bank is not open the next day might be reasonable. The difference is not between knowing and not knowing but between being and not in a position reasonably to act on the assumption that the bank will be open.

This fact is given in perception, in the presence of an appropriate perceptual-recognitional ability. It is what grounds the judgement that the tank is half-full. But it can do that only if the subject assumes something to the effect that:

(2) this reading indicates that the fuel tank is half-full.

A suitably equipped subject seeking to know the level of fuel will presume this to be so and thus accept that:

(3) the fuel tank is half-full.

The indicator assumption (2) might seem to be epistemologically problematic. Yet there can be little reasonable doubt that when we judge that the tank is half-full on the basis of the reading, we act on the assumption that the reading indicates (signifies, means) that the tank is half-full. The question is what puts us in a position to treat the reading as such an indicator. The standard way to deal with this—what I shall call *the standard model*—has it that we are entitled to rely on (2) provided that we have sufficiently strong evidence justifying belief in a suitable covering generalization. The generalization might be that when the fuel gauge reads half-full the tank is half-full, or it might be some qualified version of this, for instance, that nearly always when the fuel gauge reads half-full the tank is half-full. But now, on the assumption that the best evidence we are likely to have for a suitable covering generalization will give this generalization a more or less high degree of support, but will fall short of establishing its truth, the standard model is incompatible with the perspective that I am presenting. That is simply because it threatens to undermine the idea that when one knows the matter is settled. For if (2) depends on evidence that merely gives the relevant covering generalization a high degree of support, but does not establish its truth, then it follows that (2) is not settled, and nor is (3). Both would inherit the uncertainty attached to the covering generalization.

There are ways to try to defuse the problem. It might argued that the evidence we have for some generalizations does not merely lend those generalizations a greater or lesser degree of support—it can establish that those generalizations are true. It is doubtful that this strategy will work for all cases of knowledge from indicator phenomena. In any case, we run into a deeper problem. There is little reason to think we routinely have evidence that so much as lends a high degree of support to a suitable covering generalization, never mind evidence adequate for knowledge of the generalization. In the case in hand you are unlikely to have such evidence for every car you drive such that you can come to know about the approximate level of fuel in its tank by reading the gauge.[5] If one were convinced that the standard model is the only game in town then one might try either to mount a case for thinking that we have good enough evidence for the generalization after all, or to show that most of us who think we can tell how much fuel is left in our fuel tanks cannot tell this. Neither option is attractive. The latter would lead to wide-ranging scepticism about the availability of knowledge from indicators. The former requires some implausible finessing about when we have evidence available to us. (See further in §7.4.) I am going to focus on developing a conception of knowledge from indicators that avoids the problem posed by the assumption that independent evidence is needed for a covering generalization and that I take to be in any case realistic.

§7.3. Recognitional Abilities Again

At the heart of the conception proposed here is the notion of a way of telling. In perceptual cases we tell that something is such-and-such from its appearance. In the simplest indicator cases two ways of telling are in play. For instance, we tell by perception that the fuel gauge displays a reading of half-full and from that we tell that the tank is half-full. In this case there is recognition at two levels: (i) we perceptually recognize what the gauge reads (the reading displayed); (ii) we recognize the significance of its reading as it does with respect to level of fuel (what the reading indicates as to level of fuel).

Talk of recognition in connection with (ii) seems entirely appropriate. This is not to retreat from the idea that an inference in the abstract sense (like (1)–(3) in the previous section) is in play. It is in play in the sense that we take in that the gauge reads half-full, that this indicates that the tank is half-full, and we understand these to entail that the tank is half-full. Yet no reasoning need have occurred if that entails making a transition from a belief or set of beliefs to a further belief. It is quite natural to talk of seeing that the tank is half-full just because at the level of phenomenology the judgement that it is half-full is an immediate response to what is seen.[6] Nonetheless, the distinction between perceptual knowledge of the sort I have been discussing and knowledge from indicators remains. When you tell by looking that the flowers in the vase are

---

[5] Compare this remark from Ernest Sosa: 'Take the gauges that we face as driver of a late-model car. Most of us have a paltry conception of them as little more than screens, displays, that keep us informed about the amount of fuel in our tank, our speed, the rpm of our motor, etc. We take the display to be part of a fuller instrument that reliably delivers its deliverances. But who knows how the display on our dashboard reliably connects with its subject matter?' (Sosa 2006: 117–18).

[6] Dretske (1969) calls this secondary epistemic seeing.

roses you see the roses and see them to be roses. When you tell from the fuel gauge reading how much fuel is in the tank you do not see the tank and so do not see it to be anything. Related to this is the fact that knowledge of the quantity of fuel that is gained from looking at the gauge is evidence-based in a way that the perceptual knowledge considered in Chapter 6 is not. We see what the gauge reads and in most cases rightly treat that as something that gives us a reason to take it that the tank is half-full. This is essential to the explanation of the knowledge in this case. By contrast, when we visually recognize a goldfinch in the garden, no fact as to the features of the goldfinch need play a role in the explanation of the knowledge—we simply see that the bird is a goldfinch, albeit that we tell that it is a goldfinch from its appearance. In what follows I shall often wish to compare or contrast indicator cases, in which the indicator is perceived and its significance recognized, and cases of perceptual knowledge that do not involve basing a judgement on some more basic fact, for instance, cases of visually recognizing a bird as being of some kind. I shall take the latter to be cases of *basic perceptual knowledge* or *basic perceptual recognition*, and I shall refer to the recognitional abilities in play in these cases as *basic perceptual-recognitional abilities*.

The similarities between basic perceptual recognition and recognition of the significance of indicators are striking:

(a) Basic perceptual-recognitional abilities are abilities with respect to favourable environments. Favourable environments for the ability to tell by looking that something is a chair are ones in which there is a range of appearances that are distinctive of chairs in that with a high degree of reliability possession by something of any such appearance indicates that it is a chair. Likewise, the ability to tell that deer have passed along a path from the fact that prints of a certain appearance are on the path is likewise an ability with respect to favourable environments—ones in which with a high degree of reliability the presence of such prints indicates that deer have recently passed.

(b) Our perceived knowledge from indicators is no more 'blind' than is basic perceptual knowledge. The gamekeeper who tells that deer have passed from the tracks on the path knows what he is doing and is in a position to explain that the presence of those tracks clinches it that deer have passed. This is possible because the gamekeeper has a perspective on deer and the traces they leave—an understanding of these matters that enables him to make sense of what he is doing when making judgements as to the passage of deer. He learns not just to call the tracks deer tracks but to treat the presence of those tracks as a clinching reason to take it that deer have recently passed by. So when he spots the right tracks he can properly take the matter to be settled.

(c) Basic perceptual-recognitional abilities and abilities to recognize the significance of indicators are akin to practical skills. Learning to ride a bicycle requires one to try to do so in advance of being able to. Perhaps with the help of some initial support from someone else, one learns the trick of maintaining one's balance through appropriate adjustments to the handlebars and shifts in one's body. Experience through trial and error shapes what one does so that it becomes an ability to ride the bicycle. Success in this endeavour comes to be routine so that failure requires some explanation—unexpected obstacles, holes in the road, etc. Learning visually to recognize thrushes requires one to get the hang of correctly judging that this or that bird is or is not a thrush. Experience through trial and error is important here too. One has to make attempts, and will sometimes judge correctly, in advance of reaching the stage at which one counts as having acquired the ability to recognize thrushes by sight. A child might initially mistake female blackbirds for thrushes but then, on being corrected, learn not to judge a bird to be a thrush unless it has a light breast with prominent spots. As the child's judgement becomes more and more sensitive to the appearance that is distinctive of thrushes it comes to have the relevant ability to tell. At that stage failure requires some explanation as due to, for instance, inattention, or relying on a look that is not good enough. Similar considerations apply to the case of learning to tell that deer have recently passed. One has to learn to identify tracks of the right configuration, and learn when they are relatively fresh. One might do these things with the help of verbal or written instruction or by observation of deer and of the tracks that they make. However one learns, experience shapes one's sensitivity to the distinctive features of deer tracks and one comes to have a way of telling that deer have recently passed from their tracks. At that stage, nearly every time one goes in for telling that deer have recently passed in this way one succeeds in doing so. As before, failure requires special explanation.

(d) Our basic perceptual knowledge does not depend on our having evidence for generalizations that connect possession of certain types of appearance with the presence of objects belonging to a certain kind or possessing a certain property. Rough-and-ready generalizations might well be part of our picture of the world. For instance, the ability to recognize zebras by sight is likely to be associated with willingness to accept that things that look like *this* (pointing to a zebra or some representation of a zebra) are zebras. But there is no reason to think that our acceptance of such a generalization is grounded in evidence adequate for knowledge. This is just as well since there is little reason to think that we have evidence adequate for this purpose. What have we ever done to test whether things that look like zebras really are? We have simply encountered zebras or representations of zebras and learned to call animals with the appropriate appearance zebras. This is a clue to the character of such knowledge: it does not depend on our having established the truth of some covering generalization but on the exploitation of a sensibility that has been inculcated and honed by experience. A similar story is just as plausible for knowledge from indicators.[7] Those who can tell that deer have recently passed from prints on a path need not have tested any generalization linking these prints with deer. What matters is whether they can do the business. The test for being able to tell whether or not deer have passed from the presence of tracks of the right configuration is, roughly speaking, that (a) you nearly always get it right when you try, (b) you rarely withhold a judgement when aiming to judge either way in conditions conducive to correct judgement, and (c) that when you judge incorrectly, or withhold judgement, in conditions conducive to correct judgement, some explanatory factor is in play, such as distraction.

This comparison between basic perceptual recognition and the double-layered recognition in perceptual indicator cases—recognition of the presence of the indicator phenomenon and recognition of its significance—highlights the practical character of the skills involved and spotlights a role for experience in knowledge-acquisition that is easy to overlook. I mean the role of experience in shaping a sensibility and thereby inculcating and refining a way of telling.

There are relatively straightforward cases of being justified in believing something on the basis of evidence *e* with respect to which the following conditions are satisfied: (i) one knows that *e* exists; (ii) *e* provides one with a reason to believe the thing in question; (iii) one believes it for that reason. How exactly (iii) should be understood is a matter of dispute. I shall take it that the cases in which it is clear that a subject believes something for a reason

---

[7] I do not wish to suggest that appearances are not indicators, but for knowledge from indicators to be acquired the indicators need not be registered as indicators at the level of judgement.

provided by evidence *e* are ones in which the subject believes *in view of* e *and on account of* e*'s existence*. This condition might be satisfied because the evidence is literally in view or otherwise perceptible, or it might be because the evidence is remembered and the memory of it sustains the knowledge. I am strongly inclined to think that unless conditions (i)–(iii) are met we do not have a case of believing for a reason as we would ordinarily understand it. I shall not argue that here. Rather, I shall take these conditions to provide at least a partial characterization of *a* sense in which a belief can be justified on the basis of evidence. I shall call it *the clear sense*. My principle concern is to clarify the distinction between the role of experience in contributing to justification in this clear sense and the role of experience in forming and honing a recognitional ability. This will be crucial for the development of a plausible alternative to the standard model of knowledge from indicators. I also wish to resist a tendency to stretch the notions of reason and evidence to do work that I think is better done by other tools.

Even granted that the ability to tell from the wetness of surfaces that it has rained recently is a practical ability, it is natural to ask: 'What justifies us in thinking that the wetness of surfaces indicates that it has recently rained?' I suggest that we should not take for granted that to make sense of our having the ability in question we must view it as resting upon possession of an independent, evidence-based, justification for believing that the wetness of surfaces indicates that it has recently rained. Informing our ability to tell is an understanding that this sort of wetness (at least nearly always) has a certain significance: it indicates that it has rained recently. We need to consider the status of this understanding. I return to this matter in §7.5.

7.4. Detached Standing Knowledge

A great deal of our general knowledge of factual information does not depend on our having in view occasions on which we gleaned this information or acquired evidence that it is genuinely factual information. The knowledge I have in mind is not sustained by recollection of sources from which one gleaned it. I shall call it *detached standing* knowledge. It is standing knowledge because it is retained over a significant period of time. It is detached because one has lost touch with the sources of information from which it was gleaned. It embraces much of what is sometimes called general knowledge of, for instance, historical, geographical, and cultural facts.

What justification do I have for believing that Kuala Lumpur is the capital of Malaysia? Perhaps I learned this in school. In any case, I have encountered a large number of sources of information—encyclopedias, reputable newspapers, magazines, and news broadcasts—confirming that Kuala Lumpur is indeed the capital of Malaysia. But, even though I have encountered these various confirming sources, it is not at all obvious that I now have a reason to believe this provided by evidence supplied by these sources. The conditions required for justification by evidence in the clear sense are not met. Whatever impact evidence may have had in inducing my belief as to the capital of Malaysia, it is not in view of that evidence that I now believe as I do. The evidence I might once have had is not evidence I now possess, since I do not recall it. So it is not evidence in view of which I now believe as I do. That is why this knowledge counts as detached standing knowledge. There is pressure to try to make out knowledge in this case to be evidence-based just because we need to make sense of the idea that one who has such knowledge is justified in believing that Kuala Lumpur is the capital of Malaysia. We might yield to this pressure by supposing that evidence can supply us with a reason for believing even if it is not evidence that we now have in view. (This is a kind of finessing about the availability of evidence to which I alluded towards the end of §7.2.) Some might find this entirely unproblematic. It seems to me, however, that to invoke reasons that, in the nature of the case, cannot function as recognizable reasons in our thinking is a bad move. In any case, it is not a move that needs to be made to account for the phenomena.

It is right that past experience of the sort under consideration, in the form of encounters with sources of information, can be relevant to our now having detached standing knowledge. But it does not follow that we have to view this knowledge as currently evidence-based. It is plausible that detached standing knowledge is, roughly speaking, an ability to recall known facts.

For convenience, I shall take the notion of recalling that Kuala Lumpur is the capital of Malaysia to cover cases of unprompted recollection along with both cases in which recollection is prompted by a question along the lines of 'What is the capital of Malaysia?' and cases in which recollection is prompted by a question along the lines of 'Is Kuala Lumpur the capital of Malaysia?' Experience is relevant to our having detached standing knowledge because it incorporates encounters with sources of known facts and over time forms and hones our powers of recollection of those facts. Since conditions of the sort usually taken to be necessary for knowledge, additional to true belief, are not satisfied, it might seem that this view is tantamount to reducing detached standing knowledge to true belief. That would be a misunderstanding. The claim is not that detached standing knowledge that p consists simply in a disposition to avow the truth that p, no matter how that disposition is formed. All empirical knowledge must derive from the impact of the world upon us through experience. But that impact can be of the ability-inculcating sort and it can be indirect because mediated via publicly available sources of information. Facts become known and become recorded in various sources because they are known. The sources in question are, in a sense, knowledge-incorporating because the facts are incorporated in those sources on account of being known. Those who encounter those sources acquire knowledge of the facts via the impact of those encounters upon them. Those who have a merely true belief need not have encountered knowledge-incorporating sources and so their belief need not have been instilled by the (indirect) impact of the world upon them. Suppose that through a dream I become convinced that a rare orchid with such-and-such features is located in a remote region of Indonesia and, amazingly, there is indeed an orchid with those features in that region. I do not count this as knowing that there is such an orchid in this area. When it occurs to me that there is such an orchid in that location, I am not recollecting a known fact, for it is not that I have come to know the fact via encounters with the orchid in question or with any knowledge-incorporating source.[8]

We do not blindly exercise the abilities that constitute detached standing knowledge. When I recall that Kuala Lumpur is the capital of Malaysia I recognize this fact as something I remember. This recognition puts me in a position to explain, in terms of my remembering, the manner in which I currently know this fact, though it does not put me in a position to know with any specificity how I came to know it. The recognition also puts me in a position to vouch for its being a fact that Kuala Lumpur is the capital of Malaysia, for given that I remember this, and am aware that I do, I have a clinching reason to continue to believe it to be so.

Sadly, memory is fallible and probably a lot more fallible than perception. It is relatively rare to be convinced that you saw that something was so, when you did not. It might well be a lot less rare to be convinced that you remember

---

[8] Goldman and Olsson (2009) draw attention to the fact that we are reluctant to count someone as ignorant that Vienna is the capital of Austria if he or she assents to this when asked. Assuming that we understand ignorance to be the condition of not knowing, our reluctance amounts to not being willing to deny such people knowledge. Yet we need have done nothing to satisfy ourselves that they meet the conditions that might be thought necessary for knowledge additional to true belief. Goldman and Olsson suggest that there is a sense in which knowledge just is true belief. It seems to me that our reluctance to regard those people as ignorant is explained by the fact that, in view of the public availability of knowledge about (what to us are) prominent world capitals, we assume that they have learned that Vienna is the capital of Austria via encounters with knowledge-incorporating sources. My view accounts for this without requiring us to posit a sense of 'knowledge' on which it is merely true belief. I have no problem with the idea that the dreamer with the true belief about the orchid is ignorant of the fact that makes it true. He has had no cognitive contact with the fact either directly or indirectly.

some fact when you do not. Nonetheless, people can be good at remembering facts, and good at telling what they remember. The test for their being good at remembering is whether they are good at recalling those facts. How do they tell whether or not they remember? Judging from the phenomenology of such things, it seems plausible that there is an intimate relationship between having a settled confidence that p and remembering that p. In the cases we are considering, the confidence is not based on recollection of any past experience that revealed that p but is, so to speak, self-standing. People who are good at telling what they remember in this manner are people who are such that their self-standing confidence that something is so is a highly reliable indicator that they remember that it is so. Plausibly, they have a recognitional ability that enables them to tell that they remember something from their self-standing confidence that it is so.[9] The ability in play here—to recognize what one remembers—is itself one that will have been shaped through experience: things we recollect are often confirmed; inability to recollect often gives way to finding out; when we misremember we are often corrected. It is more like the abilities in play in perceptual cases than it is like those in play in the indicator cases I have been considering: it is a judgement *from* strength of confidence rather than based in evidence to the effect that one has strength of confidence. (In a similar way one tells that the bird is a goldfinch from its appearance not because we take the appearance to be evidence.) I do not suggest that we are all good at telling what we remember from our strength of confidence. There is an analogue for the relation to a favourable environment in the basic perceptual cases and in the sorts of indicator cases already considered. One must be such that one's strength of conviction that something is so always or nearly always indicates that one remembers that it is so.

To sum up: experience bears on detached standing knowledge in two ways. First, encounters with knowledge-incorporating sources for some fact induce the ability to recall that fact—an ability that consists in knowing it. Second, those encounters, and subsequent episodes in which what one recalls is confirmed, what one misremembers is corrected, and what one has forgotten is rediscovered, reinforce or re-establish the strength of confidence from which one tells that one remembers it. So while it is true that from experience we gain this kind of knowledge, the role of experience is that of furnishing us with an ability to recall the fact or to recognize that it is a fact.

---

[9] It might be thought that there is a *constitutive* connection between having a strong conviction that p and being disposed to judge that one remembers that p when the question of whether one remembers that p arises. Even if that is so, the present concern is with how we tell and thus know, that we remember something. It is to explain this that I invoke a further recognitional ability.

I should stress that it is not part of the account I am giving that detached standing knowledge must always have its roots in episodes in which evidence-based knowledge of the fact in question was once acquired. This is just as well, since when we were young we were unable to discriminate between knowledge-incorporating sources and others and so were in no position to acquire knowledge straight off from an encounter with a source for a fact. We had to imbibe a vast amount of information without having well-grounded assurance that the sources from which we have gleaned it are trustworthy. But even at those early stages of learning, episodes in which information was conveyed to us, through instruction by parents and teachers or through reading, contributed to the experience that over a period of time furnished us with an ability to recall the fact, and that ability, I am suggesting, amounts to knowledge of the fact. Subsequent social interactions reinforce and refine such abilities, improve our abilities to detect reliable sources, and contribute to sifting out false beliefs.

7.5. Back to Knowledge from Indicators

In §7.3 I emphasized the practical character of our ability to recognize the significance of indicators but also that we need to be able to shed some light on the status of the understandings that inform our recognitional abilities. For indicator cases these are likely to include rough generalizations linking indicator phenomena to what they indicate, enabling us to explain and justify the judgements we make through exercising those abilities. Against the background of the previous section it would be convenient if we could regard ourselves as having detached standing knowledge of these generalizations, along the lines sketched in the previous section. I think that this works for some cases. For instance, the ability to tell that a helicopter in flight will fall to the ground on seeing that its rotor blades have disintegrated might be informed by knowledge that helicopters in this state will fall to the ground. But I think it would be a mistake to take this to provide the form of a general explanation of the status of these generalizations in our thinking because it is doubtful that the conditions for the relevant detached standing knowledge are always met when people have and exercise recognitional abilities.

There is a problem concerning the indeterminacy of candidate generalizations. Even in a simple case like that of telling that it has rained from the wetness of surfaces we are hard put to characterize just what sort of wetness counts in terms that are both general and specific. Yet we know it when we see it. Much the same applies to the deer-track case. Learning to tell that deer have passed is largely a matter of learning to recognize the right sort of tracks. Once you 'get your eye in' you know by looking, but it is questionable whether we have a conceptual grip of the sort to which the tracks conform, if that is understood to incorporate some specification of the features of the tracks. Why is that a problem for the account that I am resisting? The reason is that, because of its lack of specificity, accepting the generalization cannot be the psychological basis, and thus the grounding, for taking it that *those prints* are deer tracks. The psychology of the situation must account for the gamekeeper's responsiveness to the features possessed by the right kind of tracks. The proposed account in terms of a generalization requires that the generalization should highlight the relevant features: it would be a generaliza-tion to the effect that tracks with such-and-such features are deer tracks. But because of their lack of specificity they cannot fulfil this role. Nor should we expect them to. As in cases of recognizing deer as deer, the keeper deploys a way of telling that requires him to be sensitive to a certain *Gestalt*—in this case the *Gestalt* presented by the tracks. This being so, it is hard to see how acceptance of the generalization can play the epistemological role that it is supposed to.

There is another problem for the account to which I am objecting. It concerns the domain of quantification of the generalizations. Consider shepherds who can tell that sheep are nearby from the sound of bleating. They are committed to thinking that the bleating sound, with a high degree of reliability, indicates that sheep are nearby. That is part of the understanding that informs their ability. It commits them to accepting that nearly always when the bleating sound occurs sheep are nearby. On the most natural interpretation of either generalization it might conceivably be false without detriment to the ability to tell in this way that sheep are nearby. (This would be the natural interpretation if, in any environment suitable for sheep, the shepherd would, on the basis of the relevant kind of bleating, form judgements as to the nearby presence of sheep.) There being goats on some other island that make exactly the same bleating sound would no more make it false that, with respect to his island, the shepherd can tell from the bleating sound that there are sheep nearby than the existence of fake-barn territory would make it false that with respect to his home territory Barney can tell that a structure is a barn from its appearance. Since that is so, we have a very good reason to try to account for the abilities in play in indicator cases in some other way.

Just to underline the point: I am not disputing that generalizations play a role in relation to the abilities under consideration. The gamekeeper will have come to accept a rough generalization about deer tracks—that prints like *these* are deer tracks—as part of the process of acquiring the ability to recognize deer tracks. However, the test for his having command of the ability is, very roughly, his nearly always getting it right when he attempts to. (A less rough specification of conditions is given in §7.3 above.) Whether the generalization has an independent evidential support or independent standing in virtue of being detached standing knowledge is not to the point.

The generalization is an element in the gamekeeper's understanding of his environment—an understanding that informs, and thus is partially constitutive of, his ability to tell that deer have recently passed, and that enables him to make sense of his deer-stalking activity and of the judgements about deer that he makes. Acceptance of the generalization has a certain status, but this status is derived from its role in equipping him with a method of telling that deer have passed by. It is the ability so to tell that is in the explanatory driving-seat, not any independent standing of acceptance of the generalization. Nonetheless, acceptance of the generalization in this and similar cases must meet certain conditions if the subject is to count as having the recognitional ability. It matters that its acceptance is an adjunct to learning how to tell which tracks are deer tracks, because the standing of its acceptance depends on its links with the ability—on its being equipment for the exercise of the ability. It matters that the generalization is not falsified by anything in the gamekeeper's experience, since it can be responsibly accepted only if the gamekeeper is responsive to countervailing evidence.

How exactly should we characterize the relation of the subject who has the ability to a generalization that informs it of the sort under consideration? I am reluctant to say that the subject is entitled to accept the generalization, given the way in which I have linked entitlement with well-groundedness. (Though that is not to suggest that the subject is not entitled either, if that is taken to imply that there is some cognitive deficit on the subject's part.) Something like this seems to be true: it is constitutive of possession by reflective subjects of the recognitional abilities in question that those subjects should accept the relevant generalizations so long as there is no available evidence that casts doubt on them. It is not irrational for them do so in the absence of such evidence because it is not irrational to draw on the equipment you need if you are to acquire and exercise the abilities in question. Moreover, responsibly exercising the ability requires one to exploit one's existing understanding. (Recall the discussion in §6.6.)

7.6. Taking Stock

My aim throughout has been to account for how significant portions of our knowledge can be understood to have the characteristics that enable that knowledge to be of value to us in the way it is. At least part of the story of why knowledge matters to us has to do with the nature of enquiry, and in particular with the need to tell when a matter is settled. Another, related, part has to do with being able responsibly to inform others, speaking from knowledge and thus able to vouch for what we know. My accounts of perceptual knowledge, knowledge from indicators, and what I called detached standing knowledge are intended to make sense of how these modes of knowing put us in a position in which a matter can responsibly be taken to be settled and vouched for. I have been at pains to show how empirical evidence can clinch it that something is so, rather than make it merely probable. In this connection I brought out analogies between basic perceptual knowledge and knowledge from indicators. I stressed that experience can have an important role in relation to knowledge-acquisition other than that of providing us with evidence. It can instil in us detached standing knowledge, and inculcate and refine our recognitional abilities.

Where knowledge is concerned we seem to be able to glean a lot from a little. Perceptual knowledge seems problematic because it is knowledge with rich content and it seems puzzling that perceptual experience should be able to make rich facts available to us. Knowledge from indicators is problematic because it seems puzzling that we can be entitled to take indicating phenomena to indicate what they do. Detached standing knowledge seems problematic because it is unclear what supplies the justification in these matters, given that we have lost touch with the sources from which we gleaned the facts in question. I have sought to defuse the puzzles by drawing on a number of key considerations. (a) Perceptual knowledge can have rich content because we are in command of suitably sophisticated recognitional abilities that are broadly individuated. It can furnish us with justified beliefs thanks to higher-order abilities that enable us to recognize what we perceive to be so. (b) Knowledge from indicators rests on perceptual knowledge and brings into play additional abilities to recognize the significance of perceived phenomena. But we can also tell when we have exercised those abilities drawing upon the understandings that inform them. (c) Detached standing knowledge brings into play abilities to recall and recognize facts—abilities that are inculcated and honed by experience.

In the concluding chapter of this contribution I turn to consider knowledge from testimony. In many respects the epistemology of testimony is at the heart of the theory of knowledge, because it serves to highlight so much else that is crucial. The discussion will incorporate some further reflections on the value of knowledge.

8

The Social Transmission of Knowledge

8.1. Why Knowledge Matters

That knowledge matters to us is hardly disputable. As I remarked in Chapter 5, the natural way to conceive of the aim of enquiry into whether something is so is in terms of aiming to find out whether it is so. Finding out is nothing less than coming to know. Since enquiry, if only into everyday practical matters, is inextricable from human life, it cannot fail to be the case that we care about obtaining knowledge on those matters into which we enquire. There are of course areas in which the best that can be achieved is less than knowledge. This might well be the right way to think of scientific enquiry, at least when it seeks to formulate theoretically interesting generalizations. Perhaps the best that can be achieved in this area are theories that are more or less well supported by empirical evidence. In more mundane enquiries, knowledge is often obtained.

Why should it be that enquiry seeks *knowledge* rather than anything lesser? I think the best way to approach this is via the idea that an interest in the truth on some matter is bound to be an interest in knowledge on that matter. (By 'having an interest in . . .' I shall mean *being interested in or concerned about* . . . In this sense we have an interest in the truth of a matter even if we think we have the truth.) Suppose that I believe that the bank will be open on Saturday and it will be. So long as nothing induces doubt between now and Saturday I shall act on the assumption that it will be open then and use the bank as I plan to. But something might justifiably induce doubt. It might strike me that my only reason for thinking that the bank will be open on Saturday is that it was open recently on a Saturday. How do I know that it will not have changed its hours? In the circumstances, that could easily be a live question. In that case, aware of this, I would have to check to find out, that is, come to know. My interest in the truth is not fully satisfied short of knowing. My interest is an interest in knowing.

Suppose that I find out about the bank's opening hours by phoning the bank. Someone at the bank with the relevant information on such matters tells me that the bank is open on Saturday and I thereby come to know that this is so. I act accordingly. In practice I would know how I know that the bank is open for I would recall having been told by someone at the bank, but suppose that my knowledge had been blind in that I knew but with no knowledge of how I came to know nor of any clinching reason to think that I do know.[1] I would probably still act on the conviction that the bank is open on Saturday *so long as* it never occurred to me, or I were not prompted, to wonder why I am confident that this is so. But if I did come to wonder, my blind knowledge would be to no avail. Nor would it enable me responsibly to vouch for what I know. My interest is in reflectively knowing—knowing with knowledge of how I know or some clinching reason to think I do know. For then I can responsibly take the matter to be settled and, if called upon, vouch responsibly for the truth of the matter. Fortunately, it will often be the case that I have reflective knowledge. Indeed, it would be unusual for me to know that the bank is open on Saturday from having been told by the informant in the bank, yet not know that I know in virtue of having been thus told.

It might be suggested that we don't need knowledge that is reflective in that it comes with knowledge concerning that knowledge, but only a reason to think true the thing we know. At this point, though, the importance of the difference between reasons that clinch or settle that something is so and reasons that fall short of doing this becomes important. How we act depends crucially on discriminating between what is settled and what is not. Merely having some reason to think that the bank is open on Saturday will not suffice for vouching that this is so if we aim to vouch responsibly. For that, we need a reason that is clinching. Recognizing that a reason for thinking that p is clinching (settles it, establishes, that p) is tantamount to recognizing that you know that p. Testimony can sometimes supply such a reason.

A merely true belief is easily vulnerable to being undermined by the realization that it is not knowledge—that the truth of the matter has not been established. So is a justified true belief if the justification is the kind that is supposed to obtain in Gettier cases. Reverting to Plato's *Meno* example, suppose you were told that this road before you leads to Larissa by someone whom you had good reason to think trustworthy, and who is right about the road, but only because he is himself in a Gettier-type situation in relation to

[1] I take it that many theories of knowledge, for instance, reliabilist theories, countenance blind knowledge. The theory of knowledge advanced in this part of the book is compatible with there being such knowledge, though in practice, if not by necessity, much human knowledge is not blind.

the proposition in question. Perhaps he is in general reliable and is suitably discriminating about testimony, and you are justified in thinking that he has those traits. The trouble is that he was told about the road by someone who passed himself off as a reliable informant and merely guessed. You accept what you have been told and as a consequence you are now in a Gettier-type situation. If you were to become aware that you lack any good reason to think that the road before you leads to Larissa, you would not know what to think. You might not become aware of this and you might get to Larissa, acting on your belief, but the belief, though true, would not be secure since it might well become apparent that you do not know whether this road leads to Larissa. By contrast, if you knew that it does because you recall having previously taken it to Larissa then it would take a lot to dislodge your belief.

Our interest in the truth is not satisfied by a merely fleeting grasp of the truth—one that is vulnerable to being undermined. If we grasp the truth only to lapse back into suspense of judgement, while retaining our interest, the interest is clearly not satisfied. Though a belief that is vulnerable in this way might never actually be undermined, it makes sense to ensure that it is not liable to being undermined. The best way to do this, I am suggesting, is to acquire reflective knowledge. Of course, a belief that is true might be resistant to being undermined because you take yourself to know even though you do not. But, irrespective of how reasonable or otherwise the belief is, if you are basically rational, it will be vulnerable to your coming to realize that you don't know what you believe to be true. If the belief is an irrational fixation, due to some psychological pathology or manipulation by others, then the kind of interest you have in the truth is not satisfied. Your believing something true would in that case be at the price of a severe loss of autonomy. It is not just that this is too high a price to pay, though it surely is, but that the kind of interest we have depends on, and is not detachable from, our being autonomous beings, who have some control over how we think and act. If I am interested in playing tennis then I want that I play tennis from time to time through my taking steps to satisfy this desire. If I am interested in whether or not something is true my interest is in my finding out whether or not it is so, not in its coming about that I believe the truth of the matter in a manner that has nothing to do with the truth's disclosing itself to me. And it is internal to my interest that I should be able to tell whether or not it has been satisfied. My interest in the truth just *is* an interest in reflectively knowing it.

In the light of this, what should we make of the idea that knowledge has greater value than merely true belief? This much seems true. For someone with an interest in whether or not *p*, reflective knowledge whether or not *p* has a greater value than true belief on the matter simply because it meets the person's interest in a way that a merely true belief or anything else falling short of knowledge does not. For our interest in the truth of a matter is an interest in seeing that the matter is settled, so that we are in a position responsibly to terminate enquiry and vouch for the truth.

My general approach to issues about the value of knowledge contrasts with a certain methodology that has been in play in recent philosophical discussions, in which it is assumed that true belief is a fundamental good in terms of which the value of knowledge is to be explained. A problem seems to arise because if one has a true belief about something then it does not seem to matter how you came by it. In particular, that you came by it in a way that amounts to knowledge seems not to add anything to the value attached to the belief simply in virtue of being true.[2] The problem strikes me as being spurious. It is assumed that if we are to explain the value of knowledge in a way that makes truth fundamental then it must be in terms of value that true belief has *merely as such*. We have been given no reason to accept this assumption. There is no reason to assume that our interest in truth as to whether or not something is so is satisfied merely by satisfying whatever minimal standards are required for having a true belief on the matter, irrespective of the kind of grip on the truth that we have. On the approach that I am taking we do not explain the value of knowledge in terms of the value of true belief merely as such. We explain the value of reflectively knowing whether or not *p* in terms of the idea that an interest in the truth as to whether or not *p is* an interest in reflectively knowing whether or not *p*. It is understandable that theorists should have started with consideration of the value of merely true belief given that merely true belief was conceived as an ingredient of knowledge. But we should explore other ways of thinking about true belief and knowledge.

The grips that climbers have on ropes onto which that they are holding can be more or less secure. Given what grips are for—keeping one attached to the rope—it is better that they be as secure as possible, unless it becomes dangerous to hold on. Since it is internal to the interest climbers have in grasping a rope that the grasp should be secure, it would clearly be absurd to try to account for the value of their having a secure grasp in terms of the value of a grasp on the rope that is barely a grasp. Knowledge is a mode of grasping the truth, and it would be no less absurd to try to explain the value of the grasp of the truth in which knowledge consists in terms of the grasp (if that is the right word) in which a merely true belief consists. Our interest in the truth of some matter calls for a grip on the truth that is secure in the sense of

---

[2] Compare the review in Pritchard's Chapter 1 (this volume) and the framework with which Jonathan Kvanvig (2003) engages.

being resistant to being loosened. For, as I have already remarked, to lose a truth that has been grasped, while continuing to have an interest in it, leaves that interest unsatisfied. From this perspective, security of grasp of the truth is not an independent goal that provides a rationale for wanting knowledge. It is internal to what we are after when we have an interest in the truth. In the light of this it would be a mistake to suppose that, according to my account, the value of knowledge is in some way instrumental in relation to the goal of gaining some truth. Such a conception would imply that acquiring knowledge is merely a means to satisfying our interest in the truth. On my account, our interest in the truth is not detachable from our interest in knowledge—it is an interest in knowledge.[3]

Before proceeding, it is worth emphasizing that nothing in the account I have given establishes that knowledge has some value simply as knowledge, independently of its content.[4] There is interest-relative value in knowing *whether or not* p for someone with an interest in whether or not *p*. No doubt there would be value in some people's knowing whether certain things are so, irrespective of whether they have an interest in this. But again, such value is content-dependent. I am sceptical that there is any value to knowing that is content-independent, and so do not take it to be a defect of my account that it does not establish that there is such value.

The preceding discussion has a direct bearing on what knowledge is and on the shape of an adequate theory of knowledge. It should not be a mystery that reflective knowledge is often acquired. Conceptual-reductionist conceptions of knowledge make this more difficult to understand than it is because by implication they impute to enquirers and informants a grasp of what, under these conceptions, turns out to be a complex and elusive condition. Theories that are not reductionist but which shed no light on the epistemology of knowledge-ascription do little to dispel the mystery. In preceding chapters I have tried to take some of the mystery out of knowing by emphasizing that attributions of knowledge are made in the light of an understanding of familiar means of acquiring knowledge. Our general conception of knowledge is in large measure a conception of that which is gained through the deployment of ways of telling of which we have more and less specific conceptions. Less

---

[3] Plato's response to the *Meno* problem is sometimes taken to be that knowledge is more valuable from a practical point of view than merely true belief (as in Sosa 2007: ch. 4, and in Pritchard, this volume, §1.3). Knowledge surely is of value from this point of view, but on my account we should not think of the interest in the truth as being only contingently related to an interest in knowledge: interest in the truth just is interest in reflective knowledge.

[4] I take it that virtue theorists hold that knowledge has value for its own sake, irrespective of its content, as being an achievement or manifestation of competence. See Pritchard's discussion in Part I above.

specific conceptions include *telling that something is such-and-such by looking at it*. More specific conceptions include *telling that one's keys are in one's pocket by feeling them there*. (Detached standing knowledge, as conceived in §7.4, need not have been acquired by deploying a way of telling, understood as a way of acquiring knowledge. We can come to know lots of facts through having imbibed information before we were in a position to acquire knowledge of those facts. Even so, such knowledge still depends on the facts in question having been previously known by someone through the deployment of some means of telling.)

This general conception of knowledge, allied to the epistemology of basic perceptual knowledge and of knowledge from indicators, outlined in Chapters 6 and 7, helps to make sense of both self-ascriptions of knowledge and ascriptions of knowledge to others. It does so because of its emphasis on familiar modes of knowledge-acquisition of which we have an understanding. This understanding we readily exploit in thinking about what we or others know. But a crucial part of the story has not yet been explored. The transmission of knowledge from person to person is important for knowledge-acquisition, and being in a position to transmit knowledge is a major reason for caring about whether we, who aim to transmit knowledge, have the knowledge we aim to transmit. We need to consider how we can so often, so effectively, transmit knowledge. It might be wondered whether knowledge from testimony can live up the standards suggested by the other kinds of knowledge that I have considered. It is to this that I now turn.

8.2. Approaching the Epistemology of Testimony

I shall not attempt to give a fully general account of either the nature of testimony or its epistemology. I shall focus on what I shall call *straightforward* cases in which knowledge is intentionally transmitted by an informant and received by those informed. Here is such a case. In response to an enquiry from me a colleague tells me that he has just sent off to a journal a paper on a topic we have been discussing. I accept what he tells me on account of his having told me, without deliberating about the matter, weighing up evidence, and the like. I thereby come to know that he has sent off this paper. In such cases the receipt of knowledge is to all intents and purposes phenomenologically immediate. Yet the recipients are not undiscriminating. They deploy a complex range of abilities by means of which they recognize speakers as engaging in acts of telling and as being trustworthy on the matter in hand. It is clearly relevant to the smoothness of my colleague's transmission of knowledge about his paper that he knows whether or not he has sent off the paper and that I know him to be competent on this sort of matter. We can imagine circumstances in which somebody, perhaps out of embarrassment over procrastination, says that he has sent off a paper when he has not yet done so. But I could know *this* colleague well enough know that he may be trusted on this kind of thing. On other subject matters I might be more cautious. If I know that he gets mixed up over the names of actors in films, or is evasive and misleading about his personal relationships, I might not know what to make of things he says on such matters. The possibility that he is not to be relied upon for some matters need not impugn knowledge-transmission in the case in hand. The discussion in this chapter is about straightforward cases like this in which knowledge is, as we might say, conveyed with something like the immediacy with which the gamekeeper discerns from the tracks that deer have recently passed by. These are cases in which the subject accepts something to be so, and acquires knowledge, on the say-so of the informant. The problem we need to address in relation to such cases is how to make sense of the discriminative capacities of recipients given that they do not engage in deliberation, weigh up evidence, and the like.

What have come to be known as *reductionist theories of testimony* assimilate or reduce the epistemology of testimony to the epistemology of reliance on empirical evidence in general.[5] Perhaps the most natural reductionist approach is to apply to testimony what in §7.2 I called the standard model of knowledge from indicators. On this model, to be justified in taking the occurrence of some phenomenon to indicate that something is so, and to gain knowledge to that effect, we need evidence for a suitable covering generalization. For my purposes it is important not to tie the appropriateness of thinking of testimony as evidence to either reductionism in general or to the version of it that assumes the standard model of knowledge from indicators. It seems right to suppose that in the straightforward cases recipients take the informant's act of telling to indicate, and in that way be evidence for, the truth of what is told. By treating the act of telling us something in this way we commit ourselves to taking it that the informant would have told us this thing only if it were true. That commitment is readily intelligible, since in those cases, by accepting what we are told, we trust our informants to be speaking from knowledge. It is a further question whether reductionism about testimony is correct. For taking an act of telling to indicate, and to be in that way evidence for, the truth of what

[5] The term 'reductionism' applied to theories of testimony was introduced by C. A. J. Coady (1992).

is told is compatible with the anti-reductionist view that the epistemology of testimony should not be assimilated to the epistemology of empirical evidence in general. More specifically, it does not preclude there being special factors in play when knowledge is transmitted by an act of telling that are not built into the standard model.

In place of the standard model of knowledge from indicators I have proposed an account on which we deploy abilities to recognize the significance of indictor phenomena, which do not depend on having evidence for, or knowledge of the truth of, a suitable covering generalization. This is just as well, since the standard model is hard put to account for the acquisition of knowledge from testimony. When my colleague tells me that he has sent off his article, a host of cues elicit my unhesitant acceptance. Stepping back from the occasion, I could pick out factors that seem explanatorily relevant. He tells me against a background in which the information is no great surprise. He speaks in a straightforward, matter-of-fact way in circumstances in which fooling around would be out of place. Given what I know of him, it would be extraordinary if he were deliberately to deceive me on the matter and there could be little reason for him to do so. But it is quite unrealistic to suppose that on the occasion in question I would have registered such features at the level of judgement, and applied a generalization to the effect that when somebody tells me something and those features are realized then what is told is (usually?) true.⁶ The problem here is in part due to the elusiveness of the relevant features: there is little reason to suppose that we so much as register all of the relevant features at the level of judgement. There is the further question whether the sought-for generalization quantifies over people in general, people I am likely to encounter, people I know, and so on. Even if the generalization were restricted to my colleague, the problem posed by the elusiveness of the relevant features would remain. In view of these indeterminacies it seems to me doubtful that we have any very clear idea of just which generalization is required in particular cases and therefore any clear idea of what evidence the subject would need to have for any such generalization.

Given these complexities, it is not surprising that some philosophers have embraced what might be called a *defaultist stance* on testimony. The general idea is that we have a default justification for accepting testimony and should hold back only if there is some reason not to accept it.⁷ On this view, the

⁶ A recent example of an approach along these lines is Fumerton (2006).
⁷ J. L. Austin writes: 'It is fundamental in talking (as in other matters) that we are entitled to trust others, except insofar there is some concrete reason to distrust them' (1946: 82). Similar views are expressed Price (1969: 124), Burge (1993: 467), and Welbourne (2001: 104–5). Elizabeth Fricker (1994; 1995)

discriminative capacities kick in to enable us to tell when there is reason not to accept what we are told. There are three problems for any such approach. The first is that it is not clear how we are to understand the proviso to the effect that there be no reason not to accept what we are told. If it just means that we *have* no reason not to accept what we are told then it is far too permissive. We might have no reason due to carelessness or gullibility even though there are reasons of which we should have been aware. If it means that we should establish that there is no fact providing a reason not to accept what we have been told, then it is far from clear how we are supposed to satisfy this condition short of having determined that the informant is someone to be trusted on the matter in hand.[8] But that would be contrary to the spirit of the defaultist stance since it requires us to pick out the trustworthy, not just to presume trustworthiness without good reason not to. The second problem is that while it seems right that our discriminative capacities play a kind of filtering role, helping us to identify reasons not to accept what we are told, it also seems right that they have a more positive role.[9] Even in the most straightforward cases of knowledge from testimony the atmosphere of trust in which our unhesitant response is elicited prevails only because in the course of an interchange we identify the informant as someone to be trusted on the matter in hand, not just as someone we may presume to be trustworthy. This can seem problematic, because there is a real question as to whether in cases in which we gain knowledge from testimony we routinely have evidence on the basis of which we have established that the informant is trustworthy. This is where it is important to have in play the wider conception of how experience can bear on what we know that I outlined in the previous chapter. According to that conception, experience can inculcate and hone our recognitional abilities in ways that are analogous to the ways in which experience inculcates and hones practical skills like riding a bicycle: we make attempts, often get it wrong, sometimes get it right, and over a period of trial and error acquire the ability in question. (See further in §8.4.) The third, and perhaps the most serious, problem for the defaultist approach arises from the obvious need for some explanation of why acceptance is supposed to be the appropriate default stance. To invoke an epistemic principle to the effect that we are justified in accepting what someone tells us, absent reason not to do so, provides no explanation. An explanation might be sought through consideration of features of our communicative practices that impose limits on the extent to which we would end up with false beliefs

criticizes this type of position. For defence of a position that has affinities with defaultism, see Goldberg (2007).

[8] For a similar criticism, see E. Fricker (1994).   [9] The filtering role in noted in Audi (2006: 134).

if we were to follow a policy of accepting what we are told in the absence of reason not to.[10] My own account makes much of the idea that there is a linguistic practice of knowledge-transmission through telling, but I do not believe that this by itself will explain how acceptance of what we are told in the straightforward cases can be the acquisition of knowledge. In particular, I do not believe that it will explain how our being told something in those cases can settle or clinch it that what we are told is true. I return to this matter in §8.4.

When a host of factors are relevant both psychologically and epistemologically to our acquiring knowledge of some sort, yet we seem not to register those factors at the level of judgement, or at least not to the extent that would be necessary if we worked with generalizations connecting those factors with something that their presence indicates, it is a sign that we should be thinking of the possibility that the knowledge in question is recognitional and therefore a manifestation of a *sensibility*.[11] Just as in judging that a bird is a goldfinch, or that tracks are deer tracks, we respond to a certain *Gestalt*—a coalescence of features that we would be hard put to specify in detail—so in identifying someone as trustworthy on a matter we respond to a complex *Gestalt* that is similarly hard to pin down.

On the approach to the epistemology of testimony that I propose we have to figure out how the ability to identify trustworthiness interacts with the abilities we manifest in linguistic communication. It is indeed remarkable that knowledge is routinely conveyed through speech and writing when, in a sense, all that hearers and readers have to go on is the act of telling. The act of telling can be as effective as it is because it is a move in a practice concerned with conveying knowledge through linguistic communication.[12] A practice as conceived here is an activity that is essentially rule-governed, or a cluster of such activities. To participate in a practice is to be subject to its rules and to incur a commitment to following its rules. Playing a game of football is engaging in a practice. Promising and issuing an invitation are moves in a practice. To know what is going on within a practice and form reasonable expectations about how participants will behave we need to know what the practice requires of those participating and more generally what it makes sense for them to do.[13] An idealized example will serve to illustrate this.

---

[10] The accounts in Coady (1992) and Burge (1993) are along these lines.

[11] The idea of a sensibility plays a prominent role in M. Fricker (2003).

[12] The importance for the epistemology of testimony recognizing that there are distinctive communicative acts used to convey information is acknowledged and discussed in, for instance, Welbourne (1986; 2001), E. Fricker (1987), Coady (1992), Moran (2006), and Goldberg (2007).

[13] I develop an account of practices in Millar (2004): see esp. pp. 83–92 and 241–7.

Suppose that you and others share a workshop in which everybody makes things in wood. Every body works independently, following their own inclinations. They each decide what to make and how to make it. There are many different products that those in the workshop could make, many different ways in which they could design and fashion these products, and many different reasons they could have for proceeding as they do. If anyone is to know about what others are doing and why, then, at least in the early stages of the production process, they will have to consult them or in some other way gain information about their particular goals, designs, methods, and so on. In this situation the workshop is simply a shared space in which a number of people work independently, doing their own thing. Now imagine that these artisans form a woodworking community in which each agrees to make a specified range of products to specified designs using specified methods, in keeping with some overall organizational scheme. Each submits him- or herself to what is in effect a set of rules concerning which products are to be made, their design, and so forth. Each expects the others to submit, and treats breaches of the rules as calling for criticism. We now have a practice—the practice of carrying out the work of this community. The rules prevail simply because the artisans treat them as rules to which they are subject. Those who engage in the practice incur a commitment to following the rules (though they may on occasion flout them). Their shared understanding of what engaging in the work of the community commits people to—of how one is supposed to work in the community—attunes them to what is expected of them and others. The upshot is that, without knowing much, if anything, about the inclinations or predilections of the others, each can know what commitments others have incurred simply in virtue of participating in the practice. On that basis each may reasonably expect that others will by and large proceed as required by the practice. There will be a level of description at which what each artisan is doing, and the way he or she is doing it, is in large measure explicable in terms of the requirements of the practice. It is not puzzling that people should conform. As participants they have submitted themselves to the rules in play, and there would be little point in doing so if they did not by and large conform to them. When people join the workshop they are initiated into the range of products and styles and learn how to execute them. Like the others, they come to view themselves as doing the things they are doing because these are the things *to be done*—the things one incurs a commitment to doing in virtue of being a member of the community. They have a standing expectation that others will proceed in keeping with the practice, conducting their work in ways that make sense given the commitments they have incurred. That is part of their understanding of the character of the community of which they are members. Against this background their access to what others are doing is via recognition of what they are supposed to be doing. Appraisal and correction of what novices do will serve to keep the practice in play. Of course, there could be rebels who work on products or styles that are not specified, but they would not be rebels for long. Either they would be expelled or they would be seen as innovators and alter the range of specified products or styles.

The practices involved in communicating by means of a particular language include those that have to do with using words to stand for this or that and those that have to do with performing this or that speech-act. They are obviously vastly more complex than the work practice in the idealized community I have described. Those in the workshop opt into it; we do not opt into the linguistic practices associated with our native language. They represent the prescribed products and styles to themselves; we do not routinely represent to ourselves the rules implicated by our linguistic practices. But in important respects these latter practices have a role that is analogous to that of the workshop practice:

(a) The existence of the practices, and a culture of initiating others into those practices, ensures that from the earliest stages there will be shared abilities to use language and shared sensibilities deployed in responding to others' uses.

(b) The upshot of the shared abilities and sensibilities is that we do not in general approach users of our language with an interpretative problem—what to make of the sounds they utter or the inscriptions they write. Far from being radical interpreters, we are already geared up to viewing them as fellow speakers of our language and to recognizing what they are doing with the words they use: asking us this, telling us that, and so on.[14]

(c) An (at least) inchoate sense that there are right and wrong ways of using particular words and right and wrong ways of telling, asking, commanding, and performing other speech-acts serves to reinforce continuing conformity to the demands imposed by the linguistic practices in which we participate. It is easy to overlook this, because so much in our use of language and our understanding of uses of language is unreflective. It seems plausible, however, that our willingness to adjust our usage of a word, for instance, when we find that it is out of kilter with common practice testifies to our having

---

[14] The discussion in McDowell (1984) of rule-following has a bearing on this issue (see esp. §§11 and 12). Mulhall (1990: esp. ch. 4) is illuminating on the problems of explaining the understanding of utterances, on the model of interpreting sounds conceived as devoid of meaning.

a sense of correctness and incorrectness in linguistic matters.[15] There is a standing temptation to suppose that our conformity to prevailing practices can be explained simply in terms of instrumental reasoning: if we don't conform we won't understand or be understood. My point is that, thanks to the existence of practices, and our initiation into them, we need not get to the stage of engaging in such reasoning: we are instilled from the start with a sense of there being correct and incorrect ways to speak and write.

Why should we think that linguistic communication implicates practices in my sense? The matter is controversial and I shall not attempt a full answer here. The basic consideration is closely tied to (b) and (c) above. We do not have to engage in meticulous investigations of each other's patterns of speech, propositional attitudes, and interactions with the world in order to figure out what each other's utterances mean.[16] Whether dealing with friends and acquaintances or strangers, we can by and large recognize what people who speak our language are doing with the words they utter—stating this, asking that, demanding the next thing, and so on. The question is how we acquire so much from so little. It is not by working out what utterances mean from linguistic behaviour, because the stretch of behaviour that would be needed is not routinely available. But nor is it because we blindly manifest certain dispositions to respond to utterances, with no idea of why we understand utterances in the way we do. A museum attendant, whom we have never met before, utters the words, 'The museum is about to close'. We understand that he is telling us that the museum is about to close because we have appropriate recognitional abilities. Just as our ability to recognize zebras by sight is informed by an understanding that a certain visual appearance is distinctive of zebras, so the recognitional abilities in play in understanding utterances are also informed by a certain understanding. This understanding enables us to grasp that by using the words 'The museum is about to close' as on this occasion one is supposed to be telling those addressed that the museum referred to is about to close. And because there are shared practices governing such proceedings, it is true *both* that what a person is supposed to be doing with words indicates

---

[15] When corrected for misusing the term 'arthritis', Burge's (1979) patient does not respond by saying that he what he means by 'arthritis' is different. He adjusts his usage. The notion of correctness in discussions of normativity is often unclear, since it glosses over a distinction between correct use in the sense of *true application of a term* and correct use in the sense of *use in keeping with meaning*. On this, and more generally on practices as related to word-meanings, see Millar (2004: ch. 6).

[16] Arrived at independently, my view has affinities with that presented in Sandy Goldberg's recent book (2007: §2.6) in respect of its emphasis on the role of public norms in comprehending speakers about whom we know little.

with a high degree of reliability what that person is doing with them *and* that we are geared up to responding to utterances by taking for granted, in the absence of countervailing considerations, that those making the utterance are doing with the words uttered what they are supposed to be doing with them. The upshot is that a practice-theoretic account offers an epistemology of understanding utterances that accommodates the plausible hypothesis that a sense of how words are supposed to be used informs our abilities to recognize what people are actually doing with words and enables us to makes sense of how we understand utterances in the ways we do.

Reductionism about testimony assimilates the epistemology of testimony to that of empirical evidence in general. The role of practices is inconsistent with reductionism so conceived, simply because it brings into play a mode of understanding that has no echo in the epistemology of empirical evidence in general. This is the mode of understanding in play when, in virtue of being a participant in a practice, one has a grasp of how to do the things that are governed by the rules of the practice. It is this grasp that not only informs how participants proceed but which also forms the basis for understanding how people act within the practice and for anticipating what they will do within the practice. We are able to understand what people do in the business of telling and responding to acts of telling because we have an understanding of how we are supposed to go about these things and have a standing expectation that by and large people will act as they are supposed to. This understanding is exploited when, for instance, we discriminate between sayings that are acts of telling and sayings that are not acts of telling. I consider this distinction in the next section.

8.3. Telling and Informing

Telling is a distinctive communicative act. My telling you that *p* is an act of saying to you that *p* by which I give you to understand that I am informing you that *p*. Informing you that *p* is a matter of saying to you that *p*, speaking from knowledge, with the aim of bringing it about that you come to know that *p* from my saying that *p*.[17] (Acts of saying that *p* should be taken to include cases in which the informant simply says 'Yes' when asked whether *p*. Likewise, saying 'No' in response to an enquiry whether *p*, should be taken to be an act of saying that not-*p*.)

---

[17] Perhaps English allows for people to be said to inform when they do not know. But it seems to me that if so this use depends on the notion of informing as imparting what one knows.

Not all cases of saying to someone that *p* are cases of telling that person that *p*. If by way of advice I say to a colleague that he should consider pursuing some topic, I do not take myself to be informing him of anything and do not expect him to take what I say to be knowledge that I am conveying to him. My aim will be to prompt him to consider pursuing the topic. Good advice does not only specify a course of action but presents considerations in the light of which the course of action can be seen to be a good idea by the agent advised. In advising my colleague I don't wish him to consider pursuing the topic just on my say-so but because there is reason to think that his doing so would be a good idea. There are other cases in which sayings are plainly not acts of telling. I might make various assertions about the qualities of well-known political figures. These may be unqualified and uttered with great conviction, but they are expressions of opinion and perhaps anger too. In giving expression to those opinions I do not take myself, and do not expect others to take me, to be so much as attempting to impart knowledge. Those hearing what I say would not be likely to take me to be attempting to impart knowledge.[18] It is initiation into the practice surrounding informing by telling—the recognized ways of informing by telling and responding to acts of telling—that attunes us to responding to the subtle cues that mark out acts of telling from other speech-acts, like asking questions, making requests, giving orders, and expressing intentions. The upshot of our initiation into the practice is that we acquire a range of perceptual-recognitional abilities that enable us to identify what people are saying to us and tell whether or not these sayings are acts of telling. These abilities are responsive not just to the sounds people utter or the inscriptions they write, but to the manner, style, and content of the communication, characteristics of the speaker, features of the situation that provide the context of the communication, and no doubt other factors as well. Yet we do not work with lists of features that form part of a general conception of what marks a speech-act as being an act of telling. We get the hang of recognizing speech-acts as acts of telling just as we get the hang of recognizing from the style of a piece of music that it is by such-and-such composer. There are features to which we respond, yet they are elusive and at the level of judgement we certainly need not take in that they are present. This is a further case in which the model of perceptual recognitional abilities does a better job than a model on which we apply a covering generalization to a complex fact that must then be assumed to be registered at the level of judgement.

---

[18] In view of these considerations I am doubtful that there is a knowledge-rule for assertion in general, as argued in Williamson (2000: ch. 11), though I do think that there is a knowledge-rule for telling. See §8.4.

It is, of course, one thing to recognize perceptually that an act is an act of telling and another to gain knowledge of the thing told from such an act. It is to this that I turn in the next section.

8.4. Acquiring True Beliefs and Acquiring Knowledge Through Being Told

There is a sense in which any act of telling you something is *supposed* to inform you of that thing. It is supposed to in that there is a rule governing telling to the effect that you do not tell people something unless you are by that act informing them of that thing and thus speaking from knowledge. Participating in the practice incurs a commitment to following this and other rules. Felicitous telling is telling in keeping with its governing rules.[19]

The efficacy of telling as a means of informing turns on there being a shared understanding of the commitments incurred by participating in the practice. The very existence of the practice depends on there being widespread willingness to tell felicitously. It is largely thanks to the practice that telling so often commands unhesitant acceptance, without any need for deliberation, and that we so often gain true beliefs through accepting what we are told. Two further factors serve to decrease the likelihood that we shall be misled by what we are told. The first is that the common currency of vastly many transactions in which we believe what we are told is uncomplicated information that is useful for practical affairs, and which we could verify if we wished. There is a significant risk that infelicitous telling, whether through incompetence or insincerity, will be exposed. The second factor is that it will often be the case that informants are liable to incur costs if they mislead us. Either we know them personally or they form part of a wider community in which there can easily be unwelcome repercussions if deception or incompetence is exposed. These factors combine to provide an incentive to speak sincerely and from

---

[19] Jennifer Lackey's (2007*b*) cases of selfless-assertion are presented as objections to the view that there is a knowledge-rule of assertion. They might also be taken to count against a knowledge-rule for telling. Subjects in those cases occupy a role, like that of a medical practitioner, that seems to oblige them to convey something to another though they do not believe what they convey and thus do not know it. I am inclined to think that these are either infelicitous tellings or not tellings at all. The medical practitioner who unqualifiedly asserts, but does not believe, that there is no connection between the vaccine and autism, would be telling the patient this infelicitously because he gives it to be understood that he knows what he tells. (He could, after all, have said that there is no evidence whatsoever of a connection, which might have been more accurate anyway.) If a creationist science teacher is instructing students in evolutionary theory, or any theory, the act of instruction could be seen as conveying the state of play in the discipline in question, rather than as telling.

knowledge when telling. They help to secure that to a very considerable extent people will end up with true beliefs if they accept what they are told, even if they are not particularly discriminating. Yet while a policy of accepting what we are told, absent obvious reasons to doubt the trustworthiness of the informant, will result in true belief with a fairly high degree of reliability, this does not explain how it can be that someone's telling us something can settle that it is so. Against the background of discussions in earlier chapters of Part II we need such an explanation to account for the acquisition of knowledge from testimony in the straightforward cases.

I take it that someone's telling us that p can clinch it that p only if the person telling us that p is trustworthy. Being trustworthy in this respect is being sincere in telling us that p and competent with respect to whether p.[20] Competence with respect to whether p is knowing whether p, which entails knowing that p if p and knowing that not-p if not-p. Sincerity, as I shall understand it, has three strands: you are sincere in telling me that p if and only if: (i) you believe that p, (ii) you believe that you speak from knowledge, and (iii) you intend that I should come to know that p through your telling me. Condition (i) needs no explanation. The rationale of condition (ii) is provided by the nature of telling as an act by which you give it to be understood that you know. If you believe what you say, but think that your standing on the matter is less than knowledge, then you are misleading those you tell. The rationale for condition (iii) is similar. Suppose that A tells B that her (B's) husband, A's friend, is not having an affair. This is true and A knows it but maliciously aims to get B to suspect that her husband is having an affair. A's assumption is that, given their shared history, B will think that A is covering up for his friend. By telling B that her husband is not having an affair, A gives B to understand that he is informing her of this. But since informing someone is understood to be an act of intentionally conveying knowledge to that person, A's communicative act gives B to understand that he (A) intends that she should come to know that her husband is having an affair. Since A has no such intention, despite telling and speaking from knowledge, he is in that respect insincere.[21]

One of the reasons why the epistemology of testimony is problematic is that, while it seems that to acquire knowledge that p from someone's telling me that p I have to know that the person is trustworthy with respect to what he or she tells me, in many circumstances in which we acquire knowledge from testimony we are in no position to have evidence that the person is

---

[20] Both of these factors are emphasized in E. Fricker (1994), though within a somewhat different general epistemological framework.

[21] Welbourne (2001: 103) draws attention to such cases.

trustworthy. It is a step towards a plausible view to acknowledge that while the reception of knowledge in straightforward cases takes place in an atmosphere of trust, as we might say, it does not depend on having evidence establishing the informant's trustworthiness. Trust can be the upshot of exercising an ability to tell that the informant speaks the truth on the occasion in question. It is at this point that we need to draw on my discussion in the previous chapter of the way in which experience can shape abilities to acquire knowledge.

There are two main elements in the proposal I wish to make that draw upon the previous discussion. The first is that an informant's being trustworthy in telling you something stands to the ability to tell that the informant is speaking the truth in a way that is analogous to how a favourable environment stands to the ability to tell that something is the case in perceptual and (non-testimonial) indicator cases. The second is that we can acquire abilities that enable us on occasion to tell, recognitionally, that someone is speaking the truth. This is unlikely to be an ability to tell whether or not someone is speaking the truth on any conceivable subject matter, in any conceivable situational context. It is likely to be more like the ability to tell of certain manifestly orchid-like flowers that they are orchids, even if there are many orchids on which one would not pronounce or take not to be orchids.

Turning to the first of those elements, recall that to tell that something is a barn from its visual appearance, the environment in which the barn is placed must be favourable in the sense that in that environment barns have a *distinctive visual appearance* so that with a high degree of reliability a thing's having such an appearance indicates that it is a barn. In a fake-barn scenario barns do not have any distinctive visual appearance because too many of the structures that look like barns are not. With respect to such a scenario no one could have the ability to tell, and thus come to know, that something is a barn from its visual appearance. There are analogues of fake-barn scenarios for cases of telling from the occurrence of an indicator phenomenon. Recall the example of the shepherd in an environment in which a certain bleating sound is distinctive of sheep. With respect to such an environment it is possible to learn, as the shepherd has, to tell that there are sheep nearby from the sound of bleating. Suppose the shepherd to be transported to an environment superficially like his familiar environment but in which the same bleating sound could as easily have been made by goats as by sheep. In this environment the bleating sound is not distinctive of sheep: all too easily could something produce that sound and not be a sheep. With respect to such an environment, it would not be possible (in general) to tell that sheep are nearby from the sound of bleating. Now, a trustworthy person with respect to a certain subject matter is such that not easily could that person tell you something on that subject matter and speak falsely. Just as in suitable environments a suitably equipped person may take the appearance or appearances of barns at face value or a bleating sound at face value, so a person who is trustworthy with respect to a certain subject matter is such that those who are suitably equipped may take at face value that person's acts of telling on that subject matter.

Turning now to the second element of the proposal, what is crucial is that just as in perceptual and indicator cases we must have learned to tell things of a certain sort from an appearance or indicator as the case may be, so in cases of testimony we must have learned when we may accept what we are told straight off on the say-so of the informant. Part of the story is an expansion of a very simple, basic, common-sense idea. We can know people well enough to know that they are trustworthy when they tell us this or that. We can know this by experience of them that shapes the sensibility that we deploy in our interactions with them. The role of experience here is not that of supplying evidence on which we base the claim that the person is trustworthy. Indeed, the deliberate gathering and weighing up of such evidence would be out of tune with relations of intimacy and friendship. It is rather a matter of learning how to take the things the person says.

So far as sincerity is concerned, it seems pretty clear both that people can be such that always or nearly always when they tell one that something is so they believe it to be so, and intend to inform us that it is so. It is clear also that through knowing such people, thus encountering their various modes of acting, feeling, and thinking, one can, without serious risk, properly deal with them in an atmosphere of trust, at least up to sincerity. Trust can, of course, be betrayed. It is possible for people to seem to be trustworthy when they are not and possible for generally trustworthy people to lapse on occasion. But the possibility that people who seem untrustworthy are not is no more reason to be sceptical about knowledge of a known person's trustworthiness than the possibility of there being mules disguised as zebras provides a reason to be sceptical about being able to tell by looking that an animal is a zebra on the plains of Africa. And the rare lapses of a trustworthy person are no more reason to be sceptical about the possibility of telling that that person is sincere on a given occasion than the insertion of an artificial rose at an otherwise respectable flower show provides a reason to be sceptical about the possibility of recognizing roses at that flower show.

How do we know that people are trustworthy with respect to competence? We often approach them with the reasonable, though defeasible, presumption that they are competent on a topic if they pronounce on it. Still, as I have stressed throughout, knowing that what they say is true is a different standing from reasonably believing that what they say is true. It seems to me that we need the idea that experience inculcates and hones an ability to recognize competence. In some cases the marks of competence are not too hard to indicate, as when someone exhibiting all the signs of being able to see, and of having ordinary levels of common knowledge and understanding, tells you on looking out of the window that it has stopped raining. Sometimes it will take acquaintance with the subject to sensitize you to his or her competence on some subject matter.

All knowledge from indicators depends on ability to recognize that the indicator phenomenon has a certain significance. In the case of testimony, it is not possible to pin down in highly general terms what the indicator phenomenon is. When we are dealing with people who have an information-providing role—for instance, assistants in shops—there are approximate specifications of the indicator phenomenon of the form: 'This person, who has the role of providing information on such-and-such subject matter, tells me that p [where $<p>$ is within the domain of the subject matter in question].' When we are dealing with people we know personally and trust we can approximate to a specification of the indicator phenomenon by saying that it must have the form: 'This person, whom I know and trust on such-and-such a subject matter, tells me that p [where $<p>$ is within the domain of the subject matter in question].' These specifications are only approximate because they leave out of account the nuances of content, manner of speaking, situational context, shared background, that manifest that the speaker speaks from knowledge on the occasion in question. This, I think, reinforces a point on which I harped in discussing non-testimonial cases: while rough generalizations form part of the understanding that informs our recognitional abilities they need not have an independent epistemic standing derived from specifiable evidence or grounded in detached standing knowledge. Gaining knowledge from testimony is if anything even closer to gaining knowledge of rich facts through perception than gaining knowledge from non-testimonial indicator cases. We tell that the bird is a goldfinch from its appearance, but even if we can describe some especially salient features, our grip on its appearance is pretty much as *the appearance of a goldfinch*. In straightforward testimonial cases—cases in which we accept straight off what is said—we tell that the person is speaking truthfully from the way that the person comes over. It is fruitless to try to pin down what gives the person's utterance the ring of truth. Whether we are entitled to take the ring of truth at face value depends on the extent to which our experience has refined our discriminative powers and on the person's actually being trustworthy.

Perceptual knowledge and knowledge from (non-testimonial) indicators are possible because of a certain fit between a person and the environment.

The environment must be favourable and the person must have acquired the necessary recognitional abilities. Likewise, in the straightforward cases of knowledge from testimony on some subject matter there must be a fit between one person, the recipient, and another, the informant. Both must have a grasp of the practice of informing by telling. The informant must be trustworthy on the subject matter in question and the recipient must be equipped by experience to tell that the informant may be trusted on that matter.

The abilities we deploy in cases in which we acquire knowledge from testimony are highly specific, being responsive to a multiplicity of factors present on the occasion of telling and informed by knowledge of the informant. Informants can be fallible but, as I have stressed, it is no part of the account that, to impart knowledge, they must be trustworthy with respect to everything they tell. Despite all this, it can be that there is the right fit between the trustworthiness of the informant and the sensibility of the recipient to make knowledge-acquisition possible.

It is crucial to recall that my account applies to straightforward cases of testimony and is not intended to be a comprehensive general account of how it is possible to acquire knowledge from testimony.[22] I should also emphasize that my account does not entail that knowledge is the routine upshot of acts of telling in cases in which the testimony is accepted. Even granted that there is a practice of informing through telling, and that there would not be such a practice unless knowledge were often enough conveyed through felicitous acts of telling, there is plenty of room for cases in which recipients accept testimony but do not acquire knowledge. That is simply because there is plenty of room for insincerity and incompetence on the part of informants and plenty of room for recipients to be insufficiently discriminating with respect to who they believe. It is worth bearing in mind, too, that truthful testimony can be useful even when it does not yield knowledge and even when it does not yield belief in what one is told. When it does not yield knowledge it might yield true belief leading to successful action. When it does not yield belief at all it might nonetheless be a good practical strategy to act as if what one has been told is true for want of a better, conveniently available, way of proceeding. In the light of these considerations, I see little point in being

---

[22] There will surely be cases in which knowledge is acquired from testimony but the conditions that obtain in the straightforward cases are not met. Jennifer Lackey's (2006) consistent liar, who correctly reports things she does not believe, might be a means by which one can obtain knowledge concerning the subject matter in question. But if one can obtain knowledge from this source it is not by a routine exploitation of the practice of informing by telling and of the kind of sensibility that figures in straightforward cases.

overly exercised about whether we gain knowledge from strangers from whom we ask directions. Much will depend on the extent to which particular cases are akin to straightforward cases. Whatever we conclude about this or that case, there will always be a vast amount of useful testimony does not yield knowledge. But some of it does.

When we know that something is so on the basis of testimony in the straightforward cases, do we routinely know that we know? Is it any more difficult to know that we know in these cases than in, for instance, perceptual cases? It is not clear that it is. We can be good at identifying trustworthy informants and pretty good at telling when we have done so. It is true that testimony depends on the will of the informant and on the care taken by the informant.[23] Informants can deliberately misinform, and even the trustworthy can have moments of weakness. Even so, I see no strong reason to suppose that we cannot often readily tell that we know something through being told it. The same sensibility that is engaged in acquiring the knowledge is engaged in telling that one has acquired it. The difference is that one deploys the additional ability to self-apply the concept of knowing from being told. That application has to be sensitive to the factors to which the acquisition of the first-order knowledge is sensitive. Phoned up by friends at a restaurant asking me to join them, I know from their telling me that they are there. To know that I know that they are there I simply have to reflect on how I have come to know that they are there.

Another point deserving emphasis is that it should not be taken to be a constraint on an adequate epistemology of testimony that it should make sense of how children, who lack the discriminative capacities required for identifying trustworthy sources of information, can acquire knowledge simply from the say-so of a parent or schoolteacher. From a variety of sources children uncritically and unreflectively take in elements of a picture of how the world works. In a suitably organized society much of this picture will comprise truths corresponding to widely known, publicly available facts. As I have already suggested, the experience gained in such a setting, and subsequent encounters with sources of the same facts, can furnish people with what becomes detached standing knowledge of much factual information—knowledge that they retain long after they have lost touch with the sources from which they have gleaned the information. Such knowledge can contribute to the formation of the discriminative capacities that make knowledge from testimony possible, but does not need to be explained in terms of those capacities. This serves to underline once again the importance of taking a broader view of how

---

[23] The role of the informant's will is interestingly discussed in Ross (1986) and Moran (2006).

experience can bear on the acquisition of knowledge, and of knowledge-acquisition abilities.

This approach might seem to have left the *practice* of informing by telling behind, but it has not. Acts of telling are constitutively dependent upon the practice of informing by telling. The practice provides a setting in which it is possible to learn how to modulate sayings so that they come over as tellings, and possible to learn how to discriminate tellings from other sayings. It also provides a setting in which it is understood that those who tell are supposed to speak sincerely and from knowledge. People who are trustworthy with regard to some subject matter are people who conform to the rules of the practice in what they say to others concerning that subject matter. They place a high value on behaving as one is supposed to with respect to that subject matter. The people we trust with respect to some subject matter are people whom we expect to conform to the rules with respect to that subject matter and to be good at doing so. But while the existence of the practice is a crucial part of what makes the overall environment in which we deal with testimony favourable to the acquisition of knowledge from testimony, it does not explain all that is needed for the acquisition of such knowledge. For that, we need to be good at identifying the trustworthy. I have been suggesting that recognitional abilities have a role here as well.

8.5. Access to Facts about Knowledge

Responsible enquiry and responsible informing are not aspirations that lie forever beyond our reach. We are all enquirers and regularly succeed in acquiring knowledge. We regularly tell others what we know and adjust how we communicate information depending on our assessment of our competence in relation to the matter in question. It is routine to discriminate between situations in which we know something and can vouch for it and situations in which we have at best a high degree of confidence. None of this would be so if we could not readily gain knowledge on matters that concern us and often enough readily tell that we know.

I have given outline accounts of perceptual knowledge, knowledge from indicators, knowledge from testimony, and detached standing knowledge. Central to the approach has been the rejection of conceptual-reductionist accounts of knowledge. Instead of trying to provide necessary and sufficient conditions for knowledge in terms that do not implicate the concept, I have focused on central kinds of knowledge aiming all along to do justice to how those kinds of knowledge figure in our thinking. Part of the challenge in developing these views has been to explain how it can be that when we know something the matter can be settled. The challenge is acute, since it often seems that what is available to us in cases in which knowledge is acquired cannot explain how it is *knowledge* that is acquired. The problem has the form: 'How can we get so much from so little?'[24] In perceptual cases, it is sometimes thought that what is available is an experience of a non-world-involving kind that might be had even if what it prompts us to believe were not true. Even if what is thought to be available is a worldly appearance—an appearance of something in the environment before us—zebra and barn cases can make it seem that that is not enough. In indicator cases, both testimonial and non-testimonial, it can seem that the availability of what is in fact an indictor that p is not enough to enable us to know that p, because it is unclear what entitles us to take the phenomenon to be an indicator. In responding to these challenges I have brought the notion of recognitional abilities into play both for perceptual cases and in relation to cases of recognizing the significance of non-testimonial or testimonial indicators. I have argued that whether or not we have the required abilities does not turn on there being connecting generalizations that we are antecedently entitled to accept. What is crucial is that we are in command of a way of telling with respect to the relevant environment. In straightforward cases of knowledge from testimony it matters that the informant is actually trustworthy when he or she informs us, in the manner in question, in the context in question, on the kind of subject matter in play, and so forth, and that we have acquired a suitable sensibility. The modes of sensibility that we deploy are clusters of abilities honed through our interactions with others. The notion of an ability also figured in my account of detached standing knowledge. Here the relevant ability is an ability to recall a fact—an ability that is instilled by encounters with sources of information that convey the fact.

   With regard to each of the kinds of knowledge I considered, I have argued that we commonly have access to how we know or at least to the fact that we know. On this approach, we do not think of knowledge as being built up from justified true belief plus some elusive anti-Gettier condition. Knowledge is indeed tied to justification, but the justifications are justifications that the knowledge puts in our way.

   On this approach, knowledge is not an elusive and complex condition. There are familiar and commonly acknowledged ways of telling, including the subject-matter-specific recognitional abilities that have figured so prominently in my account. Our general conception of knowledge is in large measure a conception of a condition that is acquired through the exercise of such abilities. In Chapter 5 I criticized reductive conceptual-analytical accounts of knowledge on the grounds that if any such account were plausible it should have been discovered by now. I think there is a simple and plausible explanation of why the kind of approach that I have taken has not been more widely adopted. At least part of the answer is that the view that knowledge is true belief plus the satisfaction of further conditions has seemed unavoidable, for understandable reasons. From this standpoint the philosophical effort must go into delving below knowledge-implicating states and abilities to something more basic out which they are built. Another part of the answer is that there is no doubt a suspicion that if epistemology deals primarily with knowledge-implicating states and conditions it cannot be substantive. I hope I have gone some way towards countering those suspicions in these chapters.[25]

[25] I have benefited enormously from many discussions with Adrian Haddock and Duncan Pritchard. The congenial research environment provided by my department at Stirling has done much to facilitate work on this book. I have been, as always, sensitive to the critical gaze of my colleagues at Stirling, and especially to that of Peter Sullivan. Thanks are due to Adam Carter, Matthew Chrisman, Chris Kelp, and Fiona Macpherson for comments on ideas presented here. A series of interchanges with Ernest Sosa have been invaluable in enabling me better to understand his position and to shape my own views. I am grateful to audiences at workshops and conferences associated with the project from which this book has emerged for the discussion at these events, and to audiences at St Andrews, Glasgow, Sheffield, and Manchester for their comments and criticisms.

III

KNOWLEDGE AND ACTION

Adrian Haddock

PART III

ANALYTICAL TABLE OF CONTENTS

Chapter 9: Knowledge and Justification

9.1. Introductory Remarks

A traditional conception of knowledge as true justified belief need not be vulnerable to the Gettier argument. We can see this in the case of visual knowledge.

9.2. The Modest Route

There is an account of visual knowledge which rejects the conception of justification which the Gettier argument assumes. It maintains that the justification involved in visual knowledge is not just truth-guaranteeing, but knowledge-affording.

9.3. Fool's Knowledge

Accounts according to which the justification involved in knowledge is not truth-guaranteeing falsify our ordinary conception of knowledge.

9.4. The Distinctive Value of Knowledge

A Socratic solution to the *Meno* problem for the case of visual knowledge: such knowledge is of distinctive value because it enables its possessor rationally to resist doubt, and thereby—in contrast to lesser states—enables the efficient realization of her projects. We can understand the distinctive value of visual knowledge in this way only if the justification it involves is knowledge-affording.

9.5. Fool's Justification

Perhaps justification as such is truth-guaranteeing. Perhaps considerations which are not truth-guaranteeing constitute merely apparent justifications.

9.6. Arguing from Illusion

The argument from illusion is powerless to defend the claim that justifications must be more certain than the beliefs they justify.

9.7. The Regress of Justifications

Making sense of the second-order knowledge which visual knowledge involves seems to trap us between a rock and a hard place—between the regress of justifications, and a non-normative conception of knowledge.

9.8. Concluding Remarks

A hopeless suggestion nevertheless supplies a clue about how to avoid the trap.

Chapter 10: Second-Order Knowledge

10.1. Introductory Remarks

The clue is contained in the idea of a transparent fact.

10.2. Transparency and Knowledge

We can avoid the regress of justifications without embracing the non-normative conception by seeing the second-order knowledge involved in visual knowledge as knowledge of facts which are transparent. The disjunctive conception of visual experience sheds light on such facts.

10.3. Transparency and Entitlement

The transparency of facts which constitute the content of the second-order knowledge enables us to avoid the trap, by enabling these facts to be understood not as justifications, but as entitlements.

10.4. On Trying to do Without Transparency

We need to understand the second-order knowledge as knowledge of a transparent fact if we are to avoid the trap.

10.5. Transparency and Luminosity

The claim that the second-order knowledge is knowledge of a transparent fact might appear to be undermined by Williamson's argument against luminosity. But it is not.

10.6. Non-sensible Knowledge

A famous argument for the incompatibility of externalism about content with the doctrine of privileged self-knowledge fails to generate a problem for the present account, thanks to a distinction between entitling and presupposing dimensions.

10.7. Self-knowledge

Non-sensible knowledge is a species of self-knowledge. There is a Cartesian objection to this claim, but it can be rejected.

10.8. Concluding Remarks

The category of fallible self-knowledge emerges from the previous discussion.

Chapter 11: Knowledge of Action

11.1. Introductory Remarks

The content of knowledge of one's intentional action is of the form 'I am doing such-and-such' or 'I am doing such-and-such intentionally'.

11.2. Non-sensible Knowledge of Action

Knowledge of one's intentional action is non-sensible knowledge of a transparent fact, which knowledge involves entitlement not justification.

11.3. The Two Dimensions

The distinction between entitling and presupposing dimensions can be applied to the case of knowledge of action, but needs to be handled with care.

11.4. The Distinctive Value of Knowledge of Action

Knowledge of intentional action is necessary for understanding the distinctive value of knowledge as such.

11.5. Non-observational Knowledge

The suggestion that knowledge of intentional action is a species of knowledge without observation can be understood with the help of my account of non-sensible knowledge.

11.6. Practical Knowledge and Intention

Knowledge of action is a special, because distinctly practical, species of knowledge without observation. It is special in two ways. First, it is knowledge acquired 'in intention'.

11.7. Practical Knowledge and Direction of Fit

Secondly, it has a mind-to-world *and* a world-to-mind direction of fit. The significance of a remark Anscombe attributes to Theophrastus is explained.

11.8. Concluding Remarks

Non-sensible knowledge is 'the cause of what it understands'. The appearance of a close similarity between my account of knowledge of action and Anscombe's account of practical knowledge is saved.

9

Knowledge and Justification

9.1. Introductory Remarks

Philosophers have found it natural to understand knowledge in normative terms.[1] I think we ought to understand certain species of knowledge in just this way, by understanding them as species of justified true belief.

There are explanations of beliefs which constitute knowledge—henceforth knowledgeable beliefs—which display the beliefs they explain as justified: one knowledgeably believes that things are a certain way because one's experience seems to reveal to one that things are this way, perhaps. But there are explanations which do not do this, because they apply when one knowledgeably believes that things are a certain way because of something which one does not know. Only something which one knows can figure on the right-hand side of an explanation which displays one's knowledgeable belief as justified. Knowledgeable beliefs can only be justified by something one knows.[2]

It might seem that this account imposes too stringent a requirement on knowledge. If one knows that things are a certain way then one has knowledge of one's justification. This might seem to prevent non-rational subjects (dogs, for instance) from knowing things. Consider a case of perceptual knowledge. Knowledge of one's justification is knowledge of how things stand with

---

[1] Sellars (1956) is a prominent example. Consider the following oft-cited claim: 'In characterising an episode or a state as that of *knowing*, we are not giving an empirical description of that episode or state; we are placing it in the logical space of reasons, of justifying and being able to justify what one says' (1956: 298–9). The idea that the possession of knowledge requires the ability 'to justify what one says' is central to the account developed in these chapters.

[2] Lest this seem too strong, it might be worth noting a feature of the account, alluded to in the previous footnote, which will be revealed in due course: that if something is a justification one has for a knowledgeable belief, then one ought—and so, is able—to assert this thing in response to the question 'Why do you think that?' For, as Williamson (2000) has argued, one ought to assert only what one knows; if one does not know that things are a certain way, then one ought not to assert that things are this way, but merely that it seems (or seemed) to one that things are this way—or something cognate (such as that one thinks that things are this way).

oneself: knowledge that one enjoys an experience which seems to reveal to one that things are a certain way, perhaps. Such knowledge embodies self-consciousness; here 'oneself' is (what is known as) the indirect reflexive, which is explicable in part by the difference between first-personal content expressible by something of the form 'I am a certain way', and third-personal content expressible, in my own case, by something of the form 'AH is a certain way'. The contents are distinct because it is possible for a rational and unconfused subject simultaneously to take rationally conflicting attitudes towards them (perhaps I believe that I am a certain way but refuse to believe that AH is this way, because I have temporarily forgotten that I am AH).[3] It is only content expressible by something of the form 'I am a certain way' which is proper to one's self-conscious knowledge. This is because only one self, viz., oneself, can grasp it; others can think that AH is a certain way, but only I can think that I am a certain way. We might follow Frege, and say that the concept of the first person—the sense of 'I'—is a 'particular and primitive' mode of presentation under which one can figure only in one's own thoughts (Frege 1918: 25–6). It is because non-rational subjects seem incapable of grasping this concept that they seem incapable of possessing knowledge—given the present account of knowledge as something which essentially involves justification.

But that is why it is important to insist that this is merely an account of knowledge as it is enjoyed by rational subjects like us. Our ordinary thinking about knowledge can seem to point us in two different directions. We want to credit non-rational subjects with knowledge of how things stand in their immediate environment. But we are tempted to think that knowledge essentially involves justification. One response to this putative tension is to settle for the first desire over the second, reject the account of knowledge as essentially involving justification, and put our knowledge on a par with that of cats and dogs. The other response is to plump for the second desire over the first, and declare a fraud our ordinary conception of (at least some) non-human subjects as knowing subjects. Neither response is satisfactory, but the choice appears to be forced on us. That this is merely an appearance can be acknowledged by acknowledging the truth of the following thought: there is *knowledge* the genus, of which knowledge as it is enjoyed by rational subjects is one species, and knowledge as it is enjoyed by non-rational subjects is another. The former species necessarily involves justification, but the latter species necessarily does not. No doubt there will be other differences; perhaps only knowledge of the former species involves beliefs. But this is not something we need settle here. We need only stress that, if this thought is true, then there

---

[3] See McDowell (1996: 180).

must be some conditions which are common to both species, so as to ensure that they really are species of the same genus; some sort of success condition, for example, as well perhaps as the requirement of a suitable causal connection between a suitable state of the subject and a suitable fact.

However, it is one thing to say that knowledge of the sort enjoyed by rational subjects essentially involves justification, another to understand knowledge of this sort as justified true belief. Has not Edmund Gettier taught us that knowledge cannot be *simply* justified true belief? Has he not taught us that a true justified belief might be true only by accident, and so might not amount to knowledge? So, has he not shown us that knowledge requires the satisfaction of a further condition, over and above a belief condition, a truth condition, and a justification condition, precisely so as to rule out the possibility of accidentally true justified beliefs?

This way of thinking constitutes a kind of mythology, by which contemporary epistemologists live.[4] Of course, its participants do not recognize the way of thinking as a mythology, but as something at least close to the plain truth. Its central claim—that the Gettier argument establishes that knowledge is not simply justified true belief—has acquired something of the status of a hinge proposition, upon which the 'normal science' of contemporary epistemology twists and turns. But the claim is false.

Gettier remarks that, 'in that sense of "justified" in which S's being justified in believing that P is a necessary condition of S's knowing that P, it is possible for a person to be justified in believing a proposition that is in fact false' (Gettier 1963: 121). The conclusion that knowledge is not simply justified true belief is drawn on the assumption that *this* is the sense of 'justified' which figures in the contested account. But is there any reason to think that this sense of 'justified' is essential to an account of knowledge as justified true belief? No doubt it has traditionally been assumed that it is essential. But it is not obvious that it is. Why not see it instead, not as essential to the account, but as something of which the account is best purged? Why not think that if one knows that things are a certain way then one has a belief that things are this way which *is* justified, in a sense of 'justified' in which it is *not* possible for a person to be justified in believing a proposition which is false?

The vast majority of contemporary epistemologists respond to the Gettier argument by simply rejecting the account of knowledge as justified true belief. But this is too drastic. We need only, and ought only, to reject the sense of 'justified' which this account has traditionally been assumed to involve, and

---

[4] Here is a representative selection of epistemologists who live by the mythology, from each decade since the 1960s: Gettier (1963), Sosa (1974), Peacocke (1986), De Rose (1992), and Pritchard (2005).

replace it with one more in line with our ordinary, pre-theoretical conception of knowledge (see §9.3). I think this more modest route is available. And I think it enables us to make sense of at least some varieties of knowledge of the sort which rational subjects like us enjoy.

I propose to restrict my focus not merely to perceptual knowledge, but to what is perhaps the central variety of perceptual knowledge, perhaps the central variety of knowledge *simpliciter*—visual knowledge, knowledge acquired by seeing. For most of this chapter, and all of the next, I will stay with this restricted focus, and do not intend the claims I make to extend beyond it. I will extend the focus a little towards the end of this chapter. And in the chapter entitled 'Knowledge of Action' I will extend it further, so as to take in an interesting, and somewhat neglected, variety of knowledge which the modest route helps us to understand: knowledge of one's intentional bodily action.

9.2. The Modest Route

So, what does the modest route look like?

Justified belief is belief which is justified *by* something, or *in the light of* something. On the traditional understanding of the account of knowledge as justified true belief, this 'something' is not such as to rule out the possibility that a belief justified in its light is false. With visual knowledge as our example, we can say that this 'something' will be a fact which in some way relates to the operations of our capacity for visual experience.[5] Consider a case in which one acquires the belief that there is a lemon over there. The 'something' might be the fact that one visually senses an inner object which looks like a lemon; it might be the fact that one sees an outer object which looks like a lemon; it might be the fact that one seems to see that there is a lemon over there; it might be the fact that it looks to one as if there is a lemon over there; and there are other possibilities. The point is that having one of these facts as one's justification for the belief that there is a lemon over there is compatible with the falsity of the belief at issue. So, each is able to justify belief in the way envisaged by the account of knowledge as justified true belief, traditionally understood (if it is able to justify belief at all).

---

[5] The exact way in which this fact relates to the operations of this capacity need not concern us here. But it is worth noting that it is far from obvious that these operations—visual experiences—must possess propositional content, despite its sometimes being the case that, in part because this capacity is operative, we can see that things are a certain way. Some very helpful discussion of this point may be found in Millar (2007a), and in McDowell (2008). Kant's (1997) fascinating remarks about cognition and illusion at the beginning of the Transcendental Dialectic are also highly relevant.

The modest route insists that the 'something' which justifies beliefs which constitute knowledge *is* such as to ensure that beliefs justified in its light are true. In the case in hand the 'something' would be the fact that one sees that there is a lemon over there. The point is that the presence of this fact guarantees the truth of the belief at issue: if one believes that there is a lemon over there in the light of the fact that one sees that there is a lemon over there then one's belief is true. If a justified true belief constitutes knowledge, it is justified by a fact of this sort, according to the modest route.

It is important to stress that, in the case of both the traditional understanding and the modest route, the fact which justifies one's knowledgeable belief must be a fact one knows. We might call this knowledge of one's justification in the case of visual knowledge second-order knowledge, to distinguish it from the first-order visual knowledge of the outer world for which it is required. We can bring out a consequence of this requirement by insisting that someone who knows that things are a certain way ought—and therefore is able—to answer the question 'Why do you think that things are this way?' by citing their justification for so thinking. It is a mark of knowledge which involves justification that there is point in asking this question to the person who knows. In the case of the traditional understanding, if one knows (visually) that there is a lemon over there then one ought to answer the question by saying 'I seem to see that there is a lemon over there'. And in the case of the modest route, if one knows (visually) that there is a lemon over there then one ought to answer the question by saying 'I see that there is a lemon over there'.

The modest route might seem vulnerable to the following objection. It claims that there is a sense of 'justified' in which it is not possible for a justified belief to be false. But the moral of the Gettier argument is that a true justified belief cannot constitute knowledge if it is only accidentally true. And that moral seems to be independent of the particular sense of 'justified' which Gettier employed. Let us grant the sense in which a justified belief is guaranteed to be true. It is not thereby guaranteed to be non-accidentally true. So, it is not thereby guaranteed to constitute knowledge.

But this objection is misplaced. It rests on the false assumption that, according to the modest route, if a belief is justified in the truth-guaranteeing sense, then it constitutes knowledge. In fact, the modest route does not say this. For all we have seen so far, it says only that if a belief constitutes knowledge, then it is justified in this sense. The objection mistakes a necessary condition for a sufficient condition. It can seem to raise a genuine worry nevertheless. If a belief which is justified even in this sense does not constitute knowledge, how can knowledge be simply true justified belief? Truth-guaranteeing justification does not seem to obviate the need for a further condition.

In fact, a belief which is justified in this sense *does* constitute knowledge. To have a justification in the way required for knowledge, one must know the fact which constitutes this justification. So, because the fact which justifies the belief involved in visual knowledge is the fact that one sees that things are a certain way, one knows that one sees that things are this way. And if one knows that one sees that things are this way then one knows that things are this way (by the so-called principle of closure). We can capture this thought by saying that the justification which one has for one's belief is not merely truth-guaranteeing but knowledge-affording: it ensure not merely that one's belief is true, but that it constitutes knowledge.

In insisting that justifications are knowledge-affording, the modest route aims to fix it that there is a sense of 'justified' in which it is not possible for a justified belief to fail to constitute knowledge. It is in *this* sense of 'justified' that knowledge is simply true justified belief. One knows that there is a lemon over there because one sees that there is a lemon over there; viz., one believes that there is a lemon over there in the light of the fact that one sees that there is a lemon over there, which fact is a justification, constituting the content of one's second-order knowledge, which is not merely truth-guaranteeing but knowledge-affording.

It follows from this that, if the kind of requirements which the Gettier argument considers central to knowing but external to justification really are requirements on knowing, these conditions need to be written into justification itself. Whereas that argument conceived the requirement of non-accidental truth as a further condition for knowledge, over and above the conditions of belief, truth, and justification, the modest route insists that the satisfaction of this requirement is part of what it is for the condition of justification to be satisfied. That condition is satisfied, in the visual-knowledge case, when one has the fact that one sees that things are a certain way as one's justification; viz., when one knows that one sees that things are this way. It follows that one cannot have this fact as one's justification in situations in which a belief that things are this way would be only accidentally true. Indeed, it follows that one cannot have this fact as one's justification in situations in which this belief would not constitute knowledge. (It does not follow that if one sees that things are a certain way then one knows that things are this way—as we shall more clearly see in the next chapter.)

More generally, it follows that any requirements on knowing which are external to the truth condition or the belief condition belong to the requirement of justification. For example, if responsible belief-acquisition is a requirement on knowing, then one cannot have a knowledge-affording justification for believing that things are a certain way if one is in a situation in which it would be irresponsible of one to believe that things are this way; perhaps it would be irresponsible of one to do so in this situation because a friend whom one knows to be highly reliable has told one, falsely as it happens, that things are some other way. It is perhaps tempting to think that one could have the fact that one sees that things are a certain way as one's justification in such a situation. But if the justification is knowledge-affording, one does not have this fact as one's justification in this situation; at best, one has as one's justification the fact that one seems to see that things are this way.

It is central to the account of visual knowledge as true justified belief that the justifications it involves fall within the scope of second-order knowledge; for example, having the fact that one seems to see that things are a certain way as one's justification is a matter of having second-order knowledge of this fact. It is often thought that this second-order knowledge differs fundamentally from the first-order visual knowledge it accompanies: whereas the latter is visual knowledge of how things stand in the outer world, the second-order knowledge of one's justification is privileged self-knowledge of how things stand in one's inner world.

The thought that the second-order knowledge involved in first-order perceptual knowledge is fundamentally different from the latter, in ways the expression 'privileged self-knowledge' does something to capture, is central to the modest route. The route maintains that facts which in some sense concern how things are in the outer world, such as the fact that one sees that things are a certain way, can fall within the scope of privileged self-knowledge. But it will take the remainder of these chapters to defend this claim; at present, I can offer no more than this promissory note: taking the modest route requires recognizing a category of self-knowledge which contemporary epistemology fails to recognize, and it is this recognition which enables us to see how there can be facts which are at once knowledge-affording and genuine justifications, self-known to the knower, and thereby such as to be something the knower can give in answer to the question: 'Why do you think that?'

We now have a reasonably detailed sketch of a way to hold on to the account of knowledge as justified true belief, in the case of visual knowledge, and in the face of the Gettier argument, by understanding that account in a distinctly non-traditional way. It may already be inspiring objections and questions. But before considering these I want to offer some reasons in favour of responding to the argument by taking this modest route, rather than that taken by the vast majority of contemporary epistemologists.

9.3. Fool's Knowledge

On the traditional understanding of the account of knowledge as justified true belief, one knows that things are a certain way if, and only if: first, one believes that things are this way; secondly, one's belief is true; and thirdly, one's belief is justified, in the appropriate sense of 'justified'. The standard response to the Gettier argument is to supplement this account with at least one further condition, to ensure, for instance, that one's belief is not accidentally true.

I think we should be suspicious as to whether any such supplemented account can be adequate. Once we have the modest route in focus, supplemented accounts cannot but seem to fail as accounts of visual knowledge. When compared with the account which the modest route offers, the so-called knowledge which these other accounts depict cannot but seem to be knowledge *ersatz*. And the same goes for the traditional understanding. Of course, it may be that we cannot endorse the modest route, for whatever reason; perhaps its notion of truth-guaranteeing justifications which constitute the content of our privileged self-knowledge is not one we can accept, on grounds of general coherence or otherwise. In that case we must either come up with a new account, or find reason for treating as the real thing what previously seemed *ersatz*. There is likely to be something disappointing about such a project, at least in the first instance, and that gives us some reason to see if the modest route can be satisfactorily defended.

I think it is easy to see why, compared to knowledge as depicted by the modest route, knowledge as the supplemented accounts depict it is not the genuine article. If you know that you see that there is a lemon over there, then you know that there is a lemon over there; as we might put it, there is no question for you as to whether there is a lemon over there. But if you merely know that you seem to see that there is a lemon over there, a question remains for you as to whether there is a lemon over there. There might be one over there, and perhaps there is. But because your second-order knowledge falls short of the fact that there is, it is possible, for all it tells you, that your environs are lemon-free.

In the first case, the fact that one has second-order knowledge of one's justification ensures that one has first-order perceptual knowledge of the relevant fact. That one's second-order knowledge does ensure this is, I think, part of our ordinary, pre-theoretical conception of perceptual knowledge. Claiming to have insight into the pre-theoretical may be a dangerous business. But consider an aspect of the line of thought designed to lead to scepticism about perceptual knowledge; a line of thought which we know many people find pre-theoretically tempting: our beliefs about how things are in the outer world can count as perceptual knowledge only if they can be suitably justified by our experience; but our experience is capable of misleading us as to how things are in the outer world, by presenting them as they are not; therefore, our beliefs about how things are in the outer world cannot be suitably justified by our experience. This line of thought rests on the assumption that our experience must be incapable of misleading us if it is suitably to justify our beliefs. That is part of our ordinary pre-theoretical conception of knowledge.

Non-misleading experience is experience which guarantees truth. So, if our experience must be incapable of misleading us, if it is suitably to justify our beliefs, it must also be such as to guarantee the truth of our beliefs. That it is truth-guaranteeing is part of our ordinary pre-theoretical conception of knowledge. It does not follow that we must hold on to this requirement at all costs. But there is a presumption in favour of our pre-theoretical conception of any object: we ought to hold on to as much of this conception as we can unless there is excellent reason for its abandonment.[6] There *is* excellent reason to abandon the claim that experience can suitably ground our beliefs only it is incapable of misleading us: the claim leads to scepticism. But abandoning this claim need not force us to abandon the requirement of truth-guaranteeing justification. The modest route retains this requirement. But whereas the pre-theoretical conception pictures the justification involved in perceptual knowledge as an experience available to our second-order knowledge, the modest route pictures it as a fact available to our second-order knowledge, such as the fact that one sees that things are a certain way.

In respecting this requirement, the modest route is closer to our pre-theoretical conception than the supplemented post-Gettier accounts (and the traditional understanding). Epistemologists seem to have been trained to give up both aspects of this conception: the requirement that experience not mislead, and the requirement that justification guarantee truth. Perhaps this is because these aspects are seen as inseparable. From this perspective, there is nothing fake about knowledge whose constituent justifications fall short of the known facts. But if these aspects are separated in the way I suggest, we can recover some of our pre-theoretical innocence. And once we have done that, to conceive of knowledge in the traditional or in the supplemented post-Gettier ways will seem doomed to fail. From this perspective, so-called

---

[6] Perhaps the theoretical purposes of suitably established branches of natural science provide reason to abandon our pre-theoretical conception of the objects which are its concern; see Chomsky (2000). But then I think it makes sense to insist that natural science is operating with concepts (as well as conceptions) which are different to those we pre-theoretically employ. Evidently it does not follow from this that the purposes of philosophy provide reason to do the same.

'knowledge' justified by something which does not guarantee the truth of what is believed is nothing but fool's knowledge; glittering perhaps, but not gold.

Short of reasons not to regain this aspect of our innocence, and so to take the modest route, we ought to do so. If there is excellent reason not to take the modest route, we ought not to regain our innocence. We will consider some putatively excellent reasons later in this chapter. I want now to consider another reason for favouring the modest route, which centres on a problem for making sense of the value of knowledge.

9.4. The Distinctive Value of Knowledge

When philosophers speak of the value of knowledge they have in mind its *distinctive* value. There seems to be an important connection between the value of knowledge and the content of knowledge, at least when its value is the value it has for us. Knowing that things are a certain way can be of value to us only if it matters to us whether things are this way: knowing that there is a three-leaf clover in my garden is of no value to me, because it matters not a jot to me whether there is a three-leaf clover in my garden; but knowing that there is a kingfisher in my garden is of value to me, because it does matter to me whether there is a kingfisher in my garden. But even if the value of knowledge does derive in part from the content of knowledge, the value possessed by knowledge that things are a certain way, but not by a state of mind which falls short of such knowledge, such as merely believing truly that things are this way, cannot derive from its content, because it shares this with the lesser states. The distinctive value of knowledge must derive not from its content but rather, as we might say, from its form: not from its being a case of knowing *that things are a certain way* but rather from its being a case of *knowing* that things are a certain way.

It might now be tempting to assume that the distinctive value of knowing derives simply from its membership of the genus *knowledge*. But it would be wrong to accede to this temptation without argument. Perhaps membership of certain species of knowledge (such as the species of knowledge enjoyed by rational subjects) suffices to confer a kind of distinctive value which mere membership of the genus does not suffice to confer. Perhaps there are instances of the genus which have no distinctive value because they are not of the appropriate species. In this section, I will keep the focus on visual knowledge enjoyed by rational subjects, and restrict my claims to knowledge of this species.

Philosophical thinking about the distinctive value of knowledge usually begins with reflection on a point made by Socrates in Plato's *Meno*. It is natural to think that knowledge is of value to us because having it enables us to achieve our goals. To use Socrates' example, we value knowledge of the way to Larissa because it enables us to achieve our goal of getting to Larissa. Socrates noted that this cannot explain the distinctive value of knowledge, because a mere true belief about the way to Larissa will also enable us to achieve this goal. To this it is overwhelmingly natural, and I think right, to respond that *of course* knowledge is not distinctively valuable *simply* because it enables us to achieve our goals (it would be bizarre if anyone thought it was). The distinctive value of knowledge resides in the superior way it enables us to achieve many of our goals—superior to the way in which lesser states (such as mere true belief) enable us to do so.

This superior way is nicely captured by Socrates' metaphorical conception of knowledge as involving beliefs which are tethered to the truth. We are less likely to lose hold of dogs which are tethered to posts than we are dogs which are not. So, we are less likely to lose hold of beliefs which are tethered to the truth than beliefs which are not. That it is *truth* to which our beliefs are tethered suggests that, in the case of knowledge enjoyed by rational subjects, this idea of losing hold of a belief is not a merely causal notion but a rational notion, which we might capture, less metaphorically, by saying that knowledge is rationally immune to doubt in a way in which lesser states are not. That ensures that knowledgeable beliefs are more likely than lesser states are to enable us to achieve many of our goals. And *that* is the superior way in which knowledge enables us to achieve many of our goals, in which its distinctive value resides. Consider goals whose attainment takes time, such as getting to Larissa. Someone who believes truly but does not know that *this* is the way to Larissa (to put it from the point of view of the person in question) is more likely to abandon their belief in the face of apparent reason to do so than someone who knows this. Someone who holds on to this belief is more likely to get to Larissa that someone who lets go of it. So, someone who believes truly but does not know that this is the way to Larissa is less likely to achieve the goal of getting to Larissa than someone who knows this.

But what does this rational immunity consist in? This is easy to see if we take the modest route. You believe that there is a lemon over there. And this belief constitutes knowledge because it is acquired in the light of the fact that you see that there is a lemon over there. So, you know that you see that there is a lemon over there. And because you know this, the situation you are in is one in which it is responsible of you to believe that there is a lemon over there (see §9.2). Imagine now that someone whom you know to be honest and reliable sincerely tells you—truly, as it happens—that someone they know is going around replacing a considerable number of the lemons in the vicinity for bars of soap carefully crafted so as to look like lemons (from a suitable distance). But imagine that, in spite of this, the object you see which looks like a lemon really is a lemon. It is possible that this new information changes the situation you are in, so as to make it one in which it would be irresponsible of you to believe that there is a lemon over there because you do not have the fact that you see that there is a lemon over there as your justification. But it is also possible that it does not change your situation, so that, even given the new information, it is still responsible of you to believe that there is a lemon over there, because you still have the fact that you see that there is one over there as your justification.

If the latter possibility is actualized, one can responsibly retain one's belief in the face of the putative reason to abandon it which the person you know to be honest and reliable provides. But if the former possibility is actualized, one cannot responsibly retain one's belief in the face of this. Put differently: if the latter is actualized one is entitled to retain one's belief, but if the former is actualized one is not entitled to do so. Which possibility is actualized depends on the details of the particular case. A case in which your friend is atypically but heavily drunk is pretty obviously one which actualizes the latter. Arguably, a case in which none of the objects in your visual field with the look of lemons are bars of soap also belongs to this category. And, arguably, a case in which every object in your visual field with the look of a lemon—with the exception of the one you think is a lemon—is a bar of soap does not belong to this category. The point is that when the latter possibility is actualized one is entitled to disregard the putative reason for belief-abandonment, and thereby to stick to one's belief, and so to retain one's knowledge. And if one is entitled to do this, one is more likely to do so. We are rational subjects, who—for the most part—do what we are entitled to do, and do not do what we are not entitled to do. That we do, and do not, do so is part of what it is to be a rational subject.

It is not easy to see what this rational immunity consists in if we reject the modest route, and adopt either the traditional understanding of the account of knowledge as justified true belief or one of the supplemented accounts. You believe that there is a lemon over there. This belief is true. And this belief supposedly constitutes visual knowledge, in part because it is acquired in the light of the fact that you seem to see that there is a lemon over there and in part because some further conditions are satisfied. In this situation, you surely see that there is a lemon over there. But (and this is the crucial difference) it is no part of your possession of this knowledge that you know that you see that there is a lemon over there. If you do possess this knowledge then, from the perspective of the present understanding, this is a mere coincidence, not an essential aspect of your status as a knower.

On the modest route, the fact which justifies one in disregarding apparent justifications for suspending one's knowledgeable belief is the very fact which justifies this belief—the fact that one sees that there is a lemon over there. And, on the modest route, this fact constitutes the content of one's second-order knowledge. I am happy to grant that this fact is present even in cases of visual knowledge as this is putatively understood by the account traditionally understood, and by the supplemented accounts. But, unlike in the case of the modest route, in the case of the traditional understanding, and in the case of the supplemented accounts, there is no guarantee that this fact constitutes the content of one's second-order knowledge: perhaps it does, but equally perhaps not. There is no guarantee that one has the fact as one's justification. So, there is no guarantee that one is entitled to retain one's belief in the face of putative reason for its abandonment, because there is no guarantee that it would be responsible of one to retain it. And with that, knowledge seems to be the same as a lesser state in this respect: neither guarantees that the belief it involves is rationally immune to doubt in the way required for knowledge to be distinctively valuable.

It is sometimes said that if something of one type causes something of another type, then the correlation of the two things would be more robust than it would be otherwise. What this means is that there are a greater range of counterfactual circumstances in which the correlation obtains than there would be if the two things were merely correlated, and so not causally related. We might try to employ a similar thought to make sense of the rational immunity of knowledgeable beliefs. Beliefs which constitute knowledge are true in a greater range of counterfactual circumstances than beliefs which fall short of knowledge. A knowledgeable belief is like a loyal friend: it can be relied upon to stay true even when the going gets tough. That suffices to identify a kind of rational immunity to doubt. But it surely does not suffice to identify the kind of rational immunity which knowledgeable beliefs have for rational subjects like us. Beliefs with this kind of immunity are ones which we retain in the light of justifications. That is not to deny that knowledgeable beliefs, unlike mere true beliefs, are robust in the way identified here. But it is to insist that the explanation of why they are robust is that, in the appropriate counterfactual circumstances, we are entitled to retain them in the circumstances (which include circumstances in which we have apparent reason for abandoning our beliefs, as in the case just discussed). We would not be satisfied with mere immunity. Knowledge is of value to rational subjects like us, precisely because it confers *rational* immunity to doubt.

So, in enabling us to make sense of the rational immunity of visual knowledge, the modest route enables us to defend the Socratic response to the *Meno* problem (in the visual case). Its rational immunity to doubt, suitably understood, ensures that it enables us to achieve our goals in a way which is more efficient, because more likely to lead to their attainment, than that of lesser states, such as mere true belief. That seems to yield a way to make sense of the distinctive value of visual knowledge. And if the modest route could be extended so as to apply to every species of knowledge enjoyed by rational subjects, it would thereby seem to yield an account of such knowledge in general. I say 'seems to yield', because there are people who seemingly would think that it would not actually do so. These people purport to be persuaded that suggestions along the present lines are vulnerable to something called 'the swamping problem' (Kvanvig 2003; Zagzebski 2003).

In its initial formulation, this supposed problem was thought merely to affect reliabilism about knowledge, according to which the only difference between knowledgeable beliefs and merely true beliefs lies in the fact that the former are acquired as a result of the operation of a reliable belief-acquiring mechanism. The thought is that this difference cannot explain why knowledgeable beliefs are more valuable than mere true beliefs. A good cup of coffee produced by a reliable coffee-making machine is of no more value than a good cup of coffee produced by an unreliable machine. So, why should a true belief acquired as a result of a reliable mechanism be of any more value than a true belief acquired in an unreliable way? That is the swamping problem: the value of true belief swamps any value which might be thought to attach specifically to knowledgeable belief. A natural response is that the reliable process by which the belief is acquired confers on it a robustness which renders it immune to certain kinds of doubt, and thereby ensures that it can enable us better to achieve our goals. Perhaps that requires further argument. But there is no need for *us* to supply this argument, because, as we have seen, our very different non-reliabilist account of knowledge has the resources to explain how this robustness is possessed by knowledgeable beliefs but not by their merely true counterparts.

The swamping problem is supposed to be a problem for what Duncan Pritchard (§1.2) calls the *primary value problem*, the problem of whether knowledge is more valuable than true belief. The Socratic account of the value of knowledge which I have sketched here serves to deal not only with this value problem, but also with what Pritchard calls the *secondary value problem*, the problem of whether knowledge is more valuable than any state which falls short of knowledge. Only knowledge partakes of the kind of value outlined here, because only it guarantees the presence of the second-order knowledge necessary for the justified retention of belief in the face of apparent reason for its abandonment.

Pritchard also thinks there is a *tertiary value problem*, a problem of whether knowledge differs not merely in degree but in kind from lesser states. For Pritchard, accounting for the distinctive value of knowledge requires accounting for this qualitative difference, which in turn requires the claim that knowledge is of non-instrumental value. It might seem that what I have said here sees knowledge's value as merely instrumental, and so fails to respond to this tertiary value problem, and thereby fails to account for the distinctive value of knowledge. But it is not clear that this is correct, for three reasons.

First, it is not clear why accounting for the distinctive value of knowledge requires showing it to be qualitatively distinct in value in this way. There is no need to query Pritchard's insistence that accounting for the former must not leave it looking mysterious why epistemological discussion has focused on knowledge rather than on lesser states. That *epistemological* discussion has focused specifically on knowledge might seem to be true by definition. But whether it is or not, we ought to query Pritchard's assumption that explaining why philosophy has focused on knowledge at the expense of lesser states—assuming that it has—cannot be merely a matter of showing that knowledge is quantitatively distinct in value. Why should it seem in need of further explanation that philosophy might want to focus on the cognitive standing which stands at the apex of the continuum of value? This is of more value than lesser standings. Why is that not enough to explain our specific interest in it?

Secondly, it is worth pausing to ask what it is for something to possess instrumental value. If it is merely for something to enable us to attain a goal or goals, then knowledge does not merely posses instrumental value (according to the Socratic solution), because it does not merely enable us to attain our goals, but rather enables us to attain them in a certain valued way, viz., efficiently. Pritchard seems to understand the idea of instrumental value in a different, capacious way, to mean value which is not independent of its possessor's status as enabling the attainment of a goal or goals. Enabling us to attain our goals efficiently is a kind of instrumental value, on this way of understanding the idea. There is a question—which I shall only raise here—of whether this is too capacious an understanding of instrumental value; whether it is really a conception of value whose possession depends on the possession of instrumental value, rather than a conception of instrumental value itself.

Thirdly, even if we grant the capacious understanding of instrumental value, it is far from obvious that the value of knowledge is merely instrumental. According to the Socratic solution, we value knowledge because knowledgeable beliefs are rationally immune to doubt. Independent of the fact that knowledge thereby enables us better to attain our goals, knowledge also serves to manifest our rationality in a distinctive way, by ensuring that a certain kind of behaviour we engage in (as it happens, that of disregarding apparent reasons to abandon our beliefs) is justified. That is something which we, as rational subjects, value. And it is something which only knowledge can yield. Knowledge thereby serves to possess a kind of distinctive value which, even on the capacious understanding outlined above, is manifestly non-instrumental. (If we can resist this capacious understanding, then we can say, simply, that one reason why the immunity which knowledge confers on beliefs is not merely of instrumental value is that it is *rational* immunity—immunity which our beliefs possess because we are entitled to possess them.) So, it seems to me far from obvious that what I have said here does not respond to the tertiary value problem (if a response is necessary). But whether it does or not, that it accounts for the distinctive value of knowledge seems assured.

Before I consider the question of how one comes to be in a position to acquire second-order knowledge of the justifications posited by the modest route, I want to mention one more reason in its favour.

9.5. Fool's Justification

The modest route maintains that the justification for the knowledgeable belief that things are a certain way must guarantee the truth of this belief. It is consistent with this that there can be a justification or a reason for a belief which is not truth-guaranteeing; the route insists merely that, if there are such reasons, they are not sufficient to justify knowledgeable beliefs. That would require us to distinguish between two different kinds of justification: truth-guaranteeing justification, and (as it were) mere justification. But perhaps we could instead distinguish between justification, and reasonableness—something which casts beliefs in a rational light but falls short of justification. Each of these possibilities is consistent with the modest route. But I would like to say something here in favour of the second (even though it does not suffice to impugn the modest route to criticize the second; readers interested only in impugning are advised to skip to the next section).

It can seem that reasons or justifications for belief must be truth-guaranteeing. A reason or justification which does not guarantee the truth of the belief that things are a certain way—such as the justification constituted by the fact that one seems to see that things are this way—can at best be a reason or justification for the different belief that things *might* be this way (or perhaps for the belief that things are likely to be this way).

Someone who knows that they see that things are a certain way would be justified in believing that they are this way. But would someone who merely knows that they seem to see that they are this way be justified in sticking their neck out this far? They would be justified in sticking their neck out a bit—in believing that they might be this way, perhaps even that it is likely that they are this way. But because, for all they know, things might not be this way, how can they be justified in believing that this is the way things are?

Of course, we can explain why someone believes that things are a certain way by adverting to the fact that they seem to see that they are this way. That is an explanation which displays their belief as intelligible, perhaps in some cases understandable, perhaps even in some cases excusable. Certainly, it 'shows rationality in operation' (McDowell 2008: 257); it is not a merely causal explanation of the sort we might express by saying that a bridge collapses because of a structural defect.[7] But it can seem that it does not display their belief as in any sense justified. We might put the point by saying that the fact that one seems to see that things are a certain way is never a reason to believe that things are this way, but merely a reason to believe that things might be this way (perhaps with reasonable likelihood).

I think these remarks state truisms, an aspect of our pre-theoretical innocence which, once recovered, presents so-called justifications which are not truth-guaranteeing as, at best, fool's justifications. Missing the truisms, or not recognizing them as such, has a number of possible sources, one of which is the blunt thought that *surely* a belief can be justified even if it false. (Other sources will be considered as we proceed.)

It is a trivial consequence of these putative truisms that this thought is false. But even though a false belief cannot be justified, of course one can think that a false belief which one has is justified. One thinks that one sees that there is a lemon over there, and so one believes that there is a lemon over there. As it happens, one's belief is false. One did not see that there is a lemon over there. So, one did not believe that there is a lemon over there in the light of a justification constituted by the fact that one sees that there is a lemon over there, because there is no such fact. One can say that one acquires the belief because one *thinks* that one sees that there is a lemon over there, or because one seems to see that there is a lemon over there. But these

---

[7] This example is borrowed from Davidson (1963).

explanations do not display one's belief as justified. The fact that one thinks that one sees that things are a certain way can no more justify one in believing that they are this way than the fact that one seems to see that they are this way. However, the explanations do display one's belief as rationally intelligible. It is reasonable for one to believe that there is a lemon over there because one thinks that one can see that there is. Perhaps one might be able to go on, in certain cases, by saying that because the lighting conditions were normal, and because one had no reason to believe that there were any bars of soap, carefully crafted so as to look like lemons, in the vicinity, one cannot be criticized, on grounds of negligence or inattention or hastiness, for taking it that one does see that there is a lemon over there. One's belief would be in this way blameless.

So, even if the thought that false beliefs can be justified is false, there is truth in its vicinity: false beliefs can be rationally intelligible, and even on occasion blameless.

The conviction which this thought underwrites is also potentially under-written by the further thought that justifications cannot guarantee the truth of the beliefs they justify. Dislodging this further thought is a central task of these chapters. Someone in its grip will wish to controvert the point which I think is a truism (viz., that justifications must be truth-guaranteeing). I only hope that the naturalness of the point will help to cast suspicion on the thought, at least for those not in its grip. And I hope the process of dislodging which these chapters set in train will help to reveal the point to be the reminder of the obvious which I think it is.

9.6. Arguing from Illusion

The modest route controverts the principle that justifications must always be more certain than the beliefs they justify. It is possible to be certain that one seems to see that things are a certain way, but less certain as to whether things are this way—less certain about the truth of the belief that they are this way. But it is not possible to be certain that one sees that things are a certain way but less certain as to whether things are this way. If one's mind is made up about the former, then one's mind is made up about the latter. So, the fact that one sees that things are a certain way cannot be a justification for believing that things are this way, if the principle is true.

But is the principle true? Well, let me consider a putative reason for thinking that it is true, which is supplied by a version of the argument from illusion.

There are at least two versions of this argument. The version which interests me is concerned with the epistemological significance of visual experience.[8]

The argument might be expressed as follows. We can distinguish between deceptive and non-deceptive cases: a non-deceptive case is one in which one sees that things in the outer world are a certain way; a deceptive case is one in which one seems to see that things in the outer world are a certain way, when in fact they are not. Deceptive cases are always possible when it comes to the outer world. It follows, according to the argument, that justifications for belief must be present in deceptive and non-deceptive cases alike. So, the fact that one seems to see that things are a certain way can constitute a justification for believing that things are this way. But the fact that one sees that things are a certain way cannot constitute a justification for believing that they are this way, because even though this fact is present in a non-deceptive case, in a deceptive case it is necessarily absent.

The upshot of the argument is that justifications cannot rule out the possibility of false beliefs about the outer world, because justifications which did that could not be present in deceptive cases. Justifications must always leave room for the possibility that the beliefs they justify are false. So, one must always be more certain of a justification than one is of the belief it justifies. The argument constitutes a defence of the principle, if it is sound. But is it sound? Why should we think that justifications for belief must be present in deceptive and non-deceptive cases alike? Why not think instead that there can be justifications which are present only in non-deceptive cases?[9] Why does the argument miss, or dismiss, this possibility? Well, there are a number of possible explanations, some of which will be considered as we proceed, and one of which, plausibly, is this: it is because the argument assumes that justifications must conform to the principle that justifications must always be more certain than the beliefs they justify. Only those facts which can be present in deceptive and non-deceptive cases alike can constitute justifications which conform to this principle. So, the fact that one sees that things are a certain way cannot, because it does not.

Of course, in the present dialectical context the argument cannot appeal to this principle in defence of its conclusion. The context is one in which we are looking for a reason to accept the principle. So, unless the argument can defend its crucial inferential step without appealing to the principle—the step from the fact that there are deceptive cases to the claim that justifications must be capable of being present in deceptive cases—it cannot serve to provide the

---

[8] The other version is concerned with the phenomenal character of visual experience. A discussion of both versions of the argument may be found in Haddock and Macpherson (2008*b*).

[9] See McDowell (1982: esp. 385–94).

reason we are looking for, viz., a reason to endorse the principle. Perhaps there are other dialectical contexts in which this appeal is justified, such as those in which we have independent reason to accept the principle. But in the present context it is not. Pending a defence of the argument which does not make the appeal, the argument is powerless to offer a defence of the principle.[10]

It might be thought that the principle can be defended simply by reflecting on our ordinary practice of giving and asking for reasons. If we are in doubt as to whether something is so, our doubt will not be assuaged by the production of a reason which entails that this is so, because our doubt will apply equally to this reason; consequently, justifications for beliefs cannot carry this entailment. But this argument is flawed on two counts.

First, it *is* possible to assuage doubt by producing a truth-guaranteeing reason. Imagine a case in which, early one morning, I tell my friends that the Prime Minister has been in Edinburgh today, and they are suspicious of this claim because they heard nothing about it on yesterday's news, and didn't watch, or listen to, or otherwise become informed of what was on the news today. But imagine that I then tell my friends that I have just been informed by a news programme that the Prime Minister is in Edinburgh today, perhaps by saying 'I just heard it on the news'. (As with justifications constituted by the fact that I see that things are a certain way, justifications constituted by the fact that I have been informed that things are a certain way are truth-guaranteeing, and so knowledge-affording.) My friends' doubt is now assuaged.

Secondly, there is no reason to think that all justifications must assuage doubt in this way. When we ask someone 'Why do you think that?' our desire might be merely to find out whether the person knew in one way rather than another; we are in no doubt that they know it, we just want to find out how they acquired their knowledge. That is part of our ordinary practice of giving and asking for reasons.

As yet, then, we have no reason to accept the principle, and so, because we have no reason to accept it, no reason to accept that the problem is a real problem. We are free to proceed to another, more serious concern

9.7. The Regress of Justifications

The modest route maintains that the possession of visual knowledge that things are a certain way requires that one possesses second-order knowledge of the

---

[10] Such a defence might well employ some of the objections I consider, and rebut, in the next chapter—objections which target the claim that we enjoy privileged self-knowledge of the truth-guaranteeing justifications involved in visual knowledge.

fact which justifies the belief which this knowledge involves—the fact that one sees that things are this way. But knowledge in general requires justification, or so it seems. So, the question arises: what is the justification required for the possession of the second-order knowledge that one sees that things are this way?

We have compared two different conceptions of the justification knowledge requires. According to the first conception, the justification does not guarantee the truth of the belief it justifies. But according to the second conception, it does guarantee this. The justification is constituted, in the case of visual knowledge, by the fact that one seems to see that things are a certain way (on the first conception), and by the fact that one sees that things are a certain way (on the second).

A proponent of the second conception might suppose that we can make sense of the justification required for the second-order knowledge by simply extending this conception to the second-order level. To see that things are a certain way is to be (visually) aware that things are a certain way; to enjoy first-order awareness in the visual mode. The analogue would be to enjoy second-order awareness in what presumably would be a non-visual mode; to be (non-visually) aware that one sees that things are a certain way. So, the extension would maintain that the possession of knowledge that one sees that things are a certain way requires that one knows the fact which justifies the belief which this knowledge involves—the fact that one is (non visually) aware that one sees that they are this way.[11]

Before we even open the question of what exactly this second-order non-visual awareness is, we face the worry that this extension of the conception to the second-order level generates a regress. It is part of the idea of knowledge as true justified belief that one must know the fact which constitutes one's justification for the belief which knowledge involves. So, in the extension, one knows the fact that one is aware that one sees that things are a certain way. And now the question arises: what is the justification required for possession of knowledge of this fact—the fact that one is aware that one sees that things are this way? We could extend the conception to the third-order level, and say that the possession of knowledge that one is aware that one sees that things are this way requires that one knows the fact which justifies the belief which this knowledge involves—the fact that one is (presumably non-visually) aware that one is (non-visually) aware that one sees that things are this way. But the futility of doing so is manifest, because a question of the same form as before will arise again, and again, *ad infinitum*. It will seem that to know one thing I must know an infinite number of things.

---

[11] See e.g. Peacocke (2009) for a version of this thought.

We need to block the regress, or better, not embark on it at all. The obvious way to do so is to restrict the scope of the overall conception of knowledge as true justified belief. Some species of knowledge fall within the scope of the overall conception, but some do not. Centrally, the second-order knowledge that one sees that things are a certain way, which is required for visual knowledge that they are this way, falls outside of its scope. Possessing this second-order knowledge does not involve believing that one sees that they are this way in the light of a justification one has for this belief. It is knowledge, which does not involve justification.

But this raises the further question: how should we understand the second-order knowledge, if not as involving justification? It can seem that there is only one answer. One knows that one sees that things are a certain way if, and only if: first, one believes that one sees that things are this way; second, one's belief is true; and third, one's belief is acquired in some way, of which one may well be ignorant. In other words, the only answer a non-normative conception of knowledge, which rips apart the connection between first-order knowledge and second-order knowledge of the justification.[12]

It is natural, at least for those not yet seduced, to baulk at such a conception of knowledge. How can beliefs for which one has no justification—indeed, which one has no idea how one acquired—possibly constitute knowledge? It might be responded that, difficult as this may be, we must accept that these beliefs can constitute knowledge. But the cases which are usually cited to establish this point are of no relevance to us; they concern things like knowledge of one's own name, and knowledge of when the Battle of Hastings took place,[13] both of which fall outside our concern with visual knowledge. As a matter of fact, I think we should reject the non-normative conception *tout court* when it comes to making sense of the knowledge enjoyed by rational animals; but this is not the occasion to defend this point.[14] (The considerations adduced in §9.3 are relevant, however.)

I do not think there is any reason to resist the natural baulking which the non-normative conception inspires. But that is cold comfort in the present context, where this conception seems to offer our only release from the regress of justifications. We seem to be caught between a rock and a hard place: here

---

[12] This is a deliberately broad specification of the non-normative conception. Evidently a traditional reliabilist account of knowledge would count as a version of the conception on this specification. As would a version of the account often attributed to Williamson (2000). In its application to the case of visual knowledge, this account would say that one knows that things are a certain way because one sees that things are this way. But it would deny that one needs to know that one sees that things are this way in order to acquire knowledge in this way.

[13] See Stroud (1989: 109).

[14] Alan Millar's contribution to this volume contains some of what is needed for a defence.

the regress, there the non-normative conception, with no resting-place in sight (cf. Rödl 2007: ch. 5).

9.8. Concluding Remarks

In the next chapter I will suggest a way out of this impasse. I want to end this chapter by considering an evidently hopeless suggestion regarding a way out, which nevertheless supplies a clue to the way out I will propose.

Imagine we insist that the fact that one seems to be aware that one sees that things are a certain way constitutes one's justification for believing that one seems to be aware that one sees that things are this way. And imagine we insist that this knowledge does not involve justification. But instead of embracing the non-normative conception, we say the following: one knows that one seems to be aware in this way if one seems to be aware in this way. That is, if one seems to be aware in this way then one not only believes that one does so but knows that one does so. As we might say, the knowledge that one seems to be aware in this way is knowledge of a transparent fact, because it is not possible for the fact that one seems to be aware in this way to be present without one knowing that it is.

This conception is not the non-normative conception of knowledge. That conception assumes that the truth condition for knowledge can be satisfied without the satisfaction of the belief condition. In the case of knowledge of a transparent fact, the satisfaction of the former condition entails the satisfaction of the latter; that one believes that one seems to be aware that one sees that things are a certain way is a simple consequence of its being the case that one seems to be aware that one sees that things are this way. This suggestion seems to be similar to the non-normative conception, in that it seems not to involve a justification condition; the fact that one seems to be aware in this way does not seem to be a justification for believing that one seems to be aware in this way, because it does not seem to be something we can cite in answer to a suitable 'why' question; if someone tells you that they seem to be aware that they see that things are a certain way, it would be odd for you to ask them why they think this, because they have already told you why they think it—they think it because they seem to be aware that they see that things are a certain way. However, the suggestion is distinct from the non-normative conception in not denying, but providing for, knowledge of the way in which one acquires this knowledge. According to the suggestion, the fact that one seems to be aware in this way suffices for one to know that one seems to be aware in this way. If one knows that one seems to be aware in this way, then one has knowledge of the fact in virtue of which one knows. And this is something the non-normative conception fails to provide for.

I think this suggestion offers a clue as to how to steer between the rock of the regress and the hard place of the non-normative conception. But it does not offer anything more than a clue, for two reasons. First, at best it enables us to make sense of how we know that we seem to be aware that we see that things are a certain way; but we want to make sense of how we know that we see that things are this way. Second, seeming awareness that we see that things are this way has no role to play in an account of how we know that we see that things are this way, if the arguments of this chapter are sound. That one seems to be aware that one sees that things are a certain way is not a truth-guaranteeing justification for believing that one sees that things are this way.

With this in mind, let us now unlock the clue, and see how to get beyond the present impasse.

10

Second-Order Knowledge

10.1. Introductory Remarks

We are seeking to make sense of the second-order knowledge involved in visual knowledge in a way which avoids two unacceptable possibilities.

We began with the thought that if one knows that things are a certain way, then one knows the fact which justifies one in believing that things are this way. I have argued that this justifying fact must guarantee the truth of the belief it justifies, and exemplified this claim for the case of visual knowledge: one knows (visually) that things are a certain way only if one knows that one sees that things are this way. So, the question arises: what is the justification required in order to know that one sees that things are this way? A natural answer reapplies the present conception of knowledge at the second-order level. One knows that one sees that things are this way only if one knows that one is (non-visually) aware that one sees that things are this way. But that only raises the question: what is the justification required in order to know that one is (non-visually) aware that one sees that things are this way? And it seems that so long as the present conception of knowledge remains in force, a question of this form will keep arising as we ascend up the levels. We will have embarked on a regress. And it looks as if the only way to block the regress will be to abandon the present conception of knowledge for a non-normative conception, in the case of the second-order knowledge which visual knowledge involves.

In this chapter I want to show how we can avoid this unpalatable choice between the rock of the regress and the hard place of the non-normative conception, by unlocking the clue I presented at the end of the previous chapter—that knowledge of a transparent fact is not merely knowledge of this fact, but knowledge of the fact which suffices for one to acquire this knowledge. The key to unlocking the clue is to see this fact as something which is not a justification, but nevertheless shares some of the essential features of justification. That will enable us to preserve a way of understanding the second-order knowledge which eschews the non-normative conception but does not fall into the regress.

10.2. Transparency and Knowledge

So, how exactly is the clue to be unlocked?

It can seem that the second-order knowledge involved in visual knowledge is knowledge of a transparent fact, because it can seem that if one sees that things are a certain way then one knows (visually) that things are this way. If one knows that things are a certain way, then one knows the fact which justifies one in believing that things are this way. So, it can seem that if one knows visually that things are a certain way then one knows that one sees that things are this way. And so, it can seem that if one sees that things are a certain way, then one knows that one sees that things are this way. The fact that one sees that things are a certain way can seem to suffice for the acquisition of knowledge of itself.

But this cannot be right as it stands. One can see that things are a certain way without knowing that one sees that things are this way, because one can see that things are a certain way without knowing (visually) that things are this way. Perhaps there are cases in which it would be irresponsible of one to believe that things are a certain way, even though one sees that things are this way. Perhaps there are cases in which one thinks—falsely as it happens—that one has reason not to believe that things are a certain way, even though one sees them to be this way. Perhaps there are cases in which one's paranoia puts visual knowledge beyond one's reach, even though one sees that things are a certain way. Perhaps one can see that things are a certain way but not know that they are this way because one is in a case of the sort which figures in Gettier-style arguments: a case in which one sees that there is a lemon over there, but every other object in one's visual field with the look of a lemon is merely a lemon façade, for instance.

Together, cases like this suffice to make it plausible that one can see that things are a certain way but not know that things are this way, and so not know that one sees that things are this way. But even if this is not merely plausible but the case, it does not follow that there cannot be cases in which one sees that things are this way, and thereby knows that things are this way (and so knows that one sees that they are this way) not because some further facts are present in addition to the fact that one sees that they are this way, but simply because one sees that they are. It is possible that there are cases of seeing that things are a certain way which are themselves cases of knowing (visually) that things are this way, even though there are also cases of seeing that things are a certain way which are themselves (as it were) merely cases of seeing that they are this way—cases of seeing that they are this way which are not cases of knowing (visually) that they are.

We might think that a case of seeing that things are a certain way can count as a case of knowing (visually) that they are this way because of the presence of further facts—facts whose absence is compatible with the presence of the fact that one sees that they are this way; I have in mind facts of the sort indicated two paragraphs back, whose presence is necessary for one to know (visually) that things are a certain way, such as the fact that one is not in a Getter-style case. But when I say that a case of seeing that things are a certain way can be a case of knowing (visually) that things are this way, I have something else in mind—that the case of seeing is intrinsically a case of knowing visually. Perhaps a case of seeing which is not intrinsically a case of knowing (visually) can count as such a case when the further facts are present. But it will not depend on the presence of these facts for its very identity. A case of seeing which is intrinsically a case of knowing (visually) is, on the other hand, one to the identity of which the presence of these facts is integral.

The thought here is very similar to that which lies behind the so-called disjunctive conception of visual experience, which maintains, in opposition to those theories which picture objects from the outer world as only externally related to visual experiences, that there are some visual experiences which are intrinsically cases of seeing outer objects (Snowdon 1980–1). One way to put this idea is by saying that some visual experiences of an object are intrinsically cases of seeing the object, whereas others are *merely* visual experiences of the object—visual experiences of the object which are not cases of seeing it. In disjunctive form, the idea is that a visual experience of an object is either intrinsically a case of seeing the object, or merely a visual experience of the object.[1]

I have no desire to endorse a disjunctive conception of visual experience. But I do want to endorse a disjunctive conception of cases of seeing that things are a certain way, by saying that such cases are either intrinsically cases in which one's capacity for knowing visually that things are a certain way is operative,

---

[1] Evidently the disjunctive conception of visual experience is not a reductive analysis of the concept of visual experience, because this very concept appears on the right-hand side of the disjunction (and is required to understand the left-hand side). The same point applies to the disjunctive conception which I endorse, and the concept of seeing that things are a certain way which it employs. So, Williamson's (2000) criticisms of disjunctive conceptions which aspire to disjunctive analyses do not apply to me. It would also take considerable argument to show that the criticisms of the disjunctive conception discussed by M. G. F. Martin in several papers apply to me; see the papers in the first section of Haddock and Macpherson (2008a) for some of these criticisms.

or cases in which one merely sees that things are this way—cases in which one sees that things are this way, but one's capacity for visual knowledge is not operative. Cases of seeing that things are this way which are intrinsically cases in which the capacity is operative are cases in which one knows (visually) that things are this way, and so knows that one sees that they are this way. But cases in which one sees that things are this way, but the capacity is not operative, are cases in which one does not know (visually) that things are this way, and so does not thereby know that one sees that they are this way.

I have so far put the disjunctive conception in terms of cases, but it can also be put in terms of facts, or propositions. Facts are true propositions. To say that a fact is present or absent is just a way of saying that a proposition is true or not true. With this in mind, we can put the disjunctive conception of visual experience as follows: the proposition that one enjoys a visual experience of an object is true, either because one sees the object, or because one merely enjoys a visual experience of the object. Here the disjunctive conception of visual experience offers different explanations of what makes this proposition true. We might say that propositions to the effect that one enjoys a visual experience of an object are made true, either by the fact that one sees the object, or by the fact that one merely enjoys a visual experience to this effect—so long as we forget the metaphysical baggage which the idea of being made true has accrued over the years.[2] With this in mind, I want to maintain that the proposition that one sees that things are a certain way is true, either because one's capacity for visual knowledge is suitably operative, so that one knows (visually) that things are this way, or because one merely sees that things are this way.

It is a truism that visual knowledge is a species of fallible knowledge. It might be thought that what it is for this knowledge to be fallible is for the justification it involves to fall short of the known fact. Obviously we cannot avail ourselves of this thought here. Rather, we should say that what it is for it to be fallible is for us to be fallible with respect to the actualization of the capacity to know (visually) how things are. It is possible that this capacity is not actualized, and yet we believe that we see that things are a certain way. But if the capacity is actualized, then we know (visually) that things are this way, and so know that we see that things are this way. And for this reason we can say that the capacity is self-conscious, because its actualizations not only yield first-order visual knowledge, but also the second-order knowledge which visual knowledge essentially involves.

---

[2] I have in mind the theory of truth-makers endorsed by many contemporary metaphysicians. Beebee and Dodd (2005) provide an excellent overview of the contemporary debate surrounding this theory.

The content of this second-order knowledge is the fact that one sees that things are a certain way. Facts to this effect fall into two classes: those which are present because one's capacity for visual knowledge is suitably actualized, and those which are present because one merely sees that things are this way. Facts in the first class constitute the content of second-order knowledge. They are constituted by the fact that one's capacity for visual knowledge is actualized. Facts in the second class are not so constituted. For this reason, we might say that facts in the first class are transparent, whereas facts in the second class are opaque. The presence of a first class fact guarantees that a suitably placed subject has knowledge of it, precisely because of how it is constituted.

So, we can say that the second-order knowledge involved in visual knowledge is knowledge of a transparent fact—the fact that one sees that things are a certain way. And we can say that, by contrast, the visual knowledge itself is knowledge of a non-transparent fact—the fact that things are this way. This contrast is manifest in the different answers one ought to give to the question: 'Why do you think that?' If what one thinks constitutes the content of one's visual knowledge, it does not suffice to answer this question simply to cite this content; one must add 'and I see that things are this way'. But if what one thinks constitutes the content of one's second-order knowledge—the second-order knowledge involved in one's visual knowledge—then it *does* suffice to answer this question to cite *this* content; there is no need to add, or to say, anything else. There is no need to add 'and it is transparent', or to say 'The fact that I see that things are this way is constituted by the fact that I know visually that things are this way'.

Of course, one *could* say the latter in response to the question in the second-order case. But in the same way, one *could* also say it in response to the question in the first-order visual case, if one so desired. So, a difference between the responses remains. If what one thinks constitutes the content of one's second-order knowledge, the answer appends 'and it is transparent' to this very content. But if what one thinks constitutes the content of one's first-order knowledge, the answer appends 'and it is transparent' not to *this* very content, but to a distinct content—the content of one's second-order knowledge.

10.3. Transparency and Entitlement

We are now in a position to see how our account of the second-order knowledge involved in visual knowledge prevents us from embarking upon the regress.

We seem to embark upon the regress if we understand the second-order knowledge as true justified belief. If one has a justification for the belief which the second-order knowledge involves, it cannot simply be the fact that one sees that things are this way; it must be something which goes beyond this fact, such as the fact that one is (non-visually) aware that one sees that things are this way. And now the regress beckons. In the case of knowledge that one is (non-visually) aware that one sees that things are this way, the justification cannot simply be that one is (non-visually) aware that one sees that they are this way; it must be something which goes beyond that fact. And so on *ad infinitum*—if the conception of knowledge as true justified belief remains in force.

It seems we cannot deny this conception of knowledge by saying that the justification for a knowledgeable belief can, sometimes, simply be the content of the belief, for that seems to violate the very idea of justification. If the justification you have for a knowledgeable belief was simply the content of your belief, there would be no point in asking you the question 'Why do you think that?' for you would have already said why you think that. But perhaps we can deny this conception of knowledge by saying that, when knowledge is knowledge of a transparent fact, its content shares some of the essential features of a justification. If we can recognize the significant respects in which the content of a knowledgeable belief is the same as a justification for this belief, we will be able to say that, even though it is not a justification for the belief, it is all but a justification.

First, the justification one has for a knowledgeable belief is something one knows. In the same way, the content of a knowledgeable belief is something one knows (whether or not this content is a transparent fact).

Secondly, the justification one has for a knowledgeable belief specifies the way one acquires this knowledge. Similarly, the content of the second-order knowledgeable belief specifies the way one acquires *this* knowledge. In the case of visual knowledge, to say that one sees that there is a lemon over there is to specify the way in which one comes to know that there is a lemon over there; seeing that things are a certain way is a way of coming to know that things are this way, because it is not possible to see that things are this way but not know (visually) that they are—when the fact that one sees that they are is transparent. In the same way, to say that one sees that there is a lemon over there is to specify the way in which one comes to know that one sees that there is a lemon over there; seeing that things are a certain way is a way of coming to know that one sees that they are this way, because it is not possible to see that they are this way but not know that one sees that they are—when the fact that one sees that they are is transparent.

Thirdly, the justification one has for a knowledgeable belief entails the truth of the belief. In the same way, the content of a knowledgeable belief entails the truth of the belief. The fact that one sees that there is a lemon over there entails that the belief that one sees that there is a lemon over there is true.

Fourthly, the justification of a knowledgeable belief guarantees that the belief constitutes knowledge—when the justification is a transparent fact. In the same way, the content of a knowledgeable belief guarantees that the belief constitutes knowledge—when the content is a transparent fact.

These commonalities do not suffice to show that the content of a knowledgeable belief is a justification for this belief—when the content is a transparent fact. But they do show that it is at least very like a justification for a belief. We can exploit this similarity for our present purpose of avoiding both the rock of the regress and the hard place of the non-normative conception. The content of a knowledgeable belief is not a justification for this belief (when the content is a transparent fact). But it is an *entitlement* to the belief (when it is transparent). That is not to say that justifications are not entitlements to the beliefs they justify. All justifications are entitlements. But not all entitlements are justifications. There is a kind of knowledgeable belief which is less than true justified belief, but more than knowledgeable belief as the non-normative conception understands it, because it is knowledgeable belief which one is entitled to have but not justified in having (on the conception of entitlement outlined here).

This parenthetical remark is necessary because it is, of course, possible to speak of knowledge as involving entitlement but not justification without embracing the conception of entitlement I have in mind, but rather, say, the conception offered by Tyler Burge (2003). But endorsing Burge's conception would amount to endorsing a version of the non-normative conception, as I understand that here, because it awards no essential role to knowledge of the entitlement. To say that one has an entitlement in Burge's sense is merely to say that one is in the right circumstances. That one is in these circumstances is something of which one may or may not be apprised. When it comes to avoiding the rock and the hard place, a conception on these lines is of no help.

Contrast the conception I have in mind. It does award an essential role to knowledge of the entitlement: if one has second-order knowledge that one sees that things are a certain way, then one knows the fact which constitutes an entitlement to the belief this knowledge involves. *Contra* the non-normative conception, knowledgeably believing something requires knowledge of one's entitlement to believe this thing. We can thereby seem to embark on the regress. However, one does not need a justification in order to have an entitlement. And one has an entitlement to believe that one sees that things are a certain way simply in knowledgeably believing that one sees that things are this way, because this entitlement is nothing but the fact that one sees that things are this way. So, we avoid the rock (the regress) *and* the hard place (the non-normative conception).

Wittgenstein famously remarked: 'To use an expression without justification does not mean to use it without right' (1978: VII-30). That is a version of the point I am making here. The fact that one has no justification for a knowledgeable belief does not entail that one has no right to the belief. One does, and in the second-order case it is the content of the knowledgeable belief which supplies this right, because this content is a fact which guarantees that the belief of which it is the content is knowledgeable. That is just a way of saying that the fact which comprises this content is an entitlement, but not a justification.

This enables us to say that knowledge, as it is enjoyed by rational subjects, is not always true justified belief. Sometimes it is true entitled belief—true belief for which one has an entitlement which might, but might not, be a justification. It is a justification in the case of visual knowledge, but not in the case of the second-order knowledge which visual knowledge involves.

10.4. On Trying to do without Transparency

The rest of this chapter is devoted to considering, and to trying to calm, concerns which my account of the second-order knowledge involved in visual knowledge may engender.

It is taken for granted that one knows that things are a certain way only if one believes that things are this way in the light of a suitable entitlement. So, it is taken for granted that one has second-order knowledge that one sees that things are a certain way only if one believes that one sees that things are this way. I have suggested that we understand the entitlement which constitutes *this* belief as knowledge as consisting, simply, in the fact that one sees that things are this way. And I have stressed that understanding this fact as an entitlement goes together with understanding the knowledge it constitutes as transparent—as sufficient for one to acquire this knowledge. But it might be thought that a possibility is being missed here: that the entitlement is not the fact that one sees that things are a certain way but the fact that one knows that one sees that things are this way. That fact constitutes one's belief as knowledgeable, but not as knowledge.

The supposed advantage of this suggestion is that it does not involve transparency. The fact that one knows that one sees that things are a certain way, rather than merely the fact that one sees that things are this way, suffices to constitute the belief that one sees that things are this way as knowledgeable. But this fact does not suffice to constitute the belief that one knows that one sees that things are this way as knowledge. And nor is it any part of the suggestion that the fact that one sees that things are a certain way suffices to ensure that one knows that one sees that things are. Knowledge, at least at this second-order level, is not a species of belief, but a mental state in its own right.[3] What is more, because the fact that one knows that one sees that things are this way is distinct from the content of one's knowledgeable belief, there seems no obstacle to understanding this fact not as a mere entitlement but as a fully fledged justification. Of course, one might want to know more about what it means to say that knowledge is a mental state in its own right. But even if one failed to illuminate that conception, one might think that it costs less to accept it in all its darkness than to understand this knowledge as knowledge of a transparent fact. The suggestion might still seem to retain the upper hand.

But the suggestion is hopeless. It inherits all the flaws of a conception of second-order knowledgeable belief as grounded in the fact that one enjoys non-visual awareness. According to the suggestion, the entitlement one has in the case of the knowledgeable belief that one sees that things are a certain way is the fact that one knows that one sees that things are this way. Of course, one has *that* fact as one's entitlement only if one knows it, and so only if one has a knowledgeable belief with the fact as its content to which one is suitably entitled. So, the question arises: what entitles one to the belief that one knows that one sees that things are this way? To apply the suggestion to this, the second-order level, would be to say that the entitlement one has to *this* belief is the fact that one knows that one knows that one sees that things are this way. And of course, one has *that* fact as one's entitlement only if one knows it. We have embarked on another regress. We could block it by applying my own suggestion to the second-order level: one's entitlement to believe that one knows that one sees that things are this way is, simply, the fact that one knows that one sees that they are this way. But then we have lost the supposed advantage, because that requires us to understand *this* fact as transparent. Transparency reappears at the second-order level.

This argument presupposes that if one has knowledge then one has a corresponding knowledgeable belief to which one is entitled. Of course, one could reject the presupposition. But to do so would be to embrace a

---

[3] Obviously this is inspired by Williamson (2000).

non-normative conception of knowledge, according to which one can enjoy knowledge even if one lacks second-order knowledge of what entitles one to the corresponding belief. And that will take us back to the hard place.

Let us now consider another apparent, and apparently more serious, objection.

10.5. Transparency and Luminosity

Timothy Williamson argues against the thesis of luminosity—the thesis that there are conditions which one knows to obtain whenever they obtain. It can seem that my claim that there are facts which are transparent is committed to this thesis.

A condition is not the potential content of a belief, because it is not a proposition. Conditions do not differ if a subject can simultaneously take rationally conflicting attitudes towards them, but merely if there are situations in which one obtains, and the other does not. Unlike propositions, conditions can be presented to us in different ways. But this difference is said to make no difference here. As Williamson (2000: 94–5) explains, we can assume 'a context in which the only relevant presentation of the condition C is as the condition that one is F [so that] knowing that C obtains can be identified with knowing that the condition that one is F obtains, which in turn is only trivially different from knowing that one is F'.

So, as Williamson puts it: '[a] condition C is defined to be luminous if and only if (L) holds:

> For every case α, if in α C obtains, then in α one knows that C obtains.' (ibid. 95).

Even if we grant the assumption which is supposed to make it harmless to speak of knowing that conditions obtain, it is not clear that I am committed to the thesis of luminosity. For Williamson, if a condition is luminous, then whenever it obtains a suitably placed subject knows that it obtains. But for me, there may be cases in which a condition which is capable of being luminous obtains but the suitably placed subject does not thereby know that it obtains.

I would like to follow Williamson in my use of the expression 'case'. But it is not entirely clear how he uses this expression. He says that 'a case is a possible total state of a system, the system consisting of an agent at a time paired with an external environment' (ibid. 52). That would suggest that a case α is distinct from a case β, if α is the case at one time, and β the case at another. But when

Williamson develops his anti-luminosity argument, he implies that the same case can be the case at different times, when he speaks of cases $a_0 \ldots a_n$ where a_0 is the case at dawn and a_n the case at noon. It seems clear from the details of his example that the conditions which obtain in the various cases recorded by the symbol 'a' pertain to the same subject. So, it seems that Williamson distinguishes between cases which are distinct with respect to subject, and cases which are distinct with respect to time. We might employ what I take to be his symbolism, and use different Greek letters to register the former, and subscripts to register the latter. So, cases a_0 and a_n are distinct with respect to time but not to subject and cases a_0 and β_0 differ with respect to subject but not to time.

Williamson's definition, by means of (L), in effect says that, if condition C obtains in any case pertaining to a single subject, then the subject in question knows that C obtains. It follows from this that, if C is luminous, then there cannot be two cases pertaining to a single subject, in one of which C obtains, and the subject knows that it obtains, and in another of which C obtains, but the subject does not know that it obtains. This is not how I understand luminous conditions. I understand them along the lines of a disjunctive conception. Let us say that condition C obtains if, and only if, either one's capacity for knowledge of a certain sort is operative, which operation ensures that one knows that C obtains, or C merely obtains, viz., C obtains *full stop*—perhaps one knows that C obtains, but equally perhaps not. We can distinguish between two classes of conditions, the members of the first of which are constituted by the condition recorded on the left-hand side of the disjunction, and the members of the second of which are constituted by the condition recorded on the right-hand side of the disjunction. A condition C which belongs to the first class is luminous, viz., is such that one knows it obtains whenever it obtains. But a condition C which belongs to the second class is not luminous, viz., is not such that one knows it obtains whenever it obtains. With this in mind, let us replace (L) with the following (L*):

> For some cases a^*, if in a^* C obtains, then in a^* one is in a position to know that C obtains.

(L*) says that if in certain cases pertaining to a single subject C obtains, then the subject in question knows that C obtains. The cases in question are those in which C is constituted by the condition recorded on the left-hand side of the disjunction. It is possible to say that a condition C is defined as luminous if, and only if (L*) holds. It is also possible to say, perhaps more intuitively, that a condition C is luminous in cases a^*, and only in cases a^*—only in cases in which C is constituted by the operation of one's capacity for knowledge of the appropriate sort. To say the latter is to say that condition C counts as a luminous condition in (and only in) those cases a^*. To say the former is to say that a condition C counts as luminous if, and only if there are, as it were, cases in which it counts as luminous (in the previous sense of luminous). In what follows, I will stay with the seemingly more intuitive way of speaking.

With this in mind, let us see how Williamson's argument works against luminosity, as he understands it. And then let us see why it does not apply to me, once we replace (L) with (L*). That will allow us to draw a moral from Williamson's argument—to see it not as an argument against luminous conditions as (L*) understands them, but rather as a transcendental argument for the possibility of luminous conditions, according to which a condition of their possibility is that they are constituted in line with (L*) and not (L).

Williamson works with the example of the condition that one feels cold, which he takes to stand as good a chance of being luminous as any.

Williamson invites us to consider a morning on which one feels freezing cold at dawn, and warm at noon, but warms up so slowly in the interim 'that one is not aware of any change in [one's feelings of heat and cold] over one millisecond' (Williamson 2000: 97). He continues:

Let $t_0, t_i \ldots t_n$ be a series of times at one millisecond intervals from dawn to noon. Let a_i be the case at t_i [where] t_i [is a time] between t_0 and t_n, and suppose that at t_i one knows that one feels cold. Thus one is at least reasonably confident that one feels cold, for otherwise one would not know. Moreover, this confidence must be reliably based, for otherwise one would still not know that one feels cold. Now at t_{i+1} one is almost equally confident that one feels cold, by the description of the case. So if one does not feel cold at t_{i+1}, then one's confidence at t_i that one feels cold is not reliably based, for one's almost equal confidence on a similar basis a millisecond later that one [feels] cold is mistaken.

We arrive at this conditional:

(1_i) If in a_i one knows that one feels cold, then in a_{i+1} one feels cold.

If the condition that one feels cold is luminous, then the following conditional follows from (L):

(2_i) If in a_i one feels cold, then in a_i one knows that one feels cold.

Now suppose:

(3_i) In a_i, one feels cold.

By *modus ponens*, (2_i) and (3_i) yield this:

(4_i) In a_i, one knows that one feels cold.

By *modus ponens*, (1_i) and (4_i) yield this:

> (3_{i+1}) In a_{i+1}, one feels cold.

By repeating the argument from (3_i) to (3_{i+1}) *n* times, we reach this:

> (3_n) In a_n, one feels cold.

But (3_n) is certainly false, for a_n is at the end of the time period, when one does not feel cold.

Williamson proceeds to reason that, because the argument is sound, and because premises $(1_i) \ldots (1_{n-1})$ are true, premises $(2_i) \ldots (2_{n-1})$ must be false. And because, 'by construction of the example' (Williamson 2000: 98), these premises are true if the condition that one feels cold is luminous, the condition is not luminous.

This is a compelling argument. But it does not touch my position, as we shall now see.

The first thing to do is to replace (L) with (L*). Whereas Williamson defines his target as the claim that the condition that one feels cold is effectively the condition C which is the concern of (L), my position can be put by saying that the condition that one feels cold is effectively the condition C which is the concern of (L*). Premise (1_i) is unaffected by this replacement. But premise (2_i) does not follow from the relevant assumptions. Given that the condition that one feels cold is effectively the condition C which is the concern of (L*) and not (L), we rather have (2_i^*):

> (2_i^*) If in a_i^* one feels cold, then in a_i^* one knows that one feels cold.

But now with (2_i^*) in place of (2_i), we do not have (4_i), because it does not follow from (2_i^*) and (3_i). (3_i) is not the antecedent of (2_i^*). Of course, we can rectify this by replacing (3_i) with (3_i^*), viz., by assuming that one is in a case in which the condition that one feels cold is luminous:

> (3_i^*) In a_i^*, one feels cold.

Now (4_i^*) will follow from (2_i^*) and (3_i^*):

> (4_i^*) In a_i^*, one knows that one feels cold.

But the problem now is that (1_i) and (4_i^*) will not yield (3_{i+1}). We can rectify this by replacing (1_i) with (1_i^*):

> (1_i^*) If in a_i^* one knows that one feels cold, then in a_{i+1} one feels cold.

But now, of course, the problem is that we cannot repeat the argument from (3_i^*) to (3_{i+1}) once, let alone n times, because (3_{i+1}) is not the antecedent of (2_{i+1}^*). Of course, we could rectify this by replacing (1_i^*) with (1_i^{**}):

(I_i^{**}) If in a_i^* one knows that one feels cold, then in a_{i+1}^* one feels cold.

So, we not have (3_{i+1}) but rather (3_{i+1}^*):

(3_{i+1}^*) In a_{i+1}^* one feels cold.

But now the question arises as to why we should accept premise (1_i^{**}). (2_i^*) is compulsory given (L^*). (3_i^*) is just a harmless assumption. And (1_i^*) is surely true. Knowledge must meet the requirement of being reliably based whether or not the condition of which it is knowledge is luminous. And it is not an obstacle to its meeting this requirement that the condition which one knows to obtain (at t_i) is luminous, and the condition which obtains (at t_{i+1}) is not luminous. The important thing is that at each millisecond the condition that one feels cold obtains. In some cases, the condition is luminous. In other cases, it is not luminous. The property of being luminous is like the property of obtaining at one time rather than another—a property which the condition instantiates in some cases but not in others. So, there is no need to accept (1_i^{**}); (1_i^*) will suffice. And with (1_i^*) in place, it will not follow from (2_i^*) and (3_i^*) that one still feels cold at the end of the time period.

It is essential to my own understanding of luminosity that there are some cases under which a condition which is capable of being luminous is not luminous. Williamson's argument against what he understands by luminosity can now be seen as an argument for the claim that luminosity must be understood as I understand it, viz., in line with (L^*), rather than (L). As we might put it, it is a condition of the possibility of luminous conditions that there are cases in which conditions which are capable of being luminous are not luminous. Far from undermining the possibility of luminous conditions as I understand them, Williamson's argument tells us, in transcendental fashion, what they must be like if they are to be possible.

Williamson thinks, independently of his argument, that there are some cases in which conditions which stand as good a chance as any of being luminous obtain but the suitably placed subject does not know that they obtain. I agree with Williamson wholeheartedly on this point. However, it is tempting to think, on the basis of his argument, that there cannot be conditions which are luminous. The disjunctive conception gives the lie to this temptation, by showing that a condition, recordable by saying (for instance) that one feels cold, can be either so constituted as to be luminous, or so constituted as not to be luminous. Williamson's argument is powerless to show that there are no conditions of this sort. And conditions of this sort are the only conditions I need commit myself to, in order to make the claims I want to make about transparency. The disjunctive conception thereby shows that—significant as Williamson's argument is—it is not so significant as to vindicate this temptation.

10.6. Non-Sensible Knowledge

There is an important sense in which the second-order knowledge involved in visual knowledge is not sensible knowledge, in a broadly Kantian sense of 'sensible'. The acquisition of visual knowledge that things are a certain way requires perceptual access to the fact known. It requires a case of seeing that things are a certain way, which is constituted by the operation of a capacity for knowing (visually) that things are this way. And the entitlement required for the belief which this knowledge involves is distinct from the fact which constitutes the content of this belief—because it is not the fact that things are this way, but the fact that I see that things are this way. By contrast, the acquisition of the second-order knowledge involved in this visual knowledge does not require being sensibly aware that one sees that things are this way. And the entitlement required for the belief which this knowledge involves is not distinct from, but the very fact which constitutes the content of this belief—because it just is the fact that I see that things are this way.

The point can be put in Kantian terms. The second-order knowledge is not empirical knowledge because it is not acquired by means of sensible intuition of its object (Kant 1997).[4] Intuitions are that through which cognitions relate immediately to their objects. Cognitions are representations which are potentially either knowledgeable representations or components of knowledgeable representations. And a sensible intuition is an intuition which a subject can enjoy only if its object affects the subject's mind. So, seeing that things are a certain way might be thought of as a species of sensible intuition. We might say that the intuition involved in the second-order knowledge is non-sensible because it does not consist in *its* object affecting the mind. Rather, it consists in the mind producing its object. Knowledge that one sees that things are a certain way does not require a sensible intuition of its object—it does not

---

[4] Here 'object' means 'objective somewhat'. As I read Kant, he uses the idea of an object both in this capacious way, and in a more restricted way, to mean objects in the restricted sense of particulars; compare McDowell (1998c; 2009a: 37, n. 20).

require one to be sensibly aware that one sees that things are a certain way. Rather, it merely requires the mind to produce its object (under pressure from suitable causes, of course)—it merely requires one to see that things are a certain way.[5]

In not requiring perceptual access to the known fact, in this way, non-sensible knowledge seems as if it might also be described as non-empirical knowledge. 'Empirical' strikes a note of contingency: empirical knowledge is of the contingent, so non-empirical knowledge must be of the necessary. For this reason, I prefer the label 'non-sensible knowledge'. But because we live in an age in which the a priori is often taken to be not necessarily knowledge of necessities but 'merely' knowledge which does not derive from perceptual access,[6] I will use this label interchangeably with the label 'non-empirical knowledge'.

This feature of the conception of second-order knowledge which I advocate might seem to make it vulnerable to a line of thought which has been taken to undermine the compatibility of 'a traditional doctrine of privileged self-knowledge . . . the view that we are able to know, without the benefit of empirical investigation, what our thoughts are in our own case', with 'externalism about mental content . . . the view that what concepts our thoughts involve may depend not only on facts that are internal to us, but on facts about our environment' (Boghossian 1997: 271). The worry is that, in the context of externalism, this doctrine enables us to acquire, 'without the benefit of empirical investigation', knowledge of 'facts about our environment'. It is part of my conception of second-order knowledge that one is 'able to know, without the benefit of empirical investigation' that one sees that things in one's outer environment are a certain way. It seems to follow from this that one is also able to know, 'without the benefit of empirical investigation', that things in one's outer environment are a certain way, viz., the way one sees them to be. So, the worry ought to apply equally to my conception.

In the context of externalism, the line of thought might be expressed as follows. Assume I enjoy non-empirical knowledge that I am thinking about water. I know a priori that if I am thinking about water then there is water in the outer environment. So, I am surely in a position to reflect on the fact which I know non-empirically, and on this conditional, and thereby arrive at

---

[5] For Kant, non-sensible intuition is not of objects in space or time, because it is (what he calls) intellectual intuition, an object-generating act of apperception. The non-sensible intuition I am envisaging here is not intellectual intuition as Kant understands it; see my 'Practical Knowledge and Intellectual Intuition' (forthcoming).

[6] See many of the papers in Wright, Smith, and Macdonald (1998).

knowledge that there is water in the outer environment. But surely I cannot acquire knowledge of this fact in this way. The acquisition of knowledge of facts about the outer environment surely requires perceptual access to these facts. In which case, surely the assumption that I know non-empirically that I am thinking about water is false.

In the context of the present conception of second-order knowledge, the line of thought might be expressed as follows. Assume I enjoy non-empirical knowledge that I see that things in the outer environment are a certain way. I know a priori that if I see that things in the outer environment are a certain way then things in the outer environment are this way. So, I am surely in a position to reflect on the fact I know non-empirically, and on this conditional, and thereby arrive at knowledge that things in the outer environment are this way. But surely I cannot acquire knowledge of this fact in this way. The acquisition of knowledge of facts about the outer environment surely requires perceptual access to these facts. In which case, surely the assumption that I know non-empirically that I see that things are a certain way is false.

In both of these contexts, the argument conflates the idea of *arriving at* knowledge with the idea of *acquiring* knowledge. I can acquire knowledge of facts about the outer environment only if I am having, or have had, perceptual access to these facts. But so long as I am acquiring, or have acquired, knowledge of these facts, by means of perceptual access, I can arrive at knowledge of them by inference from knowledge which is not itself acquired by means of perceptual access. One cannot acquire knowledge of outer facts by inference from the conjunction of non-empirical knowledge and conditionals known a priori. But one can arrive at knowledge of these facts by inference in this way, so long as one has already acquired, or contemporaneously acquires, knowledge of them by the ordinary perceptual channels.

This is especially easy to see in the second context. One can have non-empirical knowledge that one sees that things are a certain way only if one has visual knowledge that things are this way. So, one can arrive at knowledge that things are this way by inference from this non-empirical knowledge and conditionals known a priori only if one has acquired, or contemporaneously acquires empirical knowledge that they are this way, by the ordinary visual channels. This can also be seen in the first context, so long as we insist, as I think we should, that one can know non-empirically that one is thinking about water only if one has acquired, or contemporaneously acquires by empirical channels, knowledge that there is water in the outer environment. That will allow us to say that one can arrive at, but cannot acquire, knowledge of the outer environment by inference from the conjunction of this non-empirical knowledge and conditionals known a priori.[7]

The mere fact that one needs to have empirical knowledge of outer facts in order to have non-empirical knowledge does not entail that these outer facts are part of one's entitlement to the beliefs involved in non-empirical knowledge. My suggestion is structurally similar to one made by Crispin Wright (1998), in a discussion of knowledge that one's feet are sore. Wright notes that it is a necessary condition of, but of course not an entitlement to, the belief involved in this knowledge that one knows that one has feet. The suggestion here is that the empirically known fact that things are this way is a necessary condition of, but not an entitlement to, the belief involved in non-empirical knowledge that one sees that things are this way. We might speak of two dimensions to non-empirical knowledge: the entitling dimension and the presupposing dimension, each of which consist of facts known. According to this suggestion, in a case of non-empirical knowledge, the fact which constitutes its content occupies the entitling dimension, and the associated empirically knowable facts occupy the presupposing dimension. The former, but not the latter, ought to be cited in answer to the question 'Why do you think that?' But when it comes to the question 'How do you know that?' perhaps it is acceptable to cite facts from both dimensions, because it is part of the explanation of how one knows non-sensibly that one sees that things are a certain way that things are this way.

We will return to this picture of two dimensions to non-empirical knowledge in the next chapter. But to conclude this chapter I would like to discuss further Boghossian's identification of 'a traditional doctrine of privileged self-knowledge [with] the view that we are able to know, without the benefit of empirical investigation, what our thoughts are in our own case'. This prompts the suggestion that we identify self-knowledge with non-empirical knowledge, as I have understood it here. I want to end by speaking in favour of this suggestion.

10.7. Self-Knowledge

One of the most striking features of recent philosophy is its attempt to rethink the boundaries of the mind. It has been said that one of the essential features of Cartesian philosophy is its picture of the mind as 'a region of reality whose

---

[7] Similar lines of thought may be found in Potter (2007), and Neta and Pritchard (2007).

layout is . . . infallibly accessible' (McDowell 1986: 211) to its subject. This is not simply the thought that every fact about the mental life of a subject is infallibly knowable by the subject. It is also the thought that there is no fact about this life which can be known by the subject only if the subject has fallible knowledge of facts which are not about this life.

There are various ways of rejecting the Cartesian picture of the mind: forms of externalism about content, disjunctive conceptions of experience, and suggestions about how we understand expressions such as 'see'. But to each it seems that a proponent of the picture has a response. One attraction of understanding self-knowledge as non-sensible knowledge is that it allows us to block this response.

In one of its forms, externalism about content is the claim that there is at least one concept which we can grasp only if we are suitably related to suitable objects in the outer environment. It seems to be a consequence of this claim that there is at least one mental state which we can enjoy only if we are suitably related to outer objects—a mental state whose content is composed of a concept of this sort. And it seems to be a consequence of *this* consequence that there is at least one fact about the mind which we can know only if we have fallible knowledge of other facts. If we know that we enjoy a mental state of *this* sort, then we know that there is, or that there has been, an object of the relevant sort in the outer environment. And because this latter knowledge concerns a fact about the outer environment, it is surely fallible.

We have already encountered the disjunctive conception of experience. There are various guises this conception may assume, some of which are metaphysical, some of which are merely epistemic.[8] But in all of its metaphysical guises, it might be said to involve the claim that there is at least one sort of experiential state which we can enjoy if, and only if, *either* there is an outer object which we perceive, *or* it is to us merely as if there is an outer object which we perceive.[9] It follows from this that there are two sub-sorts of the sort of experiential state posited by the disjunctive conception, the sort we enjoy when we perceive a relevant outer object, and the sort we enjoy when it is to us merely as if we perceive this object. One can know that one enjoys an experiential state of the overall sort without knowing how things are in the outer environment. But one can know that one enjoys an experiential state of at least the first sub-sort only if one knows how things are in the outer environment. So, it seems to be a consequence of *this* claim that there is at

---

[8] This is the view of Byrne and Logue (2008). For a development of this thought, see Haddock and Macpherson (2008*b*).

[9] See Snowdon (1980–1).

least one fact about the mind which we can know only if we have fallible knowledge of other facts.

It seems to be possible to derive this consequence without endorsing externalism about content, or the disjunctive conception by claiming, not implausibly, that the fact that one sees that things are a certain way in the outer environment is a fact about one's mind. One can know that one sees that things are a certain way in the outer environment only if one knows that things are this way in this environment. So, it seems to be a consequence of *this* claim that there is at least one fact about the mind which we can know only if we have fallible knowledge of other facts.

In the case of the first and the second of these positions, the Cartesian will either deny the position or attempt to show that it does not have the claimed consequence for the picture. In the case of the disjunctive conception, it might be denied that the fact that one enjoys an experiential state of the first sub-sort is a fact about the mind. In the case of externalism, it might be denied that states with contents composed of concepts of the posited sort are mental states properly so-called. And in the case of the third position, the Cartesian must deny its claim that facts of the relevant sort are facts about the mind.

It would beg the question raised by these denials of the Cartesian conception simply to insist that these facts cannot be about the mind because they are not infallibly accessible. That is precisely what is being denied. But it would not beg the question to insist that facts which are only fallibly accessible cannot be about the mind because they are not the potential contents of 'privileged self-knowledge'. It is a mark of facts about the mental life of a subject that they are knowable in a special way by the subject, viz., 'without the benefit of empirical investigation'. It seems right to think of this freedom from the empirical as a kind of epistemic privilege which is denied to the subject's knowledge of other facts. The distinctively Cartesian claim is that what makes for this privilege is infallibility. Only if facts about the mind are infallibly accessible are they knowable 'without the benefit of empirical investigation', and so potentially contents of 'privileged self-knowledge'.

We are in a position to resist this line of thought. We have an account of non-empirical knowledge which precisely does not understand this knowledge as infallible. It is non-empirical not because it is infallible but because its acquisition is not such as to require perceptual access to the fact known. This blocks the route from self-knowledge to infallibility which the Cartesian is trying to exploit. Short of this route, the Cartesian seems to have no choice but to make a seemingly question-begging appeal to infallibility, or to relinquish the picture. An advantage of the identification of self-knowledge with non-empirical knowledge, as I have understood it here, is that it enables the present attempt at rethinking the boundaries of the mind to resist this Cartesian counter-attack. This attempt can insist that the claim that there are facts about the mind which are knowable only fallibly does not violate any reasonable conception of these facts as the potential contents of privileged self-knowledge.

To acknowledge the conclusion I have just drawn is to acknowledge a category of knowledge which seems to be absent from much contemporary epistemological thinking. It seems to be assumed that there cannot be any such thing as a justification or an entitlement which falls within the scope of our privileged self-knowledge, but does not fall short of facts about the outer world. Failure to recognize a category of privileged self-knowledge, within whose scope entitlements of this sort fall, might lead one to reject the account of visual knowledge, and the justifications and entitlements it involves, which I recommend. But it might also lead one to think that what I mean by 'justification' or 'entitlement' is not the same as what those I have presented as my opponents (proponents of the traditional understanding of the account of knowledge as justified true belief, and the supplemented post-Gettier accounts) mean by those words. We each mean something which falls within the scope of privileged self-knowledge; but whereas it is no part of what I mean that this knowledge is always infallible, it is part of what the others mean; so, there is no real difference between us.

But there is a real difference, even given the point about a difference in meaning (which I am not sure is true). There is a category of privileged self-knowledge which I recognize. And whereas I insist that the entitlements we ought to cite in answer to suitable 'Why do you think . . .?' questions are facts which fall within the scope of this self-knowledge, my opponents insist that the entitlements are not these facts, but rather those which fall within the scope of knowledge of a more restricted sort. In this way, my account gives essential epistemic place to a category of privileged self-knowledge which does not figure in their accounts, and that alone constitutes a real difference between us.

10.8. Concluding Remarks

I want to claim that the second-order knowledge involved in visual knowledge is non-empirical, or non-sensible knowledge, and that the possibility of this sort of non-sensible knowledge establishes the possibility of privileged self-knowledge acquired 'without the benefit of empirical investigation' which is nevertheless fallible, contrary to what the Cartesian counter-attack assumes. I have no desire to claim that every species of privileged self-knowledge must be understood as non-sensible knowledge. Perhaps there are instances of infallible self-knowledge. But I do want to claim that we can understand the second-order knowledge involved in visual knowledge as non-sensible knowledge, and therefore as a species of privileged self-knowledge.

The account of non-empirical knowledge I have presented in this chapter has some interesting affinities with the account of knowledge without observation sketched by G. E. M. Anscombe in her book *Intention* (1957). Anscombe famously claimed that the knowledge we have of our intentional actions is a species of knowledge without observation, which species she characterizes as *practical* knowledge. I think we can shed some light, not only on knowledge of action, but also on Anscombe's undeniably difficult text, by understanding practical knowledge as a-special-species of non-sensible knowledge. That is the task for the next chapter.

11

Knowledge of Action

11.1. Introductory Remarks

Intentional bodily actions are akin to cases of seeing that things are a certain way, in that they can help to undermine the idea of a strict divide between the inner and the outer world.

Cases of seeing that things are a certain way constitutively depend for their existence on the existence of suitable inner items and suitable outer items—on cases of seeming to see that things are this way, and on facts to the effect that things are this way. Intentional bodily actions also constitutively depend for their existence on the existence of suitable such items—on intentions to do such-and-such, and on suitable bodily movements (amongst other things). In the previous chapter I sought to remove an obstacle to thinking of cases of seeing that things are a certain way as genuinely psychological items in their own right, by showing how they fall within the scope of a kind of privileged self-knowledge. Given their manifest similarity to these cases, I ought now to do the same for intentional bodily actions. Doing so will remove an obstacle to thinking of intentional bodily actions as genuinely psychological items in their own right.

It is natural to think that to have knowledge of one's intentional actions is to know what one is doing intentionally. But this thought needs elaboration.

I want to suggest that 'I am doing such-and-such' and 'I am doing such-and-such intentionally' are equally forms of the content of knowledge of one's intentional actions. Each form is a determination of the determinable form 'I am a certain way'. The forms are forms of content—forms of thought, or forms of judgement—not forms of words. But we may still find clues to these forms (often excellent clues) in our ways of expressing their contents in language. And it may be that these clues are not mere symptoms but criteria, because it may be that the possibility of suitably formed sentences is in some sense constitutive of the possibility of their associated thoughts.[1] There is no need to take a stand on these questions here. But for me facts are themselves thoughts of a certain sort—true thoughts, or true propositions; so, it is a way of putting my point to say that there are facts of the form 'I am doing such-and-such' and 'I am doing such-and-such intentionally'.

The forms which concern us here exhibit (what linguists call) imperfective aspect.[2] There can be times at which it is true to say that I am doing such-and-such even if there is no time at which it is true to say that I have done such-and-such. For example, there can be times at which it is true to say that I am writing a novel even if there is no time at which it is true to say that I have written a novel (perhaps my inspiration packs up, or my hard-drive). Novels come into being only when they are written. Michael Thompson has argued that, if actions are understood as particular events, actions come into being only when they are executed. It is not true to say that there is an action (of mine) of doing such-and-such until it is true to say that I have done such-and-such. Just as I can be writing a novel even though no novel emerges from the process of writing it, I can be executing an action even though no action emerges from the process of executing it.[3] If actions are understood in this way, it would be wrong to describe our topic as knowledge of action; I might well know that I am doing such-and-such even if there is no action of my doing such-and-such for me to have knowledge of. That description is correct only if the actions of which I have knowledge are suitably understood: not as events, but as processes, perhaps; or at least as episodes whose associated forms exhibit imperfective aspect; or even—as we might allow ourselves to put it—as episodes whose being is becoming, because it resides in the doing, not in the done.

So, knowledge of one's intentional actions is knowledge with first-personal propositional content of a form which exhibits imperfective aspect—'I am doing such-and-such' or 'I am doing such-and-such intentionally'.

11.2. Non-sensible Knowledge of Action

I want to suggest that we understand knowledge of intentional action as a species of non-sensible knowledge.

---

[1] See Wright (1980) for the idea of criteria. See Dummett (1993) for the idea of a constitutive connection between thought and language.

[2] By contrast, 'I have done such-and-such' exhibits perfective aspect. As I am using the notion of aspect, it applies not only to linguistic constructions but also to forms of judgement. Here I am following Thompson (2008: ch. 8). See Comrie (1976) for more on the notion.

[3] Thompson (2008: ch. 8). We might say that there are no times at which it is true to say that there is a particular action (of mine) of doing such-and-such, but false to say that I have done such-and-such.

The fact that one is doing such-and-such intentionally is a fact which is capable of being transparent, and sometimes instantiates this property. It fails to instantiate this property in cases relevantly akin to those mentioned in §10.2—when it would be irresponsible to believe that one is doing such-and-such, when one is suffering from excessive paranoia, and so on. A disjunctive conception of intentional action makes this clear. Some cases of doing such-and-such intentionally are intrinsically operations of one's capacity to know what one is intentionally doing—intrinsically cases of knowing that one is doing such-and-such intentionally. They are, as we might say, intrinsically cases of doing something not merely intentionally but knowledgeably. But other cases of doing such-and-such intentionally are not cases of knowing that one is doing such-and-such intentionally—not operations of the relevant epistemic capacity but rather, as we might say, cases of doing such-and-such merely intentionally. So, it is true that one is doing such-and-such intentionally if, and only if, either one knows that one is doing such-and-such intentionally, or one is merely doing such-and-such intentionally.[4] Put differently, the fact that one is doing such-and-such intentionally is constituted, either by the fact that one is doing such-and-such not merely intentionally but knowledgeably, or by the fact that one is doing such-and-such merely intentionally.

For this reason, we can say that some facts to the effect that one is doing such-and-such intentionally are transparent, because their presence is explained by the presence of the fact that one is doing such-and-such not merely intentionally but knowledgeably. And so, we can say that a fact which forms the content of knowledge of one's intentional action constitutes an entitlement to the belief the knowledge involves. This entitlement satisfies the four features outlined in §10.3. It is something one knows. It specifies the way one comes by the knowledge in question (one acquires knowledge that one is doing such-and-such intentionally by doing such-and-such intentionally). It guarantees the truth of the belief that one is doing such-and-such intentionally. And it guarantees that this belief constitutes knowledge, because when doing such-and-such intentionally is an operation of one's capacity for knowledge of what one is intentionally doing, it is not possible to be doing such-and-such intentionally without knowing that one is doing so.

---

[4] Assuming the acceptability of the disjunctive conception of visual experience, it is no objection to this claim that the fact which figures on the left-hand side of the disjunction entails the truth of the proposition that one is doing such-and-such intentionally; the fact that one sees an object entails the truth of the proposition that one has a visual experience of this object, and yet it figures on the left-hand side of the disjunction employed in the case of visual experience.

So, the acquisition of knowledge of what one is intentionally doing does not require perceptual access to the fact known. And the entitlement required for the belief which this knowledge involves is the very fact which constitutes its content—not a distinct fact, as in the case of sensible knowledge (see §10.6). So, the knowledge is non-sensible.

This constitutes a direct transposition of the account of non-sensible knowledge to the key of action. *Inter alia*, it enables us to avoid the following famous counterexample, due to Donald Davidson (1978: 91–2):

> It is mistake to suppose that if an agent is doing something intentionally, he must know that he is doing it . . . in writing heavily on this page I may be intending to produce ten legible carbon copies. I do not know, or believe with any confidence, that I am succeeding. But if I am producing ten legible carbon copies, I am certainly doing it intentionally.

If Davidson is right, then it is possible for someone to be doing such-and-such intentionally without knowing that they are doing such-and-such, and so without knowing that they are doing such-and-such intentionally. I agree that this is possible. I insist only that there are cases in which the act of making ten legible carbon copies is intrinsically an operation of one's capacity for knowledge of what one is intentionally doing. In such a case, one knows what one is doing simply by doing the thing intentionally. It is consistent with this that there are cases in which the act of making ten legible carbon copies is not an operation of this capacity. That is something the disjunctive conception of intentional action secures.

However, it can seem that cases in which the act of making ten legible carbon copies is intrinsically an operation of one's capacity to know what one is intentionally doing will be the exception, not the rule. One can, from this knowledge, arrive by inference at knowledge that ink is getting on to the tenth sheet of paper. The latter is surely knowledge which one can acquire only sensibly (by seeing that ink is appearing on the tenth sheet, say). And in all but exceptional cases, the last sheet will be hidden from one's sensible view. One can imagine cases in which someone else can see that ink is appearing on the tenth sheet, and this other person informs one of this as one is making the copies; perhaps the other person is wearing X-ray spectacles, or perhaps she is located underneath the tenth sheet, which is itself situated on a glass table. But clearly such cases are exceptional. Here we return to the idea of the entitling and the presupposing dimensions, which seems to be just as integral to knowledge of intentional action as it is to the second-order knowledge which visual knowledge involves.

11.3. The Two Dimensions

I introduced the distinction between entitling and presupposing dimensions in the context of discussing an argument which turns on the following thought: if one has non-sensible knowledge, then one can arrive by inference at knowledge which one can acquire only sensibly. I suggested that this thought should not trouble us if we have a firm grip on the distinction between acquiring, and arriving at knowledge. But it might seem that it is not always easy to take this sanguine attitude when it comes to non-sensible knowledge of intentional action.[5]

Consider a case, reasonably close to one described by G. E. M. Anscombe (1963: 82): you write 'I am a fool' on a whiteboard intentionally, and, as you do so, you see, and so know, that these words getting written onto the board by your hand (which you know you are moving). In this case, there seems no obstacle to you knowing non-sensibly that you are writing 'I am a fool' on the whiteboard, and then arriving by inference at knowledge that the words are getting written on the board. But now consider another case, closer to Anscombe's own: you write 'I am a fool' on the whiteboard intentionally, but with your eyes closed, so you do not see the words getting written on the board by your hand (which you know you are moving). Let us make two further assumptions about this case: first, just before you begin to write, you see, and so know that your pen is touching the whiteboard in front of you; secondly, you know that your pen works, and so know that it will work in the immediate future (we can ignore the question of how you know this, because we are only making this assumption for the sake of argument). It might seem that, even with these two other bits of knowledge in place, you cannot know that you are writing 'I am a fool on the whiteboard' when you are doing so, because if you know you are doing this, then you can arrive (by inference) at knowledge that your hand moves in the way appropriate to writing 'I am a fool'. And this knowledge has not yet been provided for. It concerns the movements of one's body, so it seems it must be known via sensible channels. But it seems there are no sensible channels which could provide for this knowledge, now that the visual, and—let us also assume—the testimonial, channels have been closed off.

Psychologists speak of proprioception, which surely gives rise to proprioceptive knowledge, just as vision gives rise to visual knowledge. Consider a case in which someone grabs on to your arm, and with it uses the pen you

[5] I would like to thank Jennifer Hornsby and John McDowell for their help with this section.

are holding to draw a circle on the whiteboard. You did not intentionally draw the circle—the other person did. But your hand still traced the circular movement, and you know that it did, by means of a capacity for knowing what your body is doing which we can think of as proprioceptive. But consider a case in which the person grabs your arm and, with it, writes 'I am a fool' on the whiteboard without telling you that this is what they are doing. Your hand once again traced the appropriate 'I am a fool' movements. But in this case you do not know that this is what your hand is doing.

In the latter case, one lacks the proprioceptive knowledge which one possesses in the former case. And it is hard to see how, in the latter case, one could possess the proprioceptive knowledge, if a sign of whether one does so is that one can possess this knowledge precisely in a case in which one does not move one's body either intentionally, or in the course of doing something intentionally. It can seem as if there is no sensible channel by means of which one knows that one's body is making the appropriate 'I am a fool' movements, now that the visual, and the testimonial, channels have been closed off. So, if we retain the assumption that one can know this only by means of sensible channels, we can seem forced to the conclusion that one cannot know that one is writing 'I am a fool' on the whiteboard—if one's eyes are closed, and no one informs you that this is what you are doing.

This seems to give us reason to question the assumption. And surely we ought to do so. To assume that one can know facts about one's body—such as facts about one's body's movements—only by means of sensible channels has the consequence that we know about our bodies in the same way that we know about the outer world; or, as a proponent of this assumption should really say, in the same way that we know about the rest of the outer world (viz., sensibly, in whole or in part). And this seems wrong. It seems wrong to think of our bodies as if they are—from an epistemic point of view—no more intimately ours than our cups of tea, or our hard-drives. One way to do justice to their being *our* bodies is to drop the present assumption.[6]

With the assumption in place, we can arrive at, but cannot acquire, knowledge of the movements of our bodies by means of an inference from the non-sensible knowledge we have of our intentional bodily actions. There now seems to be pressure to conclude that we do not have non-sensible

---

[6] Another way is considered in Haddock (2004), which develops a disjunctive conception of bodily movement, and a related conception of bodily action. The account of knowledge of bodily movement developed here, and fleshed out further in §11.6, naturally complements the account of bodily action and bodily movement developed there. See also Haddock (2010) for further discussion of disjunctive conceptions of bodily movement.

knowledge of our intentional bodily actions in cases such as the one we have just considered. However, short of this assumption, we can not only arrive at but acquire knowledge of the movements of our bodies by means of an inference from non-sensible knowledge of our intentional bodily actions. So, we can acquire knowledge that our body is making the appropriate 'I am a fool' movements by inference from our (non-sensible) knowledge that we are writing 'I am a fool' on the whiteboard. And with that, the pressure will dissolve. Of course, it does not follow from this rejection of the assumption that the fact that our body is moving in the appropriate way enters the entitling dimension when it comes to non-sensible knowledge of what we are doing. That fact remains in the presupposing dimension for this knowledge. We must not think of this dimension as exclusively occupied by facts which are only sensibly knowable.

To reject the assumption is not to deny that we have a capacity for proprioceptive knowledge. But it is to insist—to put it with an air of paradox—that much of the knowledge we have of the positions and movements of our bodies is not proprioceptive. Or at least, it is to insist—to put it without that air—that much of this knowledge is not proprioceptive in the way knowledge that our hand is tracing a circle is proprioceptive in the above case, because it is not a sign of whether we can possess knowledge of our bodily movements that we can do so in a case in which we do not move our body either intentionally or in the course of doing something intentionally. We shall return to this point in §11.5.

I do not want to deny that there can be cases in which one does something intentionally but does not know that one is doing it, because one lacks knowledge, derived from sensible channels, of the presupposed facts. Consider the case in which one is intentionally making ten legible carbon copies. If one knows that one is doing this, then one can arrive at knowledge that there is ink on the tenth sheet by inference from this knowledge. But imagine that one has not yet seen the tenth sheet, and that only when one has stopped writing does one look to see, and thereby come to know that there is ink on the tenth sheet. One did not acquire this knowledge by visual channels prior to, or contemporaneously with, one's acquisition of the non-sensible knowledge that one is making ten legible carbon copies. Perhaps one acquired it by some other route prior to, or contemporaneously with, one's acquisition of the non-sensible knowledge. And other routes are easy to find; we saw some at the end of the previous section. But when these routes are absent, we should accept that, these recherché cases aside, one does not have non-sensible knowledge that one is making ten legible carbon copies. This concession is compatible with insisting that one has plenty of non-sensible knowledge of actions which extend into the world: actions such as writing 'I am a fool' on the whiteboard, eating a lemon, writing a novel, closing a door, and even—in suitable cases—making ten legible carbon copies.

11.4. The Distinctive Value of Knowledge of Action

One striking feature of the *Meno* problem is its concern with the role of knowledge in enabling the execution of an intention, viz., the intention to get to Larissa. The Socratic solution to this problem is that, because knowledgeable beliefs are rationally immune to doubt, but lesser states are not, the former enable the efficient attainment of our goals, but the latter do not. We could put this solution by saying that knowledge enables the efficient execution of our intentions, but lesser states do not. That is one aspect of the connection between the value of knowledge and intentional action.

But I think the connection goes deeper than this. It is hard to see how knowing the way to Larissa can enable the efficient execution of the intention to walk to Larissa if one does not know that one is walking (when one is doing so). Perhaps one regularly suffers from kinaesthetic hallucinations which make it seem to one as if one is walking when in fact one is standing still. And as a result of this, perhaps one is not able to know that one is walking when one is doing so, but merely able to believe truly that one is doing so. If so, one's belief that one is walking is rationally vulnerable to doubt, because one lacks knowledge of the fact which entitles one to hold on to one's belief in the face of apparent reason for doubt—viz., the fact that one is walking. And this is likely to stymie the execution of one's intention (where this is an intention whose execution involves walking) given that one is a rational agent (see §9.5). Perhaps one will start walking very slowly and deliberately, so as to pay careful visual and tactile attention to the movement of one's legs, in order to check that one is not suffering from a hallucination. Perhaps one will stop walking altogether and fall to the ground, wrecked by the kinaesthetic crisis brought on by one's lack of this basic knowledge. And there are other possibilities.

Walking is not typically something one does by doing something else, in the teleological sense of 'by'. Of course, one does it by moving one's legs and contracting one's muscles, but typically that is 'by' in a merely causal sense. Walking is not typically informed by knowledge or belief that one does so by moving one's legs. One simply walks. If knowledge of the way to Larissa has distinctive value because it enables the efficient execution of one's intention, then basic knowledge that one is walking—as we might call it—also has distinctive value, because without it knowledge of the way to Larissa is less likely to play this enabling role.[7] That is the deeper connection between the value of knowledge, and the value of knowledge of intentional action.

In §9.4 I suggested that my account of visual knowledge enables us to make sense of the Socratic solution in this case. Central to this suggestion was that if one knows that things are a certain way then one knows that one sees that things are this way. This second-order knowledge helps to secure rational immunity for the knowledgeable belief that things are this way by entitling one to disregard at least some apparent reasons to abandon this belief. Knowledge of what one is doing intentionally neither is, nor essentially involves second-order knowledge. But this does not mean that one is not entitled to disregard putative reasons to abandon the belief involved in knowledge of this sort. The reason why the second-order knowledge helps to secure this immunity in the visual case is because it is knowledge of one's knowledge-affording entitlement. Second-order knowledge is needed for knowledge of one's entitlement in the visual case, because one's visual knowledge is not itself knowledge of this entitlement. But knowledge of one's intentional actions is itself knowledge of one's knowledge-affording entitlement—viz., of the fact that one is doing such-and-such intentionally. When that fact is one's knowledge-affording entitlement, it entitles one not only to the knowledgeable belief that one is doing such-and-such intentionally, but also to rule out apparent reasons for abandoning this belief.[8]

So, the value of knowledge in general seems to rest on the possession of knowledge of one's intentional action. And just as the modest route enables us to make sense of the value of knowledge in general, it also enables us to understand its value in cases of intentional action, by means of its idea that some cases of knowledge are themselves cases of knowledge of the entitlements to the beliefs they involve.

---

[7] Someone who doubts that knowledge that one is walking is basic knowledge is free to go back further until they hit basic knowledge proper. It remains the case that knowledge of action at the basic level is needed for knowledge to be valuable in the way specified by the Socratic solution.

[8] This is not to deny the possibility of cases in which one does not have the fact that one is doing such-and-such intentionally as one's entitlement, and so is not entitled to disregard these apparent reasons, as in cases in which one's doing such-and-such is not an operation of one's capacity for knowledge of one's intentional action.

11.5. Non-observational Knowledge

I want now to enumerate some similarities between my account of knowledge of intentional action and Anscombe's account of practical knowledge (Anscombe 1963).

The first thing to do is to show that the idea of the genus of which practical knowledge is a species—the idea of knowledge without observation, a form of knowledge which is at once fallible and non-sensible, and therefore opposed to the Cartesian counter-attack pinpointed in §10.7—matches my idea of non-sensible knowledge.

One sign of the profoundly non-Cartesian spirit of the idea of knowledge without observation is the fact that the paradigm case of such knowledge is not knowledge of one's mental states but knowledge of the position of one's limbs. Its paradigm content—the fact that one's limbs are in such-and-such a position—is not even an ostensible denizen of the Cartesian inner world. According to Anscombe, if I have knowledge without observation of this fact, there is 'just that fact and my knowledge of it, i.e. my capacity to describe my position straight off; no question of any appearance of the position to me, of any sensations which give me the position' (Anscombe 1962: 73). There is just that fact and my knowledge of it: if we look around for a fact to play the role of an entitlement to the belief the knowledge involves, the only candidate is the content of my knowledge, the fact that my limbs are in such-and-such a position. I can describe the position straight off, so I do not need a mediating entitlement, such as the fact that it appears to me as if my limbs are in such-and-such a position, or the fact that I enjoy suitable sensations which give me the position. Anscombe does not deny that suitable sensations may be causally involved in the acquisition of knowledge of this sort. But she insists that one does not acquire this knowledge by 'identifying' these sensations—viz., by judging (knowledgeably) that one has them (Anscombe 1963: 49).

There is at least one philosopher who seems unable to ascribe this position to Anscombe. Hanna Pickard claims that 'the crux of Anscombe's idea of knowledge without observation' is simply that it is non-inferential knowledge (Pickard 2004: 218). If this is right, then it is compatible with 'the crux' of Anscombe's idea that if one has knowledge without observation of the fact that one's limbs are in such-and-such a position, then there is more than just the fact and one's knowledge of it; there is also, according to Pickard, the fact that it seems to one as if one's limbs are in such-and-such a position, which fact plays the role of a non-inferential entitlement to the belief one's knowledge involves. This is clearly the exact opposite of what Anscombe actually says. So, why does Pickard think it is 'the crux' of her idea?

Attempting to elucidate the idea of knowledge with observation, Anscombe says: 'Where we can speak of separately describable sensations, having which is in some sense our criterion for saying something, then we can speak of observing that thing; but that is not generally so when we know the position of our limbs' (Anscombe 1963: 13). Here she ties down observational knowledge to justifications, or entitlements, or criteria which consist in the fact that one has 'separately describable' sensations—sensations whose intrinsic nature can be characterized in a way which does not match the content of the knowledge supposedly acquired by identifying the sensation (Anscombe 1962). For example, a sensation of one's bent knee would not be 'separately describable' if one acquired knowledge that one's knee is bent by identifying it. But a tingle in the knee would be a 'separately describable' sensation if one acquired knowledge that one's knee is bent by identifying it. Knowledge that one's knee is bent, acquired in this second way, would be knowledge with observation. However, Anscombe thinks 'it is not generally so' that knowledge of the position of one's limbs is acquired by coming to know that one has 'separately describable' sensations. So, it is 'not generally so' that knowledge of the position of one's limbs is knowledge with observation. She concludes that it is generally knowledge without observation, knowledge which is acquired not by coming to know that one has suitable sensations, but simply by coming to know the position of one's limbs. Pickard notes that this conclusion rests on the assumption that sensations must be 'separately describable'. She thereby maintains that the conclusion misses the possibility that knowledge without observation is generally acquired by coming to know that one has sensations which are not 'separately describable', such as a sensation of one's bent knee. Pickard assumes that it is a short and harmless step from acknowledgment of this possibility to the claim that knowledge of the position of one's limbs is generally acquired in the light of justifications such as the fact that it seems to one as if one's limbs are in such-and-such a position.

It is reasonable to ask why Anscombe misses the possibility of knowledge grounded in sensations which are not 'separately describable'—or, better, why she does not recognize it as a possibility. I suspect it is because she thought, at the time of writing *Intention*, that the very idea of a sensation is the idea of something which is 'separately describable'. That is essential to the sense-datum theory's idea of a sensation. Knowledge that the sky is blue is acquired by identifying, not a visual sensation of the blue sky, but (perhaps for reasons putatively provided by an experiential version of the argument from illusion)[9] a visual sensation which is 'separately describable'—a visual sensation of a blue expanse, perhaps. Anscombe tells us that she took this idea very seriously, and struggled for many years to overcome it, not rejecting it in print until eight years after the publication of the first edition of *Intention*.[10] So, it is not implausible to suppose that this theory was shaping her conception of a sensation in 1957, and with it her conception of knowledge with observation, in part because of what she tells us, and in part because it renders rationally intelligible what Pickard can only see as an ungrounded oversight.

Knowledge without observation is clearly non-sensible knowledge, because its acquisition does not involve perceptual access to the known fact. Rather there is 'just that fact and my knowledge of it, i.e. my capacity to describe my position straight off'. Anscombe speaks of a capacity to describe the position of her limbs knowledgeably. But we can speak more generally of a capacity to know the position of our limbs. There is often no need for the operation of this capacity; we often acquire knowledge of the position of our limbs derivatively from knowledge yielded by the operation of our distinct capacity to do things not merely intentionally but knowledgeably. But given this, I see no reason to deny that, in cases where we do not act intentionally but do know the position of our limbs, our knowledge is typically acquired via the operation of our 'capacity to describe [our] position straight off'. The entitlement required for the belief which this knowledge involves is the very fact which constitutes its content—not a distinct fact, as in the case of sensible knowledge. So, knowledge without observation is non-sensible knowledge.[11]

Anscombe is exactly right to claim that we have non-sensible knowledge of the position of our limbs (as we saw in §11.3 above). Her focus on bodily position and bodily movement, as a paradigm for non-observational

---

    [9] See Martin (2003).

    [10] See the introduction to Anscombe (1981). Anscombe eventually rejected the idea in her (1965) paper 'The Intentionality of Sensation: A Grammatical Feature'.

    [11] Edward Harcourt (2008) is concerned that understanding knowledge in this non-perceptual way forecloses the possibility of making sense of the possibility of illusions of bodily position. But I do not think he needs to be concerned. I understand visual knowledge as yielded by cases of seeing that things are a certain way, which are constituted by the operations of a capacity for knowing (visually) that things are this way. Evidently this understanding does not rule out the possibility of cases in which it seems to one as if one sees that things are this way, which have the potential to mislead one into thinking not only that things are this way, but also that one sees that things are this way. So, why should the present understanding of knowledge of bodily position foreclose the possibility of cases in which it seems to one as if one's body is in such-and-such a position, which cases have the potential to mislead one into thinking that this is how things are? It is worth noting that it does not manifestly follow from what I have said that one must conceive of such illusions as episodes with propositional content, as the papers cited in n. 5 of §9.2 indicate.

knowledge, is not only entirely apt, for the development of a non-Cartesian account of self-knowledge, but also entirely correct on its own terms. This is not to say that knowledge of intentional action is merely non-sensible knowledge. Knowledge of bodily position is merely non-sensible knowledge, even when it is acquired derivatively from knowledge of intentional bodily action. The second-order knowledge involved in visual knowledge is also merely non-sensible knowledge. But knowledge of intentional action has some special properties in addition to being non-sensible, which make it distinctly *practical* knowledge.

11.6. Practical Knowledge and Intention

As we have seen, practical knowledge is a species of knowledge without observation. As well as falling under this genus, it has the following two central features: first, what is known in practical knowledge is known 'in intention' (Anscombe 1963: 57); secondly, if one fails to acquire practical knowledge because of a mistake on one's part, then 'the mistake is in the performance, not in the judgment' (ibid. 82).[12]

I want to suggest that to say one knows what one is doing 'in intention' is to say that one knows what one is doing by doing it intentionally.

It is natural to find the idea of knowing what one is doing 'in intention' puzzling. Intentions are intentions to do things. So, we might think that to say that one knows what one is doing 'in intention' is to say that one is doing such-and-such intentionally by having the intention to do such-and-such. And that might seem to be the thought that if one believes truly that one is doing such-and-such in the light of the fact that one has the intention to do such-and-such, then one knows that one is doing such-and-such. It can now be tempting to cast this fact in the role of a justification for knowledge along the lines of the account favoured by most post-Gettier epistemologists: in addition to believing truly that one is doing such-and-such in the light of the fact that one has the intention to do such-and-such, it must be the case that one's true belief satisfies a further condition, or further conditions (of the sort these epistemologists specify).

The idea of knowing what one is doing 'in intention' thereby seems to push us back to an account of the sort I rejected in §§9.2–4. But perhaps there is a different way of understanding the idea on which it does not have this consequence.

---

[12] Anscombe attributes this remark to Theophrastus.

The idea of an intention is the idea of an intention to do something. It is possible to have an intention to do something without doing the thing intentionally. That can lead us to picture the intention itself as always of the same sort whether one is intentionally doing the thing or not. But this picture is quite optional. Doing something intentionally just is executing an intention to do that thing. So, why not treat an intention one is executing as an intention of one sort, and an intention one has not yet started executing as an intention of another sort? One can have an intention to do such-and-such which one has not yet started executing without doing such-and-such intentionally. But one cannot have an intention to do such-and-such which one has started executing without doing such-and-such intentionally.

There is nothing in what I have just said to raise the hackles of a philosopher who makes a point of saying that the intrinsic nature of the intention remains the same whether one is executing it or not. Such a philosopher will agree that there are particular intentions one is executing, and particular intentions one has not yet started executing. All I am saying is that we can treat those intentions one is executing as of one sort, and those intentions one has not yet started executing as of another sort. There is no need for there to be anything more to an intention's belonging to the former sort than the fact that one is executing it, and no need for there to be anything more to an intention's belonging to the latter sort than the fact that one has not yet started executing it. These are nothing but platitudes. But they nevertheless yield a different way of understanding the idea of knowing something 'in intention'.

The idea is that only intentions of the former sort, intentions one is executing, are relevant to the acquisition of practical knowledge. We might put the idea by saying that one knows that one is doing such-and-such by suitably executing an intention to do such-and-such. But we might put it in a way which brings out the connection between this way of understanding the idea and the idea as originally formulated, by saying that one knows that one is doing such-and-such by having a suitable intention to do such-and-such of a certain sort, viz., a suitable intention which one is executing. We might even give intentions of this sort a name: 'intentions in action.'

Different philosophers have put the expression 'intention in action' to different kinds of use. We might consider as an example the use to which it is put by John R. Searle (1983). Searle thinks there are intentions with different intrinsic natures. He contrasts intentions in action with prior intentions. Prior intentions are intentions to do such-and-such at a future time, whose intentional objects are actions of doing such-and-such. Intentions in action are intentions to do such-and-such at the present time, whose intentional objects are the bodily movements involved in doing such-and-such. We can illustrate Searle's thought by imagining that one acquires the intention to do such-and-such at a future time, and then at that time one starts intentionally doing such-and-such. According to Searle, just before one starts doing such-and-such, a prior intention expressible by something of the form 'I am going to do such-and-such' starts to bring about a bunch of intentions in action, each of which is directed at each of the bodily movements involved in doing such-and-such, and each of which is expressible by something of the form 'I am doing such-and-such'. The intentional action of doing such-and-such is itself a composite of these intentions in actions and the bodily movements they generate. And it is precisely on account of the presence of the former that the action they compose counts as intentional.

A comparison with Searle's use might help to explain how I am using the expression 'intention in action'. I am happy to co-opt the label 'prior intention' to refer to intentions to do such-and-such which one is not yet in the process of executing. But I see no reason to think that this label must pick out an item whose intrinsic nature differs from that picked out by 'intention in action'. I see no reason not to think that they both pick out the same item at a different stage in its history: the former picks it out when one is not yet executing it; the latter picks it out when one is executing it. In consequence, I see no need to agree with Searle that the intentional object of a prior intention differs from that of an intention in action. Whether prior, or in action, the object of an intention is simply doing such-and-such.[13] The rest of Searle's account I wish simply to ignore; whether actions are complexes composed of intentions in action and bodily movements is not something I need to consider here. But I do want to dispute that 'I am doing such-and-such' is the proper form for the expression of the content of an intention in action. I think that it is more naturally thought of as the proper form for the expression of the content of the practical knowledge which having the intention in action puts one in a position to acquire. The proper form for the expression of the content of an intention, whether prior to or in action, is simply 'to do such-and-such', as in 'I intend to do such-and-such'.[14]

So, to say one knows what one is doing 'in intention' is to say that one knows that one is doing such-and-such because one has a *suitable* intention

---

[13] We might think that a reference to time is needed in the content of the intention. And surely that is right. But there is no reason to think the concept of futurity must appear. The temporal difference between prior intentions and intentions in action resides not in their contents but in the fact that in the case of the latter, viz., when the intention is being executed, the time which figures in the content of the former is progressively receding into the past. The same is not true of the former, viz., before the intention has started to be executed; in its case, the time is still in the future. I am indebted here to 'Intention in Action', an unpublished lecture by John McDowell.

[14] There is an extended defence of this point in Thompson (2008: part 2).

in action, viz., an intention to do such-and-such which one is executing *knowledgeably*, a knowledge-guaranteeing intention-in-action. Having this intention makes the fact that one is doing such-and-such available to one as one's knowledge-guaranteeing entitlement.

This can seem to throw up a problem, which attaches to my equation of doing such-and-such intentionally with executing an intention to do such-and-such. That entails something which we might seem to have reason to reject: that if one is intentionally doing such-and-such then one has an intention to do such-and-such. David Velleman has argued that one can do such-and-such intentionally even if one does not have the intention to do such-and-such, on the grounds that believing that one will do such-and-such is required to have the intention to do such-and-such, but not to be doing such-and-such intentionally (Velleman 1989: 109–43).

There does appear to be a substantive disagreement here. But I think this appearance is illusory. I am happy to accept that there is a kind of intention which requires belief in its successful execution. But I want to insist that it is not *this* kind of intention which is presupposed to doing things intentionally. It is not a prior intention, but an intention in action, which is presupposed to this kind of doing (the claim carries no requirement that the intention one is executing comes into being prior to its execution). So, perhaps I should add: it is only a prior intention—only an intention one acquires prior to the doing—which requires belief of this sort. Or, perhaps I should say simply that neither prior intention nor intention in action of the kind I am interested in carries *this* requirement.

I am not sure that I need to choose between these ostensible alternatives. Both give a place to the kind of intention which carries this requirement. I simply offer them to readers with concerns about the claim to choose between as they wish (or not; I see no reason to choose). It is possible that supporters of the Velleman position will at this point dig in their heels, and insist that *there is only one kind of intention*, viz., that which carries this requirement. But I think the burden is now on them to show that this ambitious claim really is so—that it really is not possible to adopt the more capacious conception of intention I am offering here.

11.7. Practical Knowledge and Direction of Fit

It is a way of putting a doctrine of Anscombe's to say that, if one fails to acquire practical knowledge of what one is doing because what one is doing is neither what one intends to do nor what one believes one is doing, then 'the mistake is in the performance, not in the judgment' (Anscombe 1963: 82); but if one fails to acquire knowledge of what one is doing which is not practical knowledge but rather (what Anscombe calls) speculative knowledge, because what one is doing is neither what one intends to do nor what one believes one is doing, then the mistake is in the judgement, not in the performance.

If I have the intention to do such-and-such, and I believe that I am doing such-and-such, but in fact I am not doing such-and-such but rather something else, then I fail to acquire practical knowledge that I am doing such-and-such. Imagine that I have the intention to dispense sugar, and believe that I am dispensing sugar, but in fact am dispensing salt. And imagine that a reliable person tells me that I am dispensing salt. Now consider a pair of cases. In the first, on being told what is going on I simply modify my belief accordingly: I simply change my belief to the belief that I am dispensing salt. In the second, on being told what is going on I simply modify my behaviour accordingly: I simply stop dispensing salt, run into the kitchen, fetch the sugar-dispenser, and start intentionally dispensing sugar. In the first case, even though it is possible that I now know that I am dispensing salt, it is not possible that I now have practical knowledge that I am doing so, because I have no intention to dispense salt. But in the second case, so long as after modifying my behaviour I continue to believe that I am dispensing sugar, it is possible that I now have practical knowledge of what I am doing, because I have the intention to dispense sugar, and I am now doing so intentionally.

So, if one fails to acquire knowledge of what one is doing because what one is doing is neither what one intends to do nor what one believes one is doing, the way to help to ensure that one has practical knowledge is to modify one's behaviour accordingly; there is no need to modify one's belief. That is what it means to say that, if one fails to acquire practical knowledge because what one is doing is neither what one intends to do nor what one believes one is doing, *the* mistake is in the performance, not in the judgement (*a* mistake was in the judgement—what one believed one was doing was not something one was doing; but this was not *the* mistake). By contrast, the way to help to ensure that one has speculative knowledge is to modify one's belief accordingly; there is no need to modify one's behaviour. That is what it means to say that, if one fails to acquire speculative knowledge because what one is doing is neither what one intends to do nor what one believes one is doing, *the* mistake is in the judgement, not in the performance (*a* mistake was in the performance—one was failing to execute a relevant intention; but this was not *the* mistake).

Evidently, if one fails to execute one's intention because what one is doing is neither what one intends to do nor what one believes one is doing, there is a mistake in the performance. Indeed, here the only mistake is in the performance. There is a potential mistake in the judgement when one fails to acquire practice knowledge, because having the right belief is constitutive of having practical knowledge. There is not even a potential mistake in the judgement when one fails to execute one's intention, because having the right belief is not constitutive of executing intentions (even though it may be a useful aid in doing so). But failure to execute intentions and failure to acquire practical knowledge are alike, in that both can involve some sort of mistake in the performance.

The fact that there can be a mistake in the performance in the case of failure to execute intentions, and in the case of failure to acquire practical knowledge, might be captured by saying that intention and practical knowledge both have a world-to-mind direction of fit. But the fact that there can also be a mistake in the judgement in the latter case, but not in the former case, might be captured by saying that practical knowledge also has a mind-to-world direction of fit. Whereas an intention is only vulnerable to a mistake in the performance, and so has only a world-to-mind direction of fit, practical knowledge is vulnerable to a mistake in the judgement, as well as a mistake in the performance, and so has a mind-to-world and a world-to-mind direction of fit. Speculative knowledge, on the other hand, is the mirror-image of an intention, in that it is only vulnerable to a mistake in the judgement, and so has only a mind-to-world direction of fit.

These differences in direction of fit are reflected in the fact that whereas a belief can be true, or not true, an intention can be executed, or not, and in the process of being executed, or not. So, we might say this: the contents of beliefs have truth-conditions—conditions which are satisfied if, and only if, the beliefs are true; and the contents of intentions have execution-conditions—conditions which are satisfied if, and only if, the intentions are either executed or in the process of being executed.

Imagine a case in which one is both in the process of executing an intention whose content is of the form 'to do such-and-such', and in possession of a true belief whose content is of the form 'I am doing such-and-such'. This belief is true because one is in the process of executing this intention. So, we can say the following: the truth-condition of the content of the belief is satisfied because a suitable intention is in the process of being executed. Indeed, we can say that there is a class of contents whose truth-conditions can only be satisfied because suitable intentions are in the process of being executed—a class of contents which in this sense have truth-conditions *and* execution-conditions, because suitable beliefs are true if, and only if, suitable intentions are in the process of being executed. We might say that contents in this class have two aspects: a theoretical aspect (the aspect of truth) and a practical aspect (the aspect of execution). These are the contents of practical knowledge.

Insisting on this point is one way of keeping vivid the fact that the knowledge which one acquires by means of intentions in action is of a special, practical sort.[15]

11.8. Concluding Remarks

Anscombe remarks that practical knowledge is not 'derived from the object known' but is rather 'the cause of what it understands' (1957: 87). Here 'cause' means formal cause. Her idea seems to be that practical knowledge constitutes the fact of which it is knowledge. This is something upon which I explicitly insist, by means of the disjunctive conception of intentional action. We can make the connection between Anscombe's remark and this conception explicit, by saying that the fact which forms the content of practical knowledge—the fact that one is doing such-and-such intentionally—is itself constituted by the fact that one has (practical) knowledge that one is doing such-and-such intentionally. So, on this point, as with the others, I am at least very close to Anscombe herself.[16]

---

[15] Roger Teichmann (2009: 23) suggests two reasons why understanding the claim which is said to derive from Theophrastus as a claim about the world-to-mind direction of fit of an intention is un-Anscombian. The first reason is odd: the thing which is supposed to fit an intention is not the world, but an action. But the world includes actions, and it is those denizens which intentions are supposed to fit. No one thinks they have to fit the whole world! The second looks shallow: Anscombe speaks of utterances, rather than states (of intention). I do not speak solely of states, because when intentions are in action they are no longer states, but processes, or at least episodes of some sort. But what is the obstacle to thinking that this talk of intentions as states, processes, or episodes is not just a harmless material mode analogue to Anscombe's formal mode presentation?.

[16] There can seem to be two points of difference. First, Anscombe thinks that the fact that one is doing such-and-such intentionally is always constituted by one's practical knowledge of this fact, but I think that there are cases in which it is not so constituted. Secondly, whereas Anscombe thinks that only practical knowledge plays this constitutive role, I think that non-observational—or non-sensible—knowledge in general does so, for the facts of which it is knowledge. I think the first point is well taken, and I have no wish to deny it. But I can find no evidence to support the second. There are differences between knowledge which is practical and knowledge which is merely non-sensible, and I have tried to say what they are. But, as far as I can see, Anscombe does not think that being 'the cause of what it understands' is one of them. Anscombe introduces the idea of being such a cause in order to distinguish practical knowledge from speculative knowledge. Only on the assumption that Anscombe thinks that the non-practical species of non-observational knowledge are uniformly speculative would

We have arrived at an account of knowledge of intentional action—of practical knowledge—which sees it as a subspecies of non-sensible knowledge. It is a special subspecies, on account of its connection with intention, which ensures that its direction of fit differs from that of other subspecies. But it shares with its fellow genus-member the feature of being knowledge of a transparent fact, and therefore (as we might put it) *self-entitling*, because the entitlement to the knowledgeable belief it involves is nothing other than the fact which forms the content of this belief.

I have suggested that we think of non-sensible knowledge as at least a species of self-knowledge. That allowed me to say, at the end of the previous chapter, that we have arrived at an account of the second-order knowledge involved in visual knowledge which understands the second-order knowledge as a species of self-knowledge. I can now say the same about practical knowledge. We might say that we have arrived at an account of self-knowledge of intentional action.[17]

it follow that, in distinguishing practical knowledge from speculative knowledge by saying that the idea characterizes the former but not the latter, she is thereby saying that the idea does not characterize the non-practical species of non-observational knowledge. As far as I can see, there is nothing in Anscombe's text to support this assumption.

[17] I would like to thank the Arts and Humanities Research Council for awarding me a period of Research Leave within which the integral work for these chapters was completed. I would like especially to thank Alan Millar and Duncan Pritchard for their very helpful comments on numerous drafts, and for many helpful conversations. Special thanks are also due to John McDowell and Peter Sullivan for conversations which enabled me substantially to improve the views recorded here. Maria Alvarez, Campbell Brown, Matthew Chrisman, Ken Gemes, Lars Gundersson, Olav Gjesvik, Chris Kelp, Denis MacManus, Alex Neill, Matthew Nudds, Aaron Ridley, Ernest Sosa, Matthew Soteriou, and Candace Vogler gave me very helpful comments and criticisms on various drafts. Finally, and above all, I would like to thank Jane Calvert, for her invaluable help and support throughout the period in which these chapters were written.

Bibliography

Achinstein, P. (1983). *The Nature of Explanation*. Oxford: Oxford University Press.

Adler, J. (2006). 'Epistemological Problems of Testimony', in E. Zalta (ed.), *Stanford Encyclopedia of Philosophy*. URL: <http://plato.stanford.edu/entries/testimony-episprob/>.

Anscombe, G. E. M. (1963). *Intention* (2nd edn.). Oxford: Basil Blackwell.

—— (1962). 'On Sensations of Position', *Analysis*, 22: 55–8. Reprinted in Anscombe (1981: 71–4). Page references to reprinted version.

—— (1965). 'The Intentionality of Sensation: A Grammatical Feature', in Butler (1965: 158–80). Reprinted in Anscombe (1981: 3–20).

—— (1981). *Collected Papers*, Vol. 2. *Metaphysics and Philosophy of Mind*. Minneapolis: University of Minnesota Press

Audi, R. (2006). *Epistemology: A Contemporary Introduction to the Theory of Knowledge* (2nd edn.). London: Routledge.

Austin, J. L. (1946). 'Other Minds', *The Aristotelian Society*, Suppl. Vol., 20: 148–87. Reprinted in Austin (1979: 76–116). Page references to reprinted version.

—— (1962). *Sense and Sensibilia*. Oxford: Clarendon Press.

—— (1979). *Philosophical Papers* (3rd edn.). Oxford: Clarendon Press.

Baehr, J. (2009). 'Is There a Value Problem?', in Haddock, Millar, and Pritchard (2009: 42–59).

Baldwin, T. (ed.) (2003). *The Cambridge History of Philosophy 1870–1945*. Cambridge: Cambridge University Press.

Beebee, H. and Dodd, J. (eds.) (2005). *Truthmakers: The Contemporary Debate*. Oxford. Oxford University Press.

Boghossian, P. A. (1997/8). 'What the Externalist Can Know A Priori', *Proceedings of the Aristotelian Society*, 97: 161–75. Reprinted in Wright, Smith, and Macdonald (1998: 271–84). Page references to reprinted version.

Brady, M. S. and Pritchard, D. H. (eds.) (2003). *Moral and Epistemic Virtues*. Oxford: Blackwell.

Brogaard, B. (2007a). 'Can Virtue Reliabilism Explain the Value of Knowledge?', *Canadian Journal of Philosophy*, 36: 335–54.

—— (2007b). 'I Know, Therefore, I Understand', unpublished typescript.

Brown, J. (1998). 'Natural Kind Terms and Recognitional Capacities', *Mind*, 107: 275–303.

Burge, T. (1979). 'Individualism and the Mental', in French, Uehling, and Wettstein (1979: 73–121).

—— (1993). 'Content Preservation', *The Philosophical Review*, 102: 457–88.

—— (2003). 'Perceptual Entitlement', *Philosophy and Phenomenological Research*, 67: 503–48.

Butler, R. J. (ed.) (1965). *Analytical Philosophy—Second Series*. Oxford: Basil Blackwell.

Byrne, A. and Logue, H. (2008). 'Either/Or', in Haddock and Macpherson (2008*a*: 57–95).

Cassam, Q. (2007). 'Ways of Knowing', *Proceedings of the Aristotelian Society*, 107: 339–58.

Child, W. (1994). *Causality, Interpretation and the Mind*. Oxford: Clarendon Press.

Chisholm, R. (1977). *Theory of Knowledge* (2nd edn.). Englewood Cliffs, NJ: Prentice-Hall.

Chomsky, N. (2000). *New Horizons in the Study of Language and Mind*. Cambridge: Cambridge University Press.

Clay, M. and Lehrer, K. (eds.) (1989). *Knowledge and Scepticism*. Boulder, Colo.: Westview Press.

Coady, C. A. J. (1992). *Testimony: A Philosophical Study*. Oxford: Clarendon Press.

Comrie, B. (1976). *Aspect*. Cambridge: Cambridge University Press.

Conee, E. (2007). 'Disjunctivism and Anti-Skepticism', *Philosophical Issues*, 17: 16–36.

Craig, E. (1990). *Knowledge and the State of Nature: An Essay in Conceptual Synthesis*. Oxford: Clarendon Press.

Dancy, J. and Sosa, E. (eds.) (1992). *A Companion to Epistemology*. Oxford: Blackwell.

David, M. (2005). 'Truth as the Primary Epistemic Goal: A Working Hypothesis', in Steup and Sosa (2005: 296–312).

Davidson, D. (1963) 'Actions, Reasons, and Causes', *The Journal of Philosophy*, 60: 685–700. Reprinted in Davidson (1980: 3–9).

——(1978). 'Intending', in Yovel (1978: 41–60). Reprinted in Davidson (1980: 83–102). Page references to reprinted version.

——(1980). *Essays on Actions and Events*. Oxford: Clarendon Press.

——(1983). 'A Coherence Theory of Truth and Knowledge', in Henrich (1983: 423–38). Reprinted in LePore (1989: 307–19) and in Davidson (2001: 137–53).

——(2001). *Subjective, Intersubjective, Objective*. Oxford: Clarendon Press.

Davies, M. (2004). 'On Epistemic Entitlement: Epistemic Entitlement, Warrant Transmission and Easy Knowledge', *The Aristotelian Society*, Suppl. Vol., 78: 213–45.

DePaul, M. (2009). 'Does an Ugly Analysis Entail that the Target of the Analysis Lacks Value?', in Haddock, Millar, and Pritchard (2009: 112–38).

——and Zagzebski, L. (eds.) (2003). *Intellectual Virtue: Perspectives from Ethics and Epistemology*. Oxford: Oxford University Press.

DeRose, K. (1992). 'Contextualism and Knowledge Attributions', *Philosophy and Phenomenological Research*, 52: 913–29.

Dodd, D. (2007). 'Why Williamson Should Be a Sceptic', *The Philosophical Quarterly*, 57: 635–49.

Dretske, F. (1969). *Seeing and Knowing*. London: Routledge & Kegan Paul.

——(1970). 'Epistemic Operators', *The Journal of Philosophy*, 67: 1007–23. Reprinted in Dretske (2000: 30–47).

——(1971). 'Conclusive Reasons', *Australasian Journal of Philosophy*, 49: 1–22. Reprinted in Dretske (2000: 3–29).

—— (1992). 'Perceptual Knowledge', in Dancy and Sosa (1992: 333–8).

—— (2000). *Perception, Knowledge and Belief*. Cambridge: Cambridge University Press.

—— (2005). 'Is Knowledge Closed under Known Entailment? The Case against Closure, in Steup and Sosa (2005: 13–26).

Dummett, M. (1993). *Origins of Analytical Philosophy*. Cambridge, Mass.: Harvard University Press.

Elgin, C. (1996). *Considered Judgement*. Princeton: Princeton University Press.

—— (2004). 'True Enough', *Philosophical Issues*, 14: 113–31.

—— (2009). 'Is Understanding Factive?', in Haddock, Millar, and Pritchard (eds.) (2009: 322–30).

Feigel, H. and Scriven, M (eds.) (1956). *Minnesota Studies in the Philosophy of Science*, vol. 1. Minneapolis: University of Minnesota Press.

Ford, A., Hornsby, J., and Stoutland, F. (eds.) (forthcoming). *Anscombe's* Intention. Cambridge, Mass.: Harvard University Press.

Frege, G. (1918). 'The Thought: A Logical Inquiry' (trans. A. and M. Quinton). Reprinted in Strawson (1967: 17–38). Page references to reprinted version

French, P A., Uehling Jr , T. E., and Wettstein, H. K. (eds.) (1979). *Midwest Studies in Philosophy*, IV. Minneapolis: University of Minnesota Press.

Fricker, E. (1987) 'The Epistemology of Testimony', *The Aristotelian Society*, Suppl. Vol., 61: 57–106.

—— (1994). 'Against Gullibility', in Matilal and Chakrabarti (1994: 125–61).

—— (1995). 'Telling and Trusting: Reductionism and Anti-Reductionism in the Epistemology of Testimony', *Mind*, 104: 393–411.

Fricker, M. (2003). 'Epistemic Justice and a Role for Virtue in the Politics of Knowing', *Metaphilosophy*, 34: 154–73.

Fumerton, R. (2006). 'The Epistemic Role of Testimony: Internalist and Externalist Perspectives', in Lackey and Sosa (2006: 77–92).

Gettier, E. (1963). 'Is Justified True Belief Knowledge?', *Analysis*, 23: 121–3.

Ginet, C. (1975). *Knowledge, Perception, and Memory*. Dordecht: Reidel.

Goldberg, S. (2007). *Anti-Individualism: Mind and Language, Knowledge and Justification*. Cambridge: Cambridge University Press.

Goldman, A. (1976). 'Discrimination and Perceptual Knowledge', *The Journal of Philosophy*, 73: 771–91.

—— (1979). 'What is Justified Belief?', in Pappas (1979: 1–23).

—— (1992a). *Liaisons: Philosophy Meets the Cognitive and Social Sciences*. Cambridge, Mass.: MIT Press.

—— (1992b). 'Epistemic Folkways and Scientific Epistemology', in Goldman (1992a: 155–63).

—— and Olsson, E. (2009). 'Reliabilism and the Value of Knowledge', in Haddock, Millar, and Pritchard (2009: 19–41).

Greco, J. (1999). 'Agent Reliabilism', *Philosophical Perspectives*, 13: 273–96.

—— (2000). *Putting Skeptics in Their Place: The Nature of Skeptical Arguments and Their Role in Philosophical Inquiry*. Cambridge: Cambridge University Press.

Greco, J. (2003). 'Knowledge as Credit for True Belief', in DePaul and Zagzebski (2003: 111–34).

——(ed.) (2004). *Ernest Sosa and His Critics*. Oxford: Blackwell.

——(2007*a*). 'Epistemic Evaluation: A Virtue-Theoretic Approach', unpublished typescript.

——(2007*b*). 'The Nature of Ability and the Purpose of Knowledge', *Philosophical Issues*, 17: 57–69.

——(2007*c*). 'Worries About Pritchard's Safety', *Synthese*, 158: 299–302.

——(2008*a*). 'What's Wrong With Contextualism?', *The Philosophical Quarterly*, 58: 416–36.

——(ed.) (2008*b*). *The Oxford Handbook of Skepticism*. Oxford: Oxford University Press.

——(2009). 'The Value Problem', in Haddock, Millar, and Pritchard (2009: 313–21).

——and Sosa, E. (eds.) (1999). *The Blackwell Guide to Epistemology*. Oxford: Blackwell.

Grimm, S. (2006). 'Is Understanding a Species of Knowledge?', *British Journal for the Philosophy of Science*, 57: 515–35.

——(2009). 'Epistemic Normativity', in Haddock, Millar, and Pritchard (2009: 243–64).

Haddock, A. (2004). 'At One with Our Actions, But at Two with Our Bodies: Hornsby's Account of Action', *Philosophical Explorations*, 8: 157–72.

——(2010). 'Bodily Movements', in O'Connor and Sandis (2010).

——(forthcoming). 'Practical Knowledge and Intellectual Intuition', in Ford, Hornsby, and Stoutland (forthcoming).

——and Macpherson, F. (eds.) (2008*a*). *Disjunctivism: Perception, Action, Knowledge*. Oxford: Oxford University Press.

———— (2008*b*). 'Introduction: Kinds of Disjunctivism', in Haddock and Macpherson (2008*a*: 1–33).

——Millar, A., and Pritchard, D. H. (eds.) (2009). *Epistemic Value*. Oxford: Oxford University Press.

Harcourt, E. (2008). 'Wittgenstein on Bodily Self-Knowledge', *Philosophy and Phenomenological Research*, 77: 306–7.

Harman, G. (1973). *Thought*. Princeton: Princeton University Press.

Hawley, P. (2006). 'Scepticism and the Value of Knowledge', unpublished typescript.

Hawthorne, J. (2004). *Knowledge and Lotteries*. Oxford: Clarendon Press

——(2005). 'Is Knowledge Closed under Known Entailment? The Case for Closure', in Steup and Sosa (2005: 26–43).

Henrich, D. (ed.) (1983). *Kant oder Hegel*. Stuttgart: Klett-Cotta.

Hills, A. (2008). 'Understanding', unpublished typescript.

Hookway, C. (2003). 'How To Be a Virtue Epistemologist', in DePaul and Zagzebski (2003: 183–202).

Jones, W. (1997) 'Why Do We Value Knowledge?' *American Philosophical Quarterly*, 34: 423–40.

Kant, I. (1997). *Critique of Pure Reason* (trans. and ed. P. Guyer and A. Wood). Cambridge: Cambridge University Press.

Kaplan, M. (1985) 'It's Not What You Know That Counts', *The Journal of Philosophy*, 82: 350–63.

Kitcher, P. (2002). 'Scientific Knowledge', in Moser (2002: 385–407).

Kornblith, H. (2002). *Knowledge and its Place in Nature*. Oxford: Clarendon Press.

Kvanvig, J. (2003). *The Value of Knowledge and the Pursuit of Understanding*. Cambridge: Cambridge University Press.

—— (2005). 'Is Truth the Primary Epistemic Goal?', in Steup and Sosa (2005: 285–96).

—— (2009). 'Responses to Critics', in Haddock, Millar, and Pritchard (2009: 339–51).

Lackey, J. (2006). 'Learning from Words', *Philosophy and Phenomenological Research*, 73: 77–101.

—— (2007a). 'Why We Don't Deserve Credit For Everything We Know', *Synthese*, 158: 345–61.

—— (2007b). 'Norms of Assertion', *Noûs*, 41: 594–626.

—— and Sosa, E. (eds.) (2006). *The Epistemology of Testimony*. Oxford: Clarendon Press.

Langford, C. H. (1942). 'The Notion of Analysis in Moore's Philosophy', in Schilpp (1942: 319–42).

Lehrer, K. and Cohen, S. (1983). 'Justification, Truth, and Coherence', *Synthese*, 55: 191–207.

Leng, M., Paseau, A., and Potter, M. (eds.) (2007). *Mathematical Knowledge*. Oxford: Oxford University Press.

LePore, E. (ed.) (1989). *Truth and Interpretation. Perspectives on the Philosophy of Donald Davidson*. Oxford: Blackwell.

Lindgaard, J. (ed.) (2008). *John McDowell: Experience, Norm, and Nature*. Oxford: Blackwell.

Lipton, P. (2004). *Inference to the Best Explanation*. London: Routledge.

McDowell, J. (1982). 'Criteria, Defeasibility, and Knowledge', *Proceedings of the British Academy*, 68: 455–79. Reprinted in McDowell (1998a: 369–94). Page references to reprinted version.

—— (1984). 'Wittgenstein on Following a Rule', *Synthese*, 58: 325–63. Reprinted in McDowell (1998b: 221–62).

—— (1986). 'Singular Thought and the Extent of Inner Space', in Pettit and McDowell (1986: 137–68). Reprinted in McDowell (1998a: 228–59). Page references to reprinted version.

—— (1994) 'Knowledge By Hearsay' in Matilal and Chakrabarti (1994. 195–224). Reprinted in McDowell (1998a: 414–43).

—— (1995) 'Knowledge and the Internal', *Philosophy and Phenomenological Research*, 55: 877–93. Reprinted in McDowell (1998a: 395–413).

—— (1996). *Mind and World* (2nd edn.). Cambridge, Mass.: Harvard University Press.

—— (1998a). *Meaning, Knowledge, and Reality*. Cambridge, Mass.: Harvard University Press.

—— (1998b). *Mind, Value, Reality*. Cambridge, Mass..: Harvard University Press.

McDowell, J. (1998c). 'The Logical Form of an Intuition', *The Journal of Philosophy*, 95: 451–70. Reprinted in McDowell (2009a: 23–43). Page references to reprinted version.

—— (2003). 'Subjective, Intersubjective, Objective', *Philosophy and Phenomenological Research*, 67: 675–81. Reprinted in McDowell (2009b: 152–9). Page references to reprinted version.

—— (2008). 'Avoiding the Myth of the Given', in Lindgaard (2008: 1–4). Reprinted in McDowell (2009a: 256–72). Page references to reprinted version.

—— (2009a). *Having the World in View: Essays on Kant, Hegel, and Sellars*. Cambridge, Mass.: Harvard University Press.

—— (2009b). *The Engaged Intellect: Philosophical Essays*. Cambridge, Mass.: Harvard University Press.

Martin, M. G. F. (2003). 'Sensible Appearances', in Baldwin (2003: 519–30).

Matilal, B. K. and Chakrabarti, A. (eds.) (1994). *Knowing from Words: Western and Indian Philosophical Analyses of Understanding and Testimony*. Dordrecht: Kluwer.

Millar, A. (1991). *Reasons and Experience*. Oxford: Clarendon Press.

—— (2001). 'The Scope of Perceptual Knowledge', *Philosophy*, 75: 73–88.

—— (2004). *Understanding People: Normativity and Rationalizing Explanation*. Oxford: Clarendon Press.

—— (2005). 'Travis' Sense of Occasion', *The Philosophical Quarterly*, 55: 337–42.

—— (2007a). 'What the Disjunctivist is Right About', *Philosophy and Phenomenological Research*, 74: 176–98.

—— (2007b). 'The State of Knowing', *Philosophical Issues*, 17: 179–96.

—— (2008a). 'Perceptual-Recognitional Abilities and Perceptual Knowledge', in Haddock and Macpherson (2008a: 330–48).

—— (2008b). 'Disjunctivism and Skepticism', in Greco (2008b: 581–604).

—— (2009). 'What is it that Cognitive Abilities are Abilities to Do?', *Acta Analytica*, 24: 223–36.

—— (forthcoming). 'Knowledge and Reasons for Belief', in Reisner and Steglich-Peterson (eds.) (forthcoming).

—— Haddock, A, and Pritchard, D. H. (eds.) (2009). *Epistemic Value*. Oxford: Oxford University Press.

Moran, R. (2006). 'Getting Told and Being Believed', in Lackey and Sosa (2006: 272–306).

Moser, P. (ed.) (2002). *The Oxford Handbook of Epistemology*. Oxford: Oxford University Press.

Mulhall, S. (1990). *On Being in the World: Wittgenstein and Heidegger on Seeing Aspects*. London: Routledge.

Nagel, T. (1986). *The View from Nowhere*. Oxford: Oxford University Press.

Neta, R. (2004). 'Perceptual Evidence and the New Dogmatism', *Philosophical Studies*, 119: 199–214.

—— and Pritchard, D. H. (2007). 'McDowell and the New Evil Genius', *Philosophy and Phenomenological Research*, 74: 381–96.

Nozick, R. (1981). *Philosophical Explanations*. Oxford: Oxford University Press.

O'Brien, L. and Soteriou, M. (eds.) (2010). *Mental Actions*. Oxford: Oxford University Press.

O'Connor, T. and Sandis, C. (eds.) (2010). *The Blackwell Companion to the Philosophy of Action*. Oxford: Blackwell.

O'Hear, A. (ed.) (forthcoming). *Epistemology (Royal Institute of Philosophy Lectures)*. Cambridge: Cambridge University Press.

Parfit, D. (1984). *Reasons and Persons*. Oxford: Oxford University Press.

Pappas, G. S. (ed.) (1979). *Justification and Knowledge*. Dordrecht: Reidel.

Peacocke, C. (1986). *Thoughts: An Essay on Content*. Oxford: Basil Blackwell.

—— (2004). *The Realm of Reason*. Oxford: Clarendon Press.

—— (2009). 'Mental Action and Self-Awareness (II)', in O'Brien and Soteriou (eds.) (2009).

Percival, P. (2003). 'The Pursuit of Epistemic Good', *Metaphilosophy*, 34: 29–47. Reprinted in Brady and Pritchard (2003: 29–46).

Petersen, S. (2008). 'Utilitarian Epistemology', unpublished typescript.

Pettit, P. and McDowell, J. (eds.) (1986). *Subject, Thought, and Context*. Oxford. Clarendon Press.

Pickard, H. (2004). 'Knowledge of Action Without Observation', *Proceedings of the Aristotelian Society*, 4: 205–230.

Potter, M. (2007). 'What is the Problem of Mathematical Knowledge?', in Leng, Paseau, and Potter (2007: 16–32).

Price, H. H. (1969). *Belief*. London: Allen & Unwin.

Pritchard, D. H. (2002). 'Resurrecting the Moorcan Response to the Sceptic', *International Journal of Philosophical Studies*, 10: 283–307.

—— (2003). 'Virtue Epistemology and Epistemic Luck', *Metaphilosophy*, 34: 106–30. Reprinted in Brady and Pritchard (2003: 210–34).

—— (2005). *Epistemic Luck*. Oxford: Oxford University Press.

—— (2007*a*). 'Anti-Luck Epistemology', *Synthese*, 156: 277–97.

—— (2007*b*). 'The Value of Knowledge', in E. N. Zalta (ed.), *The Stanford Encyclopedia of Philosophy* (Fall 2008 edition). URL: <http://plato.stanford.edu/entries/knowledge-value/>

—— (2007*c*). 'Knowledge, Luck, and Lotteries', in Pritchard and Hendricks (2007: 28–51).

—— (2007*d*). 'Recent Work on Epistemic Value', *American Philosophical Quarterly*, 44: 85–110.

—— (2008*a*). 'A Defence of Quasi-Reductionism in the Epistemology of Testimony', *Philosophica*, 78. 13–28.

—— (2008*b*). 'Greco on Knowledge: Virtues, Contexts, Achievements', *The Philosophical Quarterly*, 58: 437–47.

—— (2008*c*). 'Knowing the Answer, Understanding and Epistemic Value', *Grazer Philosophische Studien*, 77: 325–39.

—— (2008*d*). 'Radical Scepticism, Epistemic Luck and Epistemic Value', *The Aristotelian Society*, Suppl. Vol., 82: 19–41.

Pritchard, D. H. (2008e). 'Sensitivity, Safety, and Anti-Luck Epistemology', in Greco (2008b: 437–55).

—— (2008f). 'Virtue Epistemology and Epistemic Luck, Revisited', *Metaphilosophy*, 39: 66–99.

—— (2009). 'Anti-Luck Virtue Epistemology', unpublished typescript.

—— (forthcoming a). 'Absurdity, *Angst* and the Meaning of Life', *The Monist*.

—— (forthcoming b). 'Apt Performance and Epistemic Value', *Philosophical Studies*.

—— (forthcoming c). 'Knowledge, Understanding and Epistemic Value', in O'Hear (forthcoming).

—— (forthcoming d). 'The Value of Knowledge', *Harvard Review of Philosophy*.

—— (forthcoming e). 'What is the Swamping Problem?', in Reisner and Steglich-Petersen (forthcoming).

—— and Hendricks, V. (eds.) (2007). *New Waves in Epistemology*. London: Palgrave Macmillan.

Pryor, J. (2002). 'The Skeptic and the Dogmatist', *Noûs*, 34: 517–49.

—— (2005). 'There is Immediate Justification', in Steup and Sosa (2005: 181–202).

Rabinowicz, W., and Roennow-Rasmussen, T. (1999). 'A Distinction in Value: Intrinsic and For Its Own Sake', *Proceedings of the Aristotelian Society*, 100: 33–49.

—— (2003). 'Tropic of Value', *Philosophy and Phenomenological Research*, 66: 389–403.

Reisner, A. and Steglich-Peterson, A. (eds.) (forthcoming). *Reasons for Belief*

Riggs, W. D. (2002). 'Reliability and the Value of Knowledge', *Philosophy and Phenomenological Research*, 64: 79–96.

—— (2003). 'Understanding Virtue and the Virtue of Understanding', in DePaul and Zagzebski (2003: 203–26).

—— (2009). 'Understanding, Knowledge, and the *Meno* Requirement Right', in Haddock, Millar, and Pritchard (2009: 331–8).

Rödl, S. (2007). *Self-Consciousness*. Cambridge, Mass.: Harvard University Press.

Rosch, E. (1978). 'Principles of Categorization', in Rosch and Lloyd (1978: 27–48).

—— and Lloyd, B. B. (eds.) (1978). *Cognition and Categorization*. Hillsdale, NJ: Erblaum.

Ross, A. (1986). 'Why Do We Believe What We Are Told?', *Ratio*, 28: 69–88.

Roth, M. D. and Ross, G. (eds.) (1990). *Doubting*. Dordrecht: Kluwer.

Salmon, W. (1989). *Four Decades of Scientific Explanation*. Minneapolis: University of Minnesota Press.

Sartwell, C. (1992). 'Why Knowledge Is Merely True Belief', *The Journal of Philosophy*, 89: 167–80.

Schilpp, P. A. (ed.) (1942). *The Philosophy of G. E. Moore*. Evanston, Ill.: Northwestern University Press.

Searle, J. (1983). *Intentionality*. Cambridge: Cambridge University Press.

Sellars, W. (1956). 'Empiricism and the Philosophy of Mind', in Feigel and Scriven (1956: 253–329).

Silins, N. (2005). 'Deception and Evidence', *Philosophical Perspectives*, 19: 375–404.

Snowdon, P. (1980–1). 'Perception, Vision, and Causation', *Proceedings of the Aristotelian Society*, 81: 175–92.

Sosa, E. (1974). 'How Do You Know?', *American Philosophical Quarterly*, 11: 113–22.

—— (1988). 'Beyond Skepticism, to the Best of our Knowledge', *Mind*, 97: 153–89.

—— (1991). *Knowledge in Perspective: Selected Essays in Epistemology*. Cambridge: Cambridge University Press.

—— (1999). 'How to Defeat Opposition to Moore', *Philosophical Perspectives*, 13: 141–54.

—— (2000). 'Skepticism and Contextualism', *Philosophical Issues*, 10: 1–18.

—— (2003). 'Relevant Alternatives, Contextualism Included', *Philosophical Studies*, 119: 35–65.

—— (2006). 'Knowledge: Instrumental and Testimonial', in Lackey and Sosa (2006: 116–23).

—— (2007). *A Virtue Epistemology: Apt Belief and Reflective Knowledge*. Oxford: Clarendon Press.

Steup, M. (ed.) (2001). *Knowledge, Truth and Duty: Essays on Epistemic Justification, Responsibility and Virtue*. Oxford: Oxford University Press.

—— and Sosa, E. (eds.) (2005). *Contemporary Debates in Epistemology*. Oxford: Blackwell.

Stich, S. (1990). *The Fragmentation of Reason*. Cambridge, Mass.: MIT Press.

Strawson, P. F. (1967). *Philosophical Logic*. Oxford: Oxford University Press.

Stroud, B. (1989). 'Understanding Human Knowledge in General', in Clay and Lehrer (1989: 31–50). Reprinted in Stroud (2000: 99–121). Page references to reprinted version.

—— (2000). *Understanding Human Knowledge*. Oxford: Oxford University Press.

—— (2004). 'Perceptual Knowledge and Epistemological Satisfaction', in Greco (2004: 164–73).

Swinburne, R. (1999). *Providence and the Problem of Evil*. Oxford: Oxford University Press.

—— (2000). *Epistemic Justification*. Oxford: Oxford University Press.

Unger, P. (1968). 'An Analysis of Factual Knowledge', *The Journal of Philosophy*, 65: 157–70.

—— (1975). *Ignorance: A Case for Scepticism*. Oxford: Clarendon Press.

Teichmann, R. (2009). *The Philosophy of Elizabeth Anscombe*. Oxford: Oxford University Press.

Thompson, M. (2008). *Life and Action: Elementary Structures of Practice and Practical Thought*. Cambridge, Mass.: Harvard University Press.

Travis, C. (2005). 'A Sense of Occasion', *The Philosophical Quarterly*, 55: 286–314.

Velleman, D. (1989). *Practical Reflection*. Princeton: Princeton University Press.

Vogel, J (1990). 'Are There Counterexamples to the Closure Principle?', in Roth and Ross (1990: 13–27).

Welbourne, M. (1986). *The Community of Knowledge*. Aberdeen: Aberdeen University Press.

—— (2001). *Knowledge*. Cheshum, Bucks: Acumen.

Williamson, T. (1995). 'Is Knowledge a State of Mind?', *Mind*, 104: 533–65.

—— (2000). *Knowledge and Its Limits*. Oxford: Oxford University Press.

Wittgenstein, L. (1958). *Philosophical Investigations* (2nd edn.). Oxford: Blackwell.
—— (1978). *Remarks on the Foundations of Mathematics*. Oxford: Basil Blackwell.
Woodward, J. (2003). *Making Things Happen: A Theory of Causal Explanation*. Oxford: Oxford University Press.
Wright, C. (1980). 'Realism, Truth-Value Links, Other Minds, and the Past', *Ratio*, 22: 112–32.
—— (1991). 'Scepticism and Dreaming: Imploding the Demon', *Mind*, 100: 87–116.
—— (1998). 'Self-Knowledge: The Wittgensteinian Legacy', in Wright, Smith, and Macdonald (1998: 13–45).
—— (2002). '(Anti-)Sceptics Simple and Subtle: G. E. Moore and John McDowell', *Philosophy and Phenomenological Research*, 65: 330–48.
—— (2004). 'On Epistemic Entitlement: Warrant for Nothing (and Foundations for Free)?', *Aristotelian Society*, Suppl. Vol., 78: 167–212.
—— Smith, B. C., and Macdonald, C. (eds.) (1998). *Knowing Our Own Minds*. Oxford: Clarendon Press.
Yovel, Y. (ed.) (1978). *Philosophy of History and Action*. Dordrecht: Reidel.
Zagzebski, L. (1996). *Virtues of the Mind: An Inquiry into the Nature of Virtue and the Ethical Foundations of Knowledge*. Cambridge: Cambridge University Press.
—— (1999). 'What Is Knowledge?', in Greco and Sosa (1999: 92–116).
—— (2001). 'Recovering Understanding', in Steup (2001: 235–52).
—— (2003). 'The Search for the Source of the Epistemic Good', *Metaphilosophy*, 34: 12–28. Reprinted in Brady and Pritchard (2003: 13–28).

Index